...s Centre LRC

What I... Theatre?

WD

What Is Theatre?
An Introduction and Exploration

John Russell Brown

Focal Press
Boston • Oxford • Johannesburg • Melbourne • New Delhi • Singapore

Focal Press is an imprint of Butterworth–Heinemann.
Copyright © 1997 by Butterworth–Heinemann
ℛ A member of the Reed Elsevier group

Cover photo: Set Design by Warren Carrie for the Alberta Theatre Projects production of *Candide* (music by Leonard Bernstein, book adapted from Voltaire by Hugh Wheeler, lyrics by Richard Wilbur, additional lyrics by Stephen Sondheim and John LaTouche), directed by D. Michael Dobbin and presented in the Martha Cohen Theatre, Calgary Centre for Performing Arts, May 27–July 21, 1990. Photo by Trudie Lee. Courtesy of Alberta Theatre Projects.

Library of Congress Cataloging-in-Publication Data
Brown, John Russell.
   What is theatre? : an introduction and exploration / John Russell Brown.
      p.   cm.
   Includes bibliographical references and index.
   ISBN 0-240-80232-2 (pbk. : alk. paper)
   1. Theatre.   2. Drama.   I. Title.
PN2037.B733   1997
792—dc20   96-41113
                                                                 CIP

British Library Cataloguing-in-Publication Data
A catalogue record for this book is available from the British Library.

The publisher offers special discounts on bulk orders of this book.
For information, please contact:
Manager of Special Sales
Butterworth–Heinemann
313 Washington Street
Newton, MA 02158–1626
Tel: 617-928-2500
Fax: 617-928-2620

For information on all Focal Press publications available, contact our World Wide Web home page at: http://www.bh.com/fp

10 9 8 7 6 5 4 3 2 1

Printed in the United States of America

Contents

List of Illustrations

Color Plates

Acknowledgments

In writing this book, I have been very aware of my debts to the many people with whom I have worked on theatre productions in the United States, England, and other countries, and to my entire theatregoing experience. I am particularly indebted to the students in Theatre 211: Introduction to Drama and Theatre at the University of Michigan, who in successive years have shared their thoughts with me and criticized mine, and also to all colleagues and students with whom I have worked on productions and in practical classes in the Department of Theatre at Ann Arbor. For all this indispensable and continuous help, I am most grateful.

After the first draft was written a number of friends and colleagues did me the great service of reading the whole manuscript or parts of it and giving me their comments and advice: Kurt Beattie, Daniel Gutstein, Christopher Kloesch, G. W. Mercier. I have also benefited from the advice of Tammy Harvey, the book's editor at Focal Press, Marie Lee, who commissioned it, and the anonymous readers whom they commissioned on my behalf. Although my book is the better for the contributions of all these readers, its faults, of course, remain my own.

A huge debt of another kind is due to the custodians of the numerous collections of illustrative material whom I have consulted, both those whose pictures I have been able to use and those who tried to provide what I sought but for various reasons were unable to do so. A writer of any book that seeks to show what theatre is must rely a great deal on this wide network of specialists who generously share their knowledge as well as make their treasures available. A special debt is due to the artists who have allowed me to use their original drawings or designs: Marjorie Bradley Kellogg, G. W. Mercier, Richard Pilbrow and his associates at Theatre Projects, and Jan Swaka. The citation of sources for the illustrations should be read not only as documentation but also as an expression of my gratitude.

The second part of this book appears thanks to the willingness of writers and artists to allow the reproduction of their writings, courtesy of their publishers. The gathering of other voices to follow mine has given me great pleasure, complementing what I wrote and providing perspectives I am not in a position to supply. I am most grateful for the generosity that has made this possible.

In some very few instances when seeking permission to reproduce writings and illustrations, I was not able to be entirely sure that I had contacted all interested parties; such omissions, if any, I greatly regret and beg indulgence. I would be grateful for information that would allow me to repair the fault in a later reprinting.

For her expert care and patience, I am greatly indebted to Maura Kelly who saw this book through its last stages towards publication.

—John Russell Brown
Ann Arbor, December 1995

Introduction

This book is about what theatre is and what it might be. It gives a great deal of information and explains many ideas, but it does not tell readers what to think. Above all other aims, I want to set readers thinking about theatre for themselves, as their view of theatre becomes wider and more complete.

Anyone can take a published play from the shelf and read the words that actors have spoken on the stage. This is a very convenient way of starting serious study of theatre and, while studying *What Is Theatre?* readers are encouraged to read, and probably reread, a number of plays, giving preference to those that can be seen in performance. Yet reading play texts alone is not enough for students who are exploring what theatre is in practical terms; nor is it easy to grasp the theatrical worth of a play simply by studying it as if it were any other book. Sitting down with a text in hand is a very different experience from seeing the same play in performance: while reading you can feel shut out from understanding, not *hearing* the different voices or the varying force of the speeches, and not *seeing* the people and events that give rise to the spoken lines of text. *What Is Theatre?* sets out to explain why this is so and to show readers how to take into account all aspects of the work that goes into putting a play on the stage.

After studying with this book, readers should find that reading a play is a more complete experience, and seeing one is more rewarding. Besides being introduced to plays and dramatists, readers will also learn about actors, directors, designers, managers, and audiences, about the various kinds of theatre buildings, stages, and technical equipment from the past and the present day, and about the organizations that support some of the most thriving theatres. Students of theatre or drama need to know how all these people and facilities function and what they contribute to the well-being of theatre. With such knowledge it becomes possible to read a play and imagine it in performance, and to judge whether a production or an actor's performance is as good as it might be.

In our study of theatre, great plays from the past make repeated appearances—plays by Shakespeare, Molière, Chekhov, Ibsen, Shaw, O'Neill, the Greek tragedians, Samuel Beckett, and other master dramatists. If readers happen to be able to see any of these in performance, the opportunity should be taken, but this is not necessary. This book is designed to be equally useful and give the same insights into the nature of theatre whatever plays its readers are able to see. The more plays seen onstage the better, because the focus of this book is directed wherever possible toward a direct experience of playgoing, but seeing only one or two should be sufficient. Any production, by a student, community, or professional company, can provide some solid ground on which to put thoughts and ideas to the test. With good fortune, some readers may see a very new play that has not yet won critical acclaim, one that is about lives very like their own or about ideas of immediate interest that were unknown to "classic" or established writers. The information and ideas in this book are applicable to all plays—the new and adventurous quite as much as the great and famous.

This is also a book about plays and theatres that its readers could not possibly have seen, because they do not exist at present. We look at what famous actors, dramatists, and directors have done in the past, but to be true to the nature of theatre, we also look at what is happening at the present time and what *may* happen in the future. One reason we need to be concerned with the here and now is that all theatre experience starts to die with the end of a performance. Critics can describe what they have seen and consult video recordings, and playgoers can remember certain moments in a play, but no one can remain in touch with the reality of a performance taking place before an audience: that experience is over once and for all at the end of the show. So although a book that introduces readers to theatre must look at past triumphs, it must also turn away from them and lead its readers to explore the theatre that they can see for themselves today, and to imagine new theatres not yet in existence.

The text falls into two halves. The first part is drawn from one person's experience and ideas and, being as short and as clear as possible, gives a wide view of theatre and how it is created. The second half is quite different in that it brings together a number of specialists to speak for themselves. Here actors, dramatists, directors, and designers give individual accounts of what they do and how they do it: for example, a manager explains how his theatre is run, and a finance director supplies figures to show how much it all costs and how it is paid for. This part of the book gives a sense of the personal and very particular involvement that is common to all theatrical work. Because theatre is such a complicated art form, these accounts are often very detailed and not always easy to understand at first reading, but with a little patience, readers should be able to explore a wide range of the fascinating activities that go into making a theatre production. Illustrations throughout the book are intended to work in much the same way; with careful study, they will reveal some of the effects achieved in particular productions, insofar as still photographs can capture them.

Among the different voices and different kinds of evidence offered, readers are invited to make their own way and find material to feed their own particular interests. Whatever their areas of study, readers should find some treatment of their special interests, as well as suggestions for further lines of inquiry. Theatre is made by a collaboration between people with very different skills and understandings, and therefore many voices and various elements of theatre making have been brought together here.

At intervals, suggestions are made about how readers might investigate further for themselves, outside of class or workshop, and so gain firsthand knowledge of what is described in the text. These notes are usually placed at the end of a section, but sometimes the text is interrupted to give readers an opportunity to experience the consequences of a point that has been made or to show alternative views. Often these paragraphs ask readers to visit a theatre, but they do not prescribe seeing any particular play and very seldom dictate what kind of play should be seen. Actual performance before an audience is the crucial experience to be explored, whether the actors are accomplished professionals or beginning students, whether the plays are serious or funny, innovative or very traditional. Obviously the better the production of its kind, the better will be the audience's experience and the more a student can benefit from it.

I

What Is Theatre?

1

Plays on Offer: A selection of theatre programs.

The Power of the Theatre

Before looking at the different parts that together make up a performance in the theatre, we will take a much wider view and ask what theatre does for an audience, what it achieves when it functions fully. Each part has to be viewed in this larger context because here will be found its justification and the measure for success. At the same time beginning with a larger view helps to define theatre over against other arts and entertainments. We will examine five aspects of the power of theatre.

Theatre Creates a Social Occasion

The next time you go to a theatre, arrive early and stand in the main lobby for five or ten minutes watching the people come in. Each of them has paid money and given his or her time to come and see the same play, but each one brings his or her own concerns along with them, thoughts that no one else will experience in exactly the same way. You can see that in their faces and in how they walk and stand around. They look at different things: toward the door, as if waiting for someone else to arrive; at pictures or posters on the walls, as if they had nothing better to do; at someone else's clothes. Some stare into the distance. They speak in very different voices, and about many different things. Some people talk a lot and others are silent, but in most people you will see a slight relaxation as they enter from outside: they have arrived, with time to spare and at the right place.

When the bell rings announcing five minutes before the play begins, you sense a change; you can hear a new sound and feel a new rhythm. People settle into their seats and, when the auditorium lights begin to dim and go out, silence and stillness herald the moment for which everyone is waiting, when the curtain will rise or an actor will walk into view. Even after I have seen a production several times, having worked on it for many weeks in rehearsal, this moment never fails to sharpen my attention. I forget the audience, their concerns and my own concerns, and wait for what is about to happen onstage, and everyone else responds in much the same way.

The difference between the intermingling individuals in the foyer and the concentrated and sometimes excited audience as the play begins is some measure of the hold theatre can have on us and of its power to create a shared experience. At

Epidaurus late on a summer afternoon, in a grand and solemn landscape some hours' journey by sea or road from Athens, an audience of eighteen thousand will sit waiting for a performance to begin in a vast open-air theatre. During the day they have journeyed through the countryside by motor coach, car, cart, or bicycle, or on foot. Some have camped on the hillside within sight of the theatre and then filed slowly along dusty paths and climbed steep banks of seats to find places high up, perhaps a hundred feet from the stage. On such occasions the silence before the play begins is profoundly impressive. One feels that the performance could become a great corporate act of affirmation and a release feelings never recognized before.

In our own far smaller theatres, the attention that each member of an audience shares can be more intense, more sharp or nervous. It can be intimate and warm, perhaps even cozy. The size of the theatre, where it is in town or in the country, its design and furnishings, the music playing before the curtain rises, the expectations of the audience—all are factors that control the kind of response that is shared in the first moment of concentration. What happens afterward the play will control: as it submits to the power of the theatre, the audience is in the hands of the actors and of everyone else who has worked on the production. Perhaps only one thing is certain about what happens next: it will be unlike anything one has experienced when one is alone.

When watching a theatrical performance, many individuals share the same experience within the same period of time, in close contact with each other, and afterward some of them may talk together about the experience. In this, theatre differs from literature or painting where one reads or sees for oneself and with few or no companions; theatre is more like music or film. One person cannot easily protest outloud against the performance of a play, or say anything at all in more than a whisper or an instinctive cry. Although some theatres encourage audiences to respond vocally and actively, when a production is good and grips attention, no one coughs or fidgets because everyone is sharing in the play. We can all be held captive by a play in performance, and, as a member of a crowd, an individual may behave in unusual ways. Without reserve or embarrassment, one person may weep at something said or done onstage, something that is not given a passing thought outside the theatre. On the other hand, an entire audience may become helpless with infectious laughter or relax together in simple happiness. Long ago St. Augustine said that theatre was like the plague: it could be caught so easily.

A reader of a novel or a poem is always able to disengage from the printed sequence of narrative or description and so escape into his or her own thoughts, but theatre is not private or "intellectual" in that way. An audience's attention is drawn forward all the time by what is happening onstage; if something is missed, there is no turning back to look it up on the printed page. This means that, unlike prose narrative, a good play can state the obvious without losing the attention of the audience, and can call upon common and basic responses without fear that they will be refused. It speaks to individuals who sit among other individuals and whose thoughts and feelings are strengthened by being shared. The difference is like that between listening to a recording in the privacy of your own room and listening to what are basically the same sounds by the same band when you are part of an enthusiastic crowd taking pleasure in the music almost as if it has taken possession of you.

A dramatist once told me that he had written a final line for his play that he had always thought very funny, right up to when the play was performed. In rehearsals its effect was a little uncertain, sometimes eliciting laughs from the few people who were watching. Then, to everyone's surprise, when it was played to a full and paying audience, the line was received in chilling silence as those very same words seemed to cut deep into the hearers' minds. Working alone on the script and sitting in at rehearsals, the author did not take into account the cumulative effects of performance and of a large number of people hearing those words together for the first time. More often the opposite is true, and at previews and first nights actors find that they have to fight against the audience's laughter, which they had in no way expected and which they now find to be destructive of the principal effects they are trying to achieve. Performance gives rise to a shared experience that goes beyond what any one person onstage or in the audience could have imagined or experienced alone.

Going to the theatre on opening night is rather like going to a party, or like giving one. The host may have little idea beforehand of how the guests will enjoy themselves, who will get along with whom, or what mood anyone is in. The guests know even less, because they have little idea of who will be there or what has been arranged for them to eat and drink, to hear, and to watch. They may have some general expectations about all these things, but no one can know beforehand exactly how host and guests will play their different parts. One of the signs of a good party is that afterward everyone wonders how it all happened and spends a good deal of time talking about it. Good theatre is very much like that.

Comparisons with other entertainments can help us to understand what happens in a theatre and nowhere else. At first it may seem to theatre's disadvantage that a play cannot be seen anywhere and at any time as a film can. But a theatre audience won't be looking at just one copy of the production sent from far afield and distributed in exactly the same form to millions of people around the world. A theatre production is never "fixed" once and for all but will be made all over again at every performance and will be slightly different each time a new audience enters the theatre and shares what is happening onstage. Unlike a film, a stage production will not be exactly the same for every audience. Often it will have been made in the town in which it is performed and within the last very few weeks, so it is able to reflect its audience's particular mind-sets and concerns. Instinctively it will change overnight if some national disaster or celebration has occurred. Theatre is more local and topical, and more responsive to its audiences, than the cinema can ever be: it provides a meeting between play and spectators, a lively public occasion.

Even very old plays can be made immediately relevant to their audience. A production of Shakespeare's *Hamlet* was performed for ten years in Moscow from 1971 to 1980, as if it had been written to depict that very time in Russia's history. In the title role of the production by Yuri Lyubimov at the Taganka Theatre was Vladimir Vysotsky, an actor who was also a singer and lyricist. His alienation from the repressive government of the day had made him a popular icon and symbol of political protest, so as Shakespeare's prince he was able to show very clearly to his audiences, in terms they immediately recognized, that an honest death was a better choice than a tortured life under oppression.

Theatre can be a social art form, a lively and powerful means of sharing ideas with thousands of people, and as a result it has been subjected to severe political censorship in certain places and at certain times. In Shakespeare's day several play-wrights, including Ben Jonson (1572-1637) and George Chapman (*ca.* 1560-1634), were put in prison for writing a play that had gotten past the official censor only to be judged unacceptable in performance. Even though it was a comedy, it still got its authors and acting company into trouble. From well before that day right down to the present time, plays have been written that have never been allowed to be performed. At the end of the twentieth century, state censorship, which was once the rule in Europe and elsewhere, is much less common, but it still exists, notably in some parts of Africa and in China. In Britain, theatre censorship was in operation until 1968; in South Korea until 1988.

Because theatre provides an occasion for a social gathering, performances that demonstrate unpalatable truths in the flesh can awaken common responses among large numbers of people. For example, Clifford Odet's *Waiting for Lefty* (1935), about a strike of New York taxi drivers, had members of its audience calling out in support of union solidarity. For some governments and other vested interests, the-atre spells trouble and needs to be controlled.

Today in the United States and other European nations, the political inten-tions of many theatres are limited to what is called "raising consciousness" about certain issues, rather than active campaigning for political action. Some compa-nies make a point of claiming that they have no political agenda so that they can attract public funding, yet few of these groups are unaware of their social role as educators and their opportunity to instigate debate about the needs and future of a rapidly changing society. In the United States every major city has at least one small theatre dedicated to African-American, Hispanic, Asian, or Native Ameri-can traditions. Similarly there are gay and lesbian theatres, theatres for children, senior citizens, or the deaf or blind, and for many other groups of people whose conditions of life are not shared by everyone else. These theatres either speak to special audiences about matters of mutual concern or make special causes and special pleasures more evident than before to audiences drawn from all parts of society.

On every side we can see evidence of the theatre's power to create a social occasion and speak directly to many people. To sit in the invariably crowded the-atres of Russia under Stalin, or of Czechoslovakia, Poland, and other Eastern European states under the Russian occupation, was an amazing experience. Despite censorship and the presence of the secret police, the theatre had a sense of common commitment that was contagious, giving the people more hope of free-dom from oppression than any other public medium on the far side of the Iron Curtain. In East Berlin, just before the Wall was pulled down in 1989, the huge public meetings that turned protest into a new force for change were organized by theatre workers who had taken the lead in exposing the inequities of state control and thus gained credibility as representatives of freedom throughout the city. You can read about this in the *Oxford Illustrated History of Theatre* (Oxford University Press).When the occupying forces left Prague in the same year, the nation chose as its new president Václav Havel, a dissident playwright whose work in theatre and whose courage while under arrest had already won for him the nation's trust and respect.

Theatre has other social roles. It can also reinforce the ideas of the powerful. In the seventeenth century, King Louis XIV of France gave special protection to

Molière, the most popular writer of comedies in his time, and in return the play-wright provided magnificent spectacles glorifying the wealth and wisdom of the monarch; he also incurred frequent criticism, his work provoking some extraordinary controversies. At all times some plays will flatter privileged audiences by showing how superior they are in lifestyle or intelligence: Nöel Coward's comedies in the 1930s and Neil Simon's in the 1960s are examples of this, flattering their well-off audiences by the elegance or wit of the play's characters, drawn from much the same sections of society. Other plays raise issues without clearly supporting either side of an argument. Such is David Mamet's *Oleanna* (1993), which depicts a case of indictable sexual harassment in such a way that both parties have received vociferous support from audiences and equally strong denunciation, according to who was in the audience and the finer points of particular stage performances.

Other plays transport entire audiences away from everyday concerns and into enjoyable and exotic fantasies by using sensational stage spectacle and irresistible music and sound. Productions of *The Phantom of the Opera*, *Cats*, and other "megamusicals" play for year after year in the biggest theatres of London and New York and are duplicated in almost every major city around the world.

Even when not successful in the usual senses of that word, theatrical productions are social occasions. In small theatres a few actors may perform a play that makes impossible demands on themselves and on their audiences, and then, in a nearly empty auditorium, the scattered members of the audience will not be able to lose themselves in the play and will, at best, sense the underlying strain felt by the actors; in such cases a shared response is very difficult to provoke and sustain, but its very absence is part of the theatre experience. When an audience is small because the play and performance require acceptance of innovative effects and an unusual degree of attention, theatregoing can provide members of the audience and the players with an extraordinary sense of mutual achievement. On such an evening, a small audience of a dozen or so people scattered in different parts of a small theatre may, in the end, find themselves immensely moved, perhaps as much by their own efforts as by the play itself. They may stay behind to applaud the skill and imagination of everyone concerned, as loudly and for as long as they can manage. Theatre is seldom for long an introverted or isolated experience.

When a play fails to win any kind of trust from its audience, the lack of a shared response can bring an unforgettable pain to the actors, who feel exposed and rejected. The experience is not so serious for the audience, but its members will feel uncomfortable and cheated. On such occasions one of the distinctive powers of theatre has been lost.

Read a play and consider how it might affect you. What would you most dislike? What would you most like? Then think of a few other people you know and consider what their reactions would be. If possible, after reading the play, see it in performance and then consider how your attitudes to it have changed, and why. Alternatively, take a few moments to watch two or three other members of the audience before, during, and after the performance of any play: Do their attitudes to the performance seem to change as yours do, or do they change in some other way? Why do you think this happened?

Theatre Holds a Mirror Up to Nature

The power of the theatre to be lifelike is easier to understand, even if it is commonly misunderstood. What happens onstage can look so very like what happens outside the theatre, in the ordinary lives of all of us, that the whole business can seem easy, as if it were something anyone could do. But convincing imitation is not easy, especially when what is shown has to draw an audience and sustain its attention.

Shakespeare had Hamlet say that the "purpose of playing" was,

> to hold as 'twere the mirror up to nature: to show virtue her own feature, scorn her own image, and the very age and body of the time his form and pressure.
>
> *Hamlet*, III, ii

What Hamlet expected the "mirror" of the stage to show was not an ordinary reflection, but one that revealed to an audience the truth about themselves: this is a magic mirror, and not always a flattering one. Hamlet had good reasons for wanting the reflection to play these particular moral and political tricks, but we should remember that it can do other tricks just as well—it can make us laugh or make us happy as well as cause us to think or grieve. The mirror of the stage reflects the real world so that it looks the same, but is in fact different—more meaningful, more enjoyable, more inspiring.

The mirror and its reflections work for an audience because what happens onstage may not only *look* real but also, in some respects, actually *is* real. A play uses the same elements as life itself: onstage there are real men, women, and children; there is talk, noise, and silence; light and darkness; movement and stillness. What is seen in the mirror may be unlikely or immediately exciting, but it will always be made of the same materials as those found in reality, and it is experienced using the same kind of consciousness: it is sensed by every means we use in lived experience. There is nothing in our world—what we experience by being alive—that cannot be placed on a stage.

No other art form can make use of anything and everything. Poetry can create an imaginary world, where the grass is greener or the sun shines more brightly, or human beings are more sensitive or passionate than in ordinary life, and it can make us see all this in our mind's eye. But poetry cannot *produce* any of this, make it actually appear before us. Arguably the world that is shown onstage can never be quite so strange or pleasurable as that evoked by poetry, but it will always be more tangible: visible, audible, almost touchable. Theatre's imitation of life is also practicable: one element cannot be allowed to develop at the expense of all the others, as in a poem, where we may concentrate attention on the brilliance of the sky or the loneliness of the poet, forgetting everything else. What we see in the theatre has natural consequences: these people breathe, their tears are wet, and their bodies shake with laughter.

Dramatists and directors can cheat by being selective in what they show us in the mirror—and sometimes they cheat a great deal—but they cannot cheat totally. If a person onstage is required to be mentally alert and excited—perhaps a scientist has just discovered a cure that will save tens of thousands of lives—that person must also show some emotional and physical reactions: the need to speak, to cry out, to move in keeping with the quickness of thought, to grasp hold of something, or perhaps to keep very still in order to contain and control a great surge of surprise and joy. The actor would be bound to express both the emotion *and* the reaction to it. ("Each action has an equal and opposite reaction" is a rule for performance, as well as for physics.) Theatre holds a mirror up to the life we live because it communicates through more than words, or music, or visual signs; its expression involves human actors who are as complicated as we are and cannot simplify or distort their performances beyond a certain point. Exactly how lifelike they are will depend on their skill and the material supplied by dramatist and director. One of the reasons we keep looking in the reflection of our lives on the stage is because this basic authenticity of means and material can communicate deeply human messages.

Usually the actor who shows us images of ourselves is seen within a setting, or "scene," chosen by a dramatist. Part of that environment is created by stage designers and technicians, but the more important part of what is seen onstage is created by the director and actors: in performance all actors onstage interact with each other, and to everything else that happens, and it is this interplay that makes evident the human interest of a play. The image in the mirror changes constantly as the characters in the play take up new relationships that offer ever new revelations of purpose and consequence. Notice that Hamlet says that an audience is shown "both form and pressure": *pressure* implies force, and *force* involves energy composed of weight and movement in time, and in such a way the dynamics of life are represented onstage. This is a prime reason for theatre's truth and power. Jean-Paul Sartre (1905-1980), the French philosopher and playwright, said in a lecture that if you want to know what theatre is,

> you must ask youself what an act is, because theatre represents the act and can represent nothing but the act. Sculpture represents the form of the body, theatre represents the act of the body. And consequently, what we want to rediscover when we go to the theatre is naturally ourselves, not ourselves as we are, more or less sentimental or more or less proud of our youth or our beauty, but ourselves as we act and as we work and as we encounter difficulties and as we are [people] who obey the rules . . . governing these actions.
>
> *Sartre on Theater*

Cinema provides a useful contrast. At first sight we might consider a film to be more lifelike than a play. Certainly it can be more accurate or complete in reproducing the actual setting of a story. Its action can take place where it naturally should, on top of a mountain, in any of the world's capital cities, or in any of its deserts. The people shown in a film may be ordinary people doing what they do in real life, and not "characters" created by actors who have been trained to simplify and enlarge certain aspects of behavior. The filmmaker can ensure that the weather supplies rain or shine, snow or baking heat. But a film shows nothing that is essentially or palpably "there": everything onscreen has only two dimensions, not three, and that is not the only difference. The distinguishing mark of cinema is the use of a camera: a film shows nothing but what the camera has seen and recorded, and it shows everything in the way the camera has seen it. At one moment a single face can fill the screen and at the next a panorama of the whole earth seen from outer space while the face, in an instant, has ceased to have any presence at all. The camera can alter the scale of anything at the director's will. The film crew can take its own time, shooting a two-hour film over the course of three months or three years, and seldom in the sequence in which the audience views it. More than this, any accident can be edited out of existence in the cutting room—any reaction from actor, dog, or machine that is not to the taste of the director. In these ways, the chosen sequence of fixed and edited images that cinema supplies is *not* reality— what is seen is a collection of two-dimensional, momentary, and independent "shots" of parts of reality. In contrast, theatre has to show all that is actually there onstage, and in one consecutive performance.

In the theatre, once a performance starts, the audience will see everything when it happens and how it happens. Although playgoers may be led to imagine that the central character has more than ordinary strength, intelligence, good looks, or good fortune, the actor who plays this role will remain basically the same throughout the performance, and whatever happens onstage will never be without some effect on the actor. Although disguised in several different ways, the actor's body will remain identical under the disguises, modified only in ways that are humanly possible. Other actors onstage in the same story will also be constant in the essentials, and the central performance will build through contact with them and with the particular audience that is watching the play on each particular night. Although the scene may change many times in the course of the play, the stage space and its relation to the audience remains constant, so the scale of the hero in regard to the surrounding world will remain basically the same too, despite temporary illusionistic effects. What may seem to be limitations of theatre in comparison with what is possible in cinema are in fact the sources of one of its great powers: these elements of theatre ensure that the mirror held up to nature represents inevitably and directly the basic facts of human life and that what is seen has, at this level, an undeniable kind of truth.

One way of understanding the essential reality of what is seen in the "mirror" of the stage is to compare watching a football game on TV with seeing it in the stadium as it is being played. While you are in front of your TV, you can see the ball at almost any time, so that you seem to be at the right place at the right time to see each exciting moment of the game; watching the screen, you have a trouble-free close-up or a wide view of the whole field, whichever seems appropriate to the program maker. When you are actually present in the stadium itself, you may miss a lot of the action, and, at times, you may have to strain to see, but then, at certain moments, everything becomes particularly vivid just because the play is close to where you are sitting or standing. You see it all, and hear it all, from your own point of view and it is up to you to see as much of the game as you can. As you share the excitement of tens of thousands of other spectators, you are actually there, and so is the game; this is how you will remember it. You can follow whichever player you wish and make your own speculations about the outcome. You are in charge as you watch the game, which is totally present before you. You are also more at its mercy than you would be were you at home in front of the TV.

When you go to the theatre, it is like being present at a game: neither you nor anyone else knows exactly what you will see. During the last moments of the play, the leading actor may show the effects of performing a long role: hair may fall over eyes, the face may be tired and yet animated; clothes are no longer neat; movements are looser, freer, more unhesitating; perhaps makeup has run and perhaps you notice this, or perhaps you do not. Compare this to how the hero or heroine appears at the end of a film: clothes and hair have been disordered just an acceptable amount, but the face is not obscured, and the whole effect has been carefully arranged and expertly processed. The scene has been composed and shot for its own sake; the actor was not taking chances, and nor will you, at the end of two consecutive hours of performance. The movie actor and director can make careful choices, and then the best of several attempts to carry them out will be chosen and perhaps altered by the editor before being printed in the final copy. The central performance is not much influenced by other actors, and the finished product is not subject to the particular accidents of the one night when you happen to see it. Compared with this, an image in the mirror of the stage is more unready and raw, and a more corporate effort shared between many differently skilled persons: in these respects too, theatre is much more like life than film is.

> *Choose a very short scene from a play you have read and read it aloud—supplying what you can of the necessary movements, thoughts, and feelings of the character. Observe how your understanding of the words changes as you add lifelike actions while reading.*

Theatre Provides a Progressive Experience

A play usually tells a story, but it need not do so. The one essential factor is development. During any performance what is onstage will change, and the audience experiences the action in the sequence in which it occurs. That may seem obvious, but its consequences during a performance need to be carefully considered.

The interest of an audience must be caught and its expectation aroused. In order for the performance to hold an audience's attention for two or three hours, that expectation has to be occasionally disappointed and fresh interest supplied. Finally, the audience must know that the drama has ended, and to effect this convincingly the various interests that have been raised must be satisfied in some way or other: there has to be a completed progression.

A painter can reveal his finished work in a moment, and although it may take a viewer considerable time to appreciate all that is in the painting, the sequence of understanding and appreciation is not within the artist's control. A novelist or poet gives his or her readers a progressive experience as they make their way though the contents of a book or poem, and this is especially true when a story is being told, but neither poet nor novelist can control the speed with which readers progress through the work or be sure that readers' attention is held without interruption. In contrast with these other artists, a dramatist does control the progress of events in real time and can alter the apparent pace at which time passes for his or her audience.

Narrative, conflict, argument, tension, climax, and development are the very stuff of dramatic energy: a play shows what *happens*, rather than what *is*. It is an art form appropriate to a civilization that is aware of change, inevitable change due to forces within society or the environment, or unexpected change brought about through the will and activity of individuals. Drama is a contemplative art, interested in how things are at any one moment, when the still moment of appreciation is presented as a culmination of active participation in events, or as a contrast to ongoing activity, or when one state of mind succeeds another. These possibilities have rarely been exploited without some other interest being present to hold the audience's attention, but such explorations of the moment can provide the most acutely sensitive of theatre experiences.

Increased awareness is one element in our enjoyment of every considerable play. An audience that is progressively involved with what happens to individual characters onstage may come to see those characters with a fuller sharing of their experience or a greater sympathy for the inner workings of their minds. In other plays the audience is encouraged to view the whole stage picture with an increasingly sharp awareness of the forces responsible for its composition and the nature of the changes it undergoes. In such plays the presentation of social groups is more significant than the portrayal of individual characters.

The progressive experience provided by theatre is not easy to understand at first, and the cumulative effect in any one play is hard to grasp until one has actually seen it performed. A few examples will show the different ways in which such an experience has been achieved.

At the end of Anton Chekhov's *Three Sisters* (1901) no single member of the cast and no single story brings the play to a conclusion: instead during the last scene each of the fourteen characters commands the audience's attention in turn. From the succession of these moments the audience gains a new understanding of why they all have come to be what they are; the focus has been widened to show the nature of an entire family of individuals and of the society in which it lives.

At the end of Samuel Beckett's *Waiting for Godot* (1953), the two characters who have been onstage almost throughout the play are alone on stage and say to each other: "Well? Shall we go?" and "Yes, let's go." At that point only stage directions follow: *"They do not move."* and *"CURTAIN."* This exactly repeats the end of the play's first act, except that the two speeches were differently assigned there. At the end of the play neither character has achieved a new ability to understand and speak of their situation; it is the audience's awareness that has progressed. The final moment reveals how little has changed and how deeply these two men are enmeshed in a common way of thinking and feeling.

At the end of Arthur Miller's *Death of a Salesman* (1949), Willy Loman's wife puts into words the consequences and meaning of his death. The audience sees no more of him, but with this speech Miller has raised in the audience's mind the wider consequences of Willy Loman's death, and he has also shown some of its effect on another character's life.

None of these endings shows in direct terms what happens at the end of one particular story. The plays have provided the audience with an experience during which understanding and sympathy have been progressively developed, and their conclusions take this process to a final reckoning. The plays have encouraged questions about why these events have occurred and what might have altered the course of events.

Telling a story can be a bait to catch the fish of whatever argument, theme, or view of the world the dramatist wants to present. Usually, however, a play involves much more than that, because drawing the audience through a sequence of events in a performance is a way of programming its consciousness. As a story is told, innumerable small entries of new material build up playgoers' capacity to respond and subsequently to understand, creating in them a consciousness that was not present at the start of the play. The audience then leaves the theatre with a heightened perception, as well as a satisfied curiosity and a new experience.

Any good play provides a completed whole to which the audience reacts. Patterns of sound and action, as they are repeated, varied, and resolved, play their part in building the experience the performance offers. Much of this effect is subliminal and far from easy to grasp, even after a performance is complete. Nevertheless the sense of progression and then of completion is often very powerful, as at the end of a symphony or a dance. A sense of triumph and pleasure can accompany the conclusion of a play, even when the conclusion involves desperate or violent events; a sense of stillness and peaceful acceptance can arise at the end of the most riotous comedy.

> *When seeing a play, write down a few one-line comments on two of the main characters at the time of the first intermission. Do the same again at the end of the play. Then observe how your ideas about the characters have changed. In a good play, the difference can be considerable and yet seem inevitable.*
>
> *Note how this exercise is different from retelling the play's story.*

Theatre Can Make Use of Words

Theatre can work without words, by use of spectacle, dance, or mime (silent and expressive actions), but many of the most successful plays use words marvelously. The greatest plays are known centuries after their first performances only through the evidence of a printed text which can record little more than what was spoken: it is this that provides sufficient material to rework the plays and bring them back to new life on the stage. Words are a vital and powerful element of theatre.

Yet the words as they appear on a page do not demonstrate their theatrical power to the fullest. Many of the elements of theatre already discussed are only hinted at in the *book of the play*, and readers need patience to acquire the skill for reading a text so that the drama implicit in the printed record comes alive in their imagination. The words need to become part of an image of living people, and in this "performance" the meanings of words may change and their effect be less predetermined.

Consider the many ways in which the simple words "Good morning" can be spoken: they can send a message that is either confident or tentative; they can suggest friendship or dependence, or servility even; they can be empty or full of meaning, ironic or directly descriptive. They may be spoken quickly or slowly, loudly or quietly, in a high or low pitch, and in each manner the effect of these words is different. The various people you meet in the morning will say these two words differently, and in so doing they will signify very different meanings. Perhaps they use other words, such as "Hi!" or "Hello!" which are like "Good morning" in meaning but significantly different in sound and implication. You, yourself, without taking particular thought, will say the two words differently depending on your mood or to whom you are speaking.

> *Tomorrow morning experiment by consciously trying a louder voice, a quicker tempo, or a higher pitch each time that you say "Good morning." You will notice that these simple adjustments will alter the effect of the words and the ways in which they are*

received. On a very small scale, you will have explored how words can take on different meanings on the stage.

A dramatist does not simply write down sentences as they are required to tell the story or to set out the argument of a play; instead he or she will have heard them spoken in the silence of his or her own mind, colored by the spoken voice appropriate to each character and influenced by the context of each momentary situation. Many dramatists say that they act out all their characters to their own satisfaction as they write. More than this, a dramatist knows that the words written down must be appropriate to the character's physical bearing, gesture, appearance, nervous tension, state of mind, position onstage, and sense of the ongoing dramatic situation, and that the choice of words must do as much as possible to suggest all this to the actor. A good dramatist imagines everything that happens onstage and provides words that will both fit in with all of this complex phenomena and help to define it, first for the actor and then for the audience. This is a prime reason why writing good plays is so very difficult and why, when care is taken by the playwright, words carry a more than usual definition of each person's involvement in the drama.

The definition given by strong and simple words is a great power in the theatre, for however complicated a particular situation, speech can clarify it and draw it forward. A single sentence, such as "I know who killed him," or "I love you," or "Look behind you," can change the effect of almost everything else that is happening: it can explain in a moment what had long been confusing or show who is in charge and who is helpless. Nothing onstage has such devastating power: to kiss or to kill, or to fall over, or to laugh or weep seldom *explains* as much or brings to the audience such a quick and efficient rush of understanding. Words are never enough to make a play, and by themselves they achieve comparatively little in the theatre, but in the fully developed staging of a story, a single word is sometimes enough to reveal an essential fact or to change everything.

Just before the outbreak of the Second World War, Oskar Wälterlin, a famous opera director, escaped the Nazis and went to neighboring Switzerland, where he took charge of a theatre in Zurich that produced plays and not operas. He explained in an interview that his sense of the political situation in Europe had led him to abandon his previous line of work:

> Opera [had] became a pointless distraction, artistry without root and aim. . . . I wanted to act and comment, if only through images and parables . . . and for that it needed the spoken word of drama.
>
> trans. Wilhelm Hortmann

A dramatist cannot make a play with words alone—good poets may be bad dramatists and often are—but in a play words can be used forcefully and brilliantly. Theatre is different from the cinema in this respect, because if the images that make up a film are to appear real to a spectator, the actors cannot use many words: the visible signs of sufficient breathing and good enunciation look ridiculous and distracting in enlarged close-up photography. In the huge visual images of film, saying little is very often more effective than saying a great deal. Besides, the kind of attention needed to respond to the ever-changing images is very different from what is needed for responding to many, subtle, or complicated words.

Figure A.1 The ancient theatre at Epidaurus, Greece. (Photograph courtesy of the Greek Tourist Board.)

Figure A.2 Twentieth-century theatre at Calgary, Alberta. The set was designed by Warren Carrie for the Albert Theatre Projects' production of Candide, directed by D. Michael Dobbin in the Martha Cohen Theatre, Calgary Centre for the Performing Arts, 1990. (Photograph by Trudie Lee; courtesy of Alberta Theatre Projects.)

Figure A.3 Contemporary Shakespeare: *Romeo and Juliet*, directed by Michael Bogdanov and designed by Chris Dyer, for the Royal Shakespeare Company, 1986. (Photograph © Joe Cocks Studio Collection, from the Shakespeare Centre Library, Stratford-upon-Avon.)

Figure A.4 Stage design for David Mamet's *American Buffalo*; sketch by Majorie Bradley Kellogg for the production at Long Wharf Theatre, New Haven, Connecticut, and on Broadway. (Reproduced by permission of the artist.)

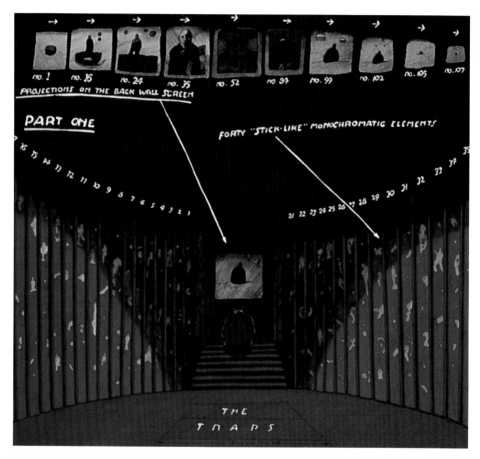

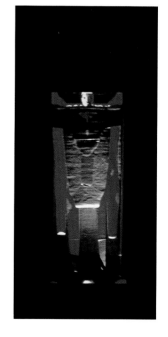

Figures A.5, A.6, A.7 *The Eyes.* A wordless play: designed and devised by Jan Swaka in the United States, with images electronically choreographed by Marc I. Rosenthal; first performed at the Arts Festival, Mito, Japan, 1993. (Photographs by Marc I. Rosenthal; courtesy of Jan Swaka.)

All the sensitivity and opulence of verbal poetry may be exploited by a dramatist, and the sharpness and excitement of verbal wit, the power of rhetoric, the fascination of storytelling and delicate description, the relentlessness of argument, the impressiveness of a thorough recounting of facts or statistics: nothing acceptable on the printed page is forbidden to drama.

By manipulating words, a dramatist can focus an audience's attention on exactly that element in a play that is important at any one moment. Usually the audience looks at whoever is speaking, so if one character dominates the talk, that person usually dominates the stage. Cunning variations on this technique have their own special effectiveness, as, for example, when the speaker is waiting for some action elsewhere on the stage and so directs the audience to look over there, or when his or her words are controlled by some silent figure at some distance away. A famous example of this second device occurs when Hamlet stands silently by while Claudius explains to everyone the cause for celebrating his wedding with Hamlet's mother. Normally the speaker dominates, but when the lead in stage dialogue passes constantly from one character to another, we can be sure that the dramatist wants to focus our attention on conflicting attitudes and argument, rather than on the development of a single point of view; in such instances the playwright probably wants the audience to be interested in theme rather than individual characters.

Occasionally what is said draws attention to what is not said. When a dominant speaker pauses and then continues as if not sure of what to say—perhaps his or her phrases are only half finished—the audience's interest is aroused about whatever silent thoughts have preceded speech or interrupted speech. If a character suddenly changes the mood or subject of talk and this is not caused by any obvious outside influence, or if his or her speech becomes agitated beyond the apparent occasion for it, the audience will again become interested in hidden thoughts and feelings, concerns that have not been expressed directly in words. In these cases the focus is said to be *subtextual*. In quite the opposite way, something said by a minor character can take attention away from the dominant figures and so direct attention to what they have not been saying. The clarity that words can have provides them, somewhat paradoxically, with the power to undermine the authority of other less stable words and their apparent meanings.

Speech is also important in a music sense, its sound being constantly changed by variations of tempo, pitch, and rhythm; this means that speech can be irresistibly musical. Because nothing is said or done to draw attention to this musical effect, playgoers are influenced without being aware, while their attention is being given elsewhere to explicit thought, feeling, or action. While words that make up a play seem devised solely to express the thoughts of characters, a verbally skillful dramatist will also give words a variable beat or rhythm, and varying textures of sound, all creating an effect on the audience's feelings and responsiveness. This hidden power of dialogue is most potent when the text is written in verse, but by varying the weight and balance of phrases and by repeating patterns of words, very similar results can be achieved with prose.

Read a play before going to see it, and make a note of two or three very short speeches that you do not quite understand. While viewing the performance, look out for the use made of these speeches when they are delivered. Alternatively, memorize a speech of five to ten lines, and while at the theatre look out for what the actor does while speaking these lines. In either case, have the words gained new meaning through this exercise?

Theatre Is Fantastic

Saying that theatre is fantastic is quite the opposite of saying that theatre "holds the mirror up to nature," yet the former is often equally true. As well as showing lives like our own and speaking our language, theatre shows us a world that never was. Like a lunatic or excited lover, and like many other kinds of artists, a dramatist can imagine all sorts of strange fictions, but what the dramatist can do and the others cannot is to transfer this fantasy into the "real" medium of theatre where an audience can experience these dreams as if they were actually happening. Many tricks can be used to represent onstage what a dramatist wants the audience to believe. With a good performance to help, good writing can almost compel the audience to believe in very unlikely fictions.

There should be a basic truth in any play, but always there will also be a basic falsity or pretense, because, in reality, the events represented in performance could not take place there and then, within that actual space and at that actual time. This contradiction is not a limitation; rather it is a springboard: the alert attention provoked by the unreal concentration of effect encourages the heightened and confident awareness that is essential for imaginative belief. By such means, theatre can make even dreams seem real.

Seldom does a play show anything exactly as it happens in ordinary life; in essential ways a play is like life, but it is also more than life—more funny, expert, beautiful, heroic, communicative; more apt and eloquent, more passionate, more considered, more amazing. Even when presenting boredom, a play can give a more crushing and more articulate sense of its hopelessness than we would ever experience in life; through subtle manipulation of tempo and rhythm, for example, the weight of boredom can be established quickly and sharply, so that the representation of boredom is *not* boring. Theatre heightens our response because it can enlarge and clarify any aspect of life. Because of this difference from life, theatre can always be entertaining: its infidelity is one of its essential powers.

Ignoring the limitations of ordinary life, theatre can present a fantastic version of life. Eric Overmyer's *On the Verge* (1986) shows three very lifelike women who climb a cliff face, change into elaborate evening dress while in the middle of the jungle, cross an ice field, and then fall into space only to recover seconds afterward; the story happens both in the nineteenth century and in the future, and at many different times in between. In Richard Nelson's *Sensibility and Sense* (1989), the three leading characters are present onstage in their early seventies and also, simultaneously, in their early twenties. As played by six actors, these three people are doubly visible to the audience but not to each other. This play is fantastic, but the events portrayed are not; throughout they bear a remarkable likeness to actual happenings.

The dramatist's handling of events in a play is often extraordinarily apt, unusual, or thought provoking, even when in other respects what happens is true to life. In Chekhov's *Three Sisters* (1901), one character likens himself to a certain

Figure 1.1 Fantasy onstage: surrounded by surrealistic jungle creatures, Cictorian time travelers take their bearings in Eric Overmyer's *On the Verge or the Geography of Yearning* at Center Stage, Baltimore, 1985. (Photograph by Richard Anderson; courtesy of Center Stage.)

dead tree, and then in the next moment the woman who is soon to be his sister-in-law says that she is going to have that very tree cut down. Improbable coincidences of this kind are frequent in theatre: the witches in Shakespeare's *Macbeth* say that Macbeth is to be Thane of Cawdor moments before messengers come from the king announcing that he has just been awarded that title. Almost anything a dramatist wants to happen can be given the illusion of happening on the stage, and what is most improbable is often that part of the play that the author cares most about and the source of the play's entertainment value.

The chief agent in realizing the dramatist's vision is the actor. Skilled at performing prodigious feats of speech and action, and equally skilled at controlling what looks like ordinary behavior, a company of actors fulfills the unusual demands of each play during the two or three hours of performance. They set their imaginations to work in harmony with the dramatist's, as do the designers and technicians, and the theatre manager who brings all the necessary objects and people together, and the director, who is in charge of everyone and makes final decisions about how things must be done. Everyone working in the theatre collaborates in creating something as complicated as life, yet something that could exist nowhere else; it is an illusionary magic.

> *Make a list of what is improbable or impossible in a play that you have read, and ask yourself why the dramatist has invented these incidents. What do these elements have to do with your enjoyment and understanding of the play?*

We say that we read a poem or novel, that we hear music, look at paintings, and watch television, but we usually say we are going to see a film or a play. The word *theatre* originally meant a "place for seeing," and that is an indication that plays have usually been more than words, and that our understanding of theatre needs to involve something more complex. We should see a theatre production as a mirror reflection of people and events, with the images changing moment by moment. Theatre is a unique art that calls for an audience to react to a lifelike experience. At its fullest power, theatre provides a shared experience that calls upon all our senses. It is a sensational medium that offers an audience an image of life possessing unusual excitement and, at times, a great and strong simplicity. When fully mobilized, the power of theatre is almost irrestible.

> *Remember as fully as you can the events shown onstage in any one play that you know well, preferably one that you have seen and greatly enjoyed. Then ask yourself how well the play used each of the five powers of the theatre that have been identified in this chapter.*

2

-I will. I'll do that. Thanks.
(turns to go, sees Betty who has just entered)
There you are.
-The system they have in this store, it drvies you
crazy. First you got to find the book. Then you
stand in one line to get a bill, you take the bill to
the cash line,you pay the cash person, then you
go back--
-Buy it at Dillons. We're g ing there next.
-We are?
-(Joe:) Actually I'm set anytime. We just have to
get Philip.
-I'll get him. I have to put these books back.
-He's up in Drama.
-Right. Be right back. (Henry goes)
(Pause)
-You didn't tell him, did you?
(he turns)
Frankie told me on the train yesterday.
-She did?
-I asked her and she told me. She had the guts to
tell me. Joe. He won't even go to his interviews.
He's dreaming. What are we supposed to do? I
don't even know where we'll live. Do you know how
much this trip has cost? Do you know why he insisted
we come?
(beat)
He was hoping-
-I know.
(beat)
Look, what do you take me for? A jerk? Betty, I
just told him. Right here, I said, Henry there is
no chance.
-You told him you hired someone.
-Yes. Of course.
(beat)
Christ. Look. I can't swear to what he heard. You
know Henry.
-I know.
-You try to be clear--
-I know.
-Sorry. I've done my bit. Don't dump shit on me.
(starts to browse)
I saved him some money on some books.
-Thanks.
-Here. I understand you like fiction. I hear it's
good. Don't have time for fiction myself. But--.
I'll buy it for you. It's only fifty p.

Author's Revisions: Richard Nelson's original typescript for *Some Americans Abroad*, as corrected during rehearsals. (Reprinted by permission of the author.)

Plays

What Is a Play?

A film shows still images on a screen, arranged so that they appear to be moving pictures, usually depicting human life; a piece of music is a sequence of chosen sounds; a painting is an image usually in two dimensions created with various paints or similar material; a poem is a collection of words in a memorable form and usually in sentences, but not necessarily written down, because poems can be carried in the head; a novel is a narrative account of fictional human experience, usually written in prose. Compared with theatre, all these arts are relatively easy to define and categorize. So how do we define a play?

"Actions imitating human life and performed, usually by human beings, before an audience, usually on a stage, and usually capable of repetition" gets somewhere near a definition, but it misses entirely the fact that a play is performed within a chosen and more or less fixed period of time. The length of performance, measured sometimes in minutes but more often in hours, is always a controlling part of the experience of a play by an audience. Samuel Beckett's *Breath* (1971) is famous for lasting only about thirty-five seconds (the single human being in this piece is never seen onstage, only heard offstage), but, on the other hand, a considerable number of plays performed in India today continue an old tradition of lasting over a period of several days, and a six-hour performance is not remarkable.

Performers are usually human, but they do not have to be. Plays have been written with parts for dogs or monkeys, and nonhuman components are not at all rare, especially if we count mechanical devices representing animals, babies, scientific instruments, trees that sprout leaves or move about the stage, and many kinds of moving scenery, together with automobiles (an early one appears in George Bernard Shaw's *Man and Superman* [1905]) or airplanes (such as the helicopter in the 1989 musical *Miss Saigon*).

Many plays are written to be performed by puppets, model human beings who may perform without their human manipulators being visible at all. Today plays are also made with high-tech equipment, mingling film with human performance, recorded sound with spoken speech. Complicated sound scores, automated moving scenery, and powerfully evocative lighting (with lasers and computerized control)

Figure 2.1   Theatre moves with the times: an automobile makes an early appearance in George Bernard Shaw's *Man and Superman* at the Criterion Theatre, London, 1911. (Photograph used by permission from the Mander and Mitchenson Theatre Collection.)

have become common in larger theatres. These plays remake life as much as they imitate it.

In trying to understand theatre, another huge consideration is the relation of a play to music. Opera and dance are theatre entertainments in which all that happens onstage is controlled by the playing or singing of music, so that music has an essential role in defining the nature of the audience's experience. But compared with theatre, which uses speech and actions taken from everyday life, opera and dance belong to different categories of art and tend to follow separate lines of development; they are close relations to theatre, but equally close to music, which seldom reflects life in any directly imitative way. Opera and dance are not within the scope of this book, which has a large enough task in introducing readers to the theatre experience. Some expertise in music is a prior requirement for anyone wishing to create dance or opera, and for anyone wishing to study them. Nevertheless music is an extension of lived experience, so it has always been one of the resources of theatre. Its power is always on call to evoke mood or express sensations beyond the reach of words, as it does in life.

In many parts of Asia and Africa, and among Native Americans, however, the different nature of opera and dance is hardly ever recognized. Music, dance, and singing are used in almost every theatre entertainment, and theatre makes little or no attempt to imitate life directly. Until comparatively recent times a lifelike theatre was inconceivable to these people, and a special term, *spoken drama*, was introduced when plays began to be based on Western models with music, song, dance, and acrobatics reduced to a minimum or banished altogether. In India, an ancient book (the *Natyasastra*, written sometime between 200 B.C. and 200 A.D.) tells the story of how the gods created theatre to offer men and women an alternative to life, one that would give more pleasure than life; the use of music arose naturally from this notion of theatre's difference from mundane existence. Western theatre, which springs from Greek, Roman, and early Christian traditions, was for centuries unaffected by the theatres of Asia, Africa, and the Native Americans, but today, as jet travel is making the world smaller, theatres of the West are gaining access to other traditions, and the value of other cultures' traditions is being more clearly recognized. The process of change is bound to be slow, and, for the time being, as with opera and dance, these theatres, which need such very special techniques and achieve unique forms of entertainment, cannot fit into this account of what has been called "Western theatre," a theatre derived chiefly from European models in which the imitation of life is a prime consideration.

To say that a play is "an action in imitation of life" is probably the most useful short description in the context of Western theatre, but this definition might suggest that a play is a permanent and self-contained construction, like a piece of sculpture or a realistic painting. But a play is both transitory and variable. Even the fixed words of a play are revalued in each production and in each performance. So we will add to the short description: a play is "an imitation of human life that is repeated by performers for an audience." Although a play text may be created once and for all, that play in performance is continually re-created and changed.

Plays are so complex and variable that they are usually defined not by what they are in performance, but by the main features of their texts. Studying plays as texts is a practical way to start to understand them.

> *After seeing a play, write down the three or four moments you chiefly remember. Then consider how much of these depend upon what the actors have said, how much on what they did, and how much on other features of the performance—story, scenery, costume, lights, music, audience.*

Varieties of Plays

Writing 2,300 years ago, Aristotle, the Greek philosopher, judged that there were two main kinds of drama: tragedy and comedy. His fragmentary analytical work, the *Poetics*, says little about comedy, except that it is a kind of drama that presents imitations of "low" characters, men and women made ludicrous through some defect or ugliness that is not painful or destructive. About tragedy he wrote much more, and his words have influenced the vast majority of subsequent critics in European-based cultures.

Aristotle wrote about the theatre in the golden age of Athens, from which the works of only four dramatists have survived—Æschylus, Sophocles, Euripides (writing tragedies), and Aristophanes (writing comedies). These men were active for little more than a hundred years, and only a handful of their plays have survived, yet even for these texts Aristotle's definitions are not wholly satisfactory. He gave "rules" for writing tragedy and defined various kinds of plot; for example:

> A perfect tragedy should . . . be arranged not on the simple but on the complex plan. It should, moreover, imitate actions which excite pity and fear, this being the distinctive mark of tragic imitation. It follows plainly, in the first place, that the change of fortune presented must not be the spectacle of a virtuous man brought from prosperity to adversity: for this moves neither pity nor fear; it merely shocks us.
>
> *Poetics*

Now, more than two thousand years later, the philosopher's confidence seems extraordinary. No one today would divide drama into two kinds or lay down laws about how to write a good tragedy: sometimes a very simple story can be presented in a noncomplex way; sometimes, indeed quite often, a good or virtuous man suffers "adversity."

Tragedy

Tragedy, over the centuries, has been variously defined as:

- a play ending in death
- a play concerned with noble persons and elevated sentiments
- a play presenting the clash between a power outside the hero, necessity, and one within, freedom—the tragedy of Fate
- a narrative about a great man brought to disaster through some fault or error—the so-called "tragic flaw"
- a narrative of prosperity for a time ending in misery—"to teach upon what rotten foundations, gilded roofs are built"
- an exposure of the moral wrongs of man and society
- a vindication of divine justice
- a collision of equally justified ethical claims.

Subtypes have been identified: sacred tragedy (especially in seventeenth-century Italy), the tragedy of blood or the revenge play (especially in Elizabethan and Jacobean England); domestic tragedy; classical, neoclassical, romantic tragedies, and so forth.

Look for a play on the library shelves that is called a tragedy on its title page. Read it, and then consider which of the descriptions or definitions given above fit it best. This means that you will need to think about the play's story and chief characters, and also about its theme or argument.

Comedy

Definitions of comedy, Aristotle's other form of drama, are just as numerous. Even the basic notion that comedy involves laughter has been questioned: during the Middle Ages, comedy was considered to be any narrative with a happy ending (as opposed to tragedy's unhappy ending), and at the beginning of the twentieth century the idea was that the highest kind of comedy should raise a smile rather than outright laughter.

Other Forms of Drama

As society has changed and new talents have entered the theatre—and also the ranks of critics—new definitions of the kinds of drama have proliferated. Somewhere around the year 1600, Shakespeare had Polonius, his experienced and self-important politician in *Hamlet*, announce that the actors who were coming to court were:

> [t]he best actors in the world, either for tragedy, comedy, history, pastoral, pastoral-comical, historical-pastoral, tragical-historical, tragical-comical-historical-pastoral, scene individable, or poem unlimited.
>
> Hamlet, II, ii

Polonius had been an amateur actor when he was at university and has a good stock of the latest critical categories. His elaboration is absurd, but it strives to account for the freedom with which dramatists were making their own rules for plays so that they would grab attention and appeal to both elite and popular audiences.

The introduction of the *history play*, coming next to the traditional tragedy and comedy in Polonius's list, foretells the three categories into which Shakespeare's plays were divided in their first collected edition of 1623. Sometimes called *chronicles*, this Elizabethan form, most persistently and brilliantly used by Shakespeare himself, was derived not from classical models, but from medieval *mystery plays*. These were performed throughout Europe in open spaces, not in theatres, and they presented the events told in the Old and New Testaments of the Bible in a series of short plays, or *pageants*. A sequence of such plays (usually called a *cycle* of plays) involved hundreds of individual characters and could take a whole day to perform in its entirety. Both religious and highly popular, the mystery plays broke almost all the rules of drama derived from pagan Greece and Rome. For example, they did not show a great man falling from prosperity to adversity, but a number of separate stories, with both upbeat and downbeat endings, which together showed the entire world as subservient to an ever-present and all-knowing God.

Defining Drama by Type

Since the Greeks, critics who have tried to define the various kinds of play have made lists very much longer than Aristotle's. To do this, they have given most attention to story, characters, and argument or theme, three of the elements that Aristotle identified as a tragedy's distinguishing features.

Some critics continued to argue that tragedy is the most important form of drama and to establish rules for writing "correct" tragedies, but their fondness for regularity has always had to give way to playwrights' new inventions, their determination to "reinvent the wheel" so that drama could do new work and keep the theatre alive in a changing world. The main reason for change has been that audiences have always had to be taken into account. Dr. Samuel Johnson (1709-1784) was a literary critic, editor of Shakespeare, and compiler of a great dictionary, but he was also a close friend of the actor-manager David Garrick and knew enough about the practicalities of theatre to have little patience with fixed definitions; as he wrote in a Prologue which Garrick was to deliver: "The drama's laws the drama's patrons give / And we that live to please must please to live." Whenever theatre is thriving, playwrights have always been up-to-date in their appeal to audiences, and therefore experimental in their choice of dramatic form. What Aristotle called "imitation" is the chief cause of this, for as people's view of life alters, so the imitation of life in the "mirror" of the stage (see discussion in Chapter 1) has to change too. Dr. Johnson saw this clearly:

> Shakespeare's plays are not in the rigorous and critical sense either tragedies or comedies, but compositions of a distinct kind; exhibiting the real state of sublunary nature, which partakes of good and evil, joy and sorrow, mingled with endless variety of proportion and innumerable modes of combination.
>
> Preface to *The Plays of William Shakespeare*

In other words, Shakespeare was more intent on showing the lunacies and conflicts of life than he was on following rules and separating good from evil, tragedy from comedy.

Why should we try to define the kinds of plays? This question must arise in view of the difficulty of doing so. The answer is that giving names to anything helps us to identify what is unique in each, so that we can respect essential qualities and recognize kinships. To illustrate the difficulties that have confronted critics through the centuries, here are some attempts to define various sorts of comedy, together with one or two examples of each type:

Old (Greek) Comedy

This usual title is unsatisfactory; perhaps *celebratory* or *festive* would serve better. In these plays contemporary people (both individuals and types), gods, and personifications, together with one or two singing, dancing, and speaking choruses, are involved in a fantastic situation, usually of a combative or ceremonious nature. By these means, the plays present a topical, social, or political issue through burlesque, parody, invective, wit, lyricism, obscenity, and argument. The action ends in revelry. A few examples of old comedy are Aristophanes' *Birds* (414 B.C.) and *Lysistrata* (411 B.C.); and Joan Littlewood's *Oh, What A Lovely War!* (1963).

New or (Later) Roman Comedy

Again, historically defined titles are unsatisfactory: perhaps *intrigue* would serve better. In Roman comedies stock characters—such as the old father, the witty servant, the shrew, or the marriageable widow—are involved ingeniously in a crisis, usually concerned with the possession of wealth, a secret, or a woman (and often all three), and always giving occasion for virtuoso displays of dexterity or wit. Sometimes the main action is interspersed with song and dance from a chorus. The play usually ends with reconciliation and revelry. Some examples include Plautus's *The Rope* (in the beginning of the second century B.C.), Ben Jonson's *The Alchemist* (1610), and Molière's *The Miser* (1668).

Comedy of Manners

A mixture of intrigue and romantic narratives provides occasions in these plays for showing examples of social behavior, often greatly exaggerated but verbally inventive and refined. Some examples of comedy of manners plays are Shakespeare's

Much Ado about Nothing (ca. 1598), Molière's *The School for Wives* (1662), William Congreve's *The Way of the World* (1700), and Oscar Wilde's *The Importance of Being Earnest* (1895).

Romantic Comedy

A romantic narrative provides opportunities for lyrical speech, song, or dance (in more musical varieties by a chorus as well as individual characters). Subsidiary incidents provide topical and burlesque humor or specialty acts. Settings are frequently magical, pastoral, or exotic. The principal characters are young, beautiful, and, finally, fortunate in love, but usually there will be one or more villainous, old, or otherwise unsympathetic characters who must be circumvented. Some examples include Shakespeare's *The Merchant of Venice* (1596-1597) and Rodgers and Hammerstein's *Oklahoma!* (1943).

Farce

In these plays a narrative (usually involving sexual encounters) develops toward violent and exaggerated activity, bringing ever-increasing complications, misunderstandings, and improbabilities. Verbally the play is often repetitive and sometimes mundane, but physically it is invariably skillful and even amazing; in both these respects it is frequently lewd. All is calculated to raise the audience's laughter and give temporary escape into irrational and fantastic behavior. Some examples are Eugène Labiche's *An Italian Straw Hat* (1851), Georges Feydeau's *A Flea in Her Ear* (1907), Michael Frayn's *Noises Off* (1982), and Neil Simon's *Rumors* (1990).

Tragicomedy

A narrative (often with both romantic and intrigue interests) that arouses both pity and fear (as "regular" tragedies are said to do) yet ends happily or has considerable comic, lyric, or otherwise happy episodes. Its plot usually provides sudden alterations of mood and marvelous or almost incredible incidents. Some examples are Shakespeare's *Cymbeline* (1609-1610), Francis Beaumont and John Fletcher's *A King and No King* (1611), and Corneille's *Le Cid* (1637).

Lists of comedies and other dramatic genres are bewildering, not least because most examples cited in them tend to be plays written centuries ago. Besides, definitions that allow a Shakespeare comedy and a twentieth-century musical to share the same label cannot account for some very obvious differences between them. Plays that have won lasting success often require double-barreled definitions as odd as those invented by Shakespeare for Polonius. Among plays of his own time, Marlowe's *Jew of Malta* is a tragical farce, or farcical tragedy; whereas John Webster's *White Devil* is a satirical tragedy or a revenge play, or a tragedy of blood, and it is also a chronicle or history play. Shakespeare's *King Lear*, perhaps the greatest tragedy ever written, is also a chronicle play, and in some scenes it is comic or, as later critics would say, expressionist. More recent dramatists have had trouble labeling their work. Chekhov called his *Cherry Orchard* a comedy and his *Three Sisters* a drama, but for *Uncle Vanya* he invented a new genre, calling the play somewhat mysteriously "Scenes from Country Life." Henrik Ibsen used "A Play" to describe *An Enemy of the People*, "A Dramatic Poem" for *Peer Gynt*, and "A Domestic Drama" for *Ghosts* (a play some later critics were to designate a tragedy).

Defining Elements of Plays

An attempt to define by story, and also by character and theme, as Aristotle and his followers have done, helps to identify what distinguishes one play from another. It leads us to consider the backbone of any performance—the play's story or imitation of an action—and also to consider who enacts that story—the play's characters. These make up the main ingredients of most plays, and to describe them is often the best way of discovering the nature of a play.

Some modern writers give little attention to story and may not reckon to create consistent characters. The ways they describe their plays through subtitles illustrate this:

> Sam Shepard, *Geography of a Horse Dreamer: A Mystery in Two Acts* (1974)
>
> Edward Bond, *The Woman: Scenes of War and Freedom* (1978)
>
> Howard Barker, *No End of Blame: Scenes of Overcoming* (1981)
>
> Tony Kushner, *Angels in America: A Gay Fantasia on National Themes* (1992)

Other dramatists, including Harold Pinter, David Mamet, Lanford Wilson, Marsha Norman, subtitle all their plays, firmly, "a play," as if disowning or defying any other description. Len Jenkin uses titles that imply that both narrative and individual characters are unimportant: one of his plays is called simply *American Notes* (1988), and another, *Poor Folk's Pleasure* (1989). The latter was published with a prefatory note:

> *Poor Folk's Pleasure* is a theatre piece for five to seven performers. These performers take on a variety of roles. . . . [In performance it] should feel like a concert for the acting company as band: a series of interconnected numbers, all coming from the same author and the same ensemble.

For such a "theatre piece," old categories do not apply and yet, taking up Len Jenkin's advice about *Poor Folk's Pleasure*, we could say that the *story* of his play is that of its actors performing a "concert," and that its *characters* are the actors taking part in various activities and wearing various disguises. At the end of the play, the audience has followed the characters' progress and is able to judge how far they have traveled. Looking for a story is a helpful way to think about any play, even when the story is not immediately apparent or its author professes to be indifferent to narrative. Seeing how the play unfolds in time and who is active in the plot—in practice, this identifies those crucial and defining elements that "give a progressive experience" to an audience.

Most plays are rooted in storytelling, and most audiences are held by it. After many years of experimenting at the International Centre for Theatre Research in Paris and other places around the world, and after working in many forms of theatre, the director Peter Brook formed the opinion that story would always provide the strongest means of shaping a play. In writing about how he had experimented in the 1960s by abandoning narrative entirely, he went on to say:

> I arrived at the conclusion that, although all kinds of other structure possibilities exist, narrative is perhaps the most powerful of them all. Even an insubstantial anecdote, if well told, can demonstrate the extraordinary power of suspense that every narrative contains.

New Theatre Quarterly VIII

Take any play and tell the main events of its story, using less than a hundred words. Then in another ten or twelve list its main characters, and in about twenty say what interests you in the story. You will have described a play by its story, characters, and theme. Does your description fit any of the kinds of play that have been discussed here?

Not everyone would agree that story has such power and that the kind of story told distinguishes one play from another.

In the present century critics have often defined plays, not by their story, characters, or themes, but by their style, their manipulation of images on the stage. We have *realist* and *naturalist* dramas, *symbolist* plays (which reject realism and naturalism in favor of representing the inner life of the mind), *melodramas* (sensational, spectacular, moralistic, sentimental), *musicals*, *mysteries*, *thrillers*: often the name is self-explanatory and is as much about content as about style.

New Genres

Three new genres that need explanation have become generally accepted.

Expressionist Plays

In this genre a sequence of scenes expresses emotional states, rather than everyday reality, and represents the nature of human life, rather than a particular story. They rely on visual effects and highly charged physical performance, rather than on conflict between characters or narrative development. Individual scenes are often short and sometimes wordless. Often one character dominates every other, and most characters are types rather than individuals. Some examples of expressionist plays are Georg Kaiser's *From Morn till Midnight* (1917); Eugene O'Neill's *The Emperor Jones* (1920) and *The Hairy Ape* (1921); and Elmer Rice's *The Adding Machine* (1923).

Epic Plays

The audience observes the epic play, rather than feeling implicated in its action and sharing the feelings of its characters. Audience members are encouraged to think, rather than to feel. Scenes contrast sharply with each other. Characters face choices. Words, music, and setting are sometimes independent of each other.

Epic theatre was a term used by Bertolt Brecht to define an "anti-Aristotelian" form of drama, one that aimed at being "non-dramatic" in most of the accepted uses of "dramatic." He developed this kind of play from fair-ground performances, earlier expressionist plays, and still older models, especially Elizabethan and Greek. His own writings fit his description better than anyone else's. Some examples include Bertolt Brecht's *The Life of Galileo* (1938 and 1947) and *Mother Courage and Her Children* (1939).

Absurdist Plays

The subject matter of absurdist plays is surreal or hallucinatory, violent, parodistic, playful, or crazy. Many of these plays are short, and most seem designed to puzzle or affront their audience. In this genre, more important than telling a story is the exploration of an intellectual idea (in this it is indebted to expressionist drama) through a series of fanciful or grotesque events.

Theatre of the Absurd was a phrase given currency by the critic Martin Esslin when he was accounting for this new genre of plays written without regard for realism or rationality, or for earlier rules of dramatic construction. Eugène Ionesco, introducing *The Chairs* (1952), said that his play progresses not through a predetermined subject and plot, but through an increasingly intense and revealing series of emotional states. Some examples of absurdist plays are Samuel Beckett's *Waiting for Godot* (1953); Edward Albee's *The Sandbox* (1959) and *The American Dream* (1960); Jean Genet's *The Screens* (1961, 1966); and Václav Havel's *Memorandum* (1965).

The Making of Plays: Recent Developments

In the second half of the twentieth century, while playwrights were exploring new subject matter and new forms in which to express their ideas, their status in the theatre was beginning to change. The separation between the author who writes a script and the director who is in charge of staging the performance is now less clear than formerly. As the whole process of production has become more complicated in technically well-equipped theatres, some playwrights have seen the need to take over the director's role in order to ensure that the original idea of their play is not obscured or destroyed during its staging. David Mamet, Sam Shepard, Maria Irene Fornes, Athol Fugard, Alan Ayckbourn, Len Jenkin, and, in his later years, Samuel Beckett have all become directors of their own work and their published scripts bear signs of this additional involvement. For example, Sam Shepard's *Fool for Love* (1983) starts with a warning: "This play is to be performed relentlessly without a break." Its stage directions give very practical details, for example:

> *She exits into bathroom, stage right, slams the door behind her. The door is amplified with microphones and a bass drum hidden in the frame so that each time an actor slams it, the door booms loud and long.*

Another development in the present century has been in an opposite direction as directors have come to take over the job of playwrights. Although in a few individual cases—notable examples are Bertolt Brecht and, in France, Roger Planchon—the one person has always combined the roles of director and dramatist, many directors have moved more gradually toward authorship. By the time that Joan Littlewood and members of the company wrote *Oh, What a Lovely War!* (1963) during rehearsals, she had already made highly effective contributions to the scripts of other authors, adding and changing as she thought best. (Shelagh Delaney's *A Taste of Honey* [1958], written when the author was seventeen years old, is an example of this kind of co-authorship.) By the late 1950s and into the 1960s plays were often being written by director-dramatists during rehearsals and before. In these dramas prescribed activity and physical images can be of more importance than the dialogue. Examples are *The Sport of My Mad Mother* (1956) and *The Knack* (1961), both the work of dramatist-director Anne Jellicoe; she did not direct the first productions herself, but both plays owe a great deal to her directing experience and to acting exercises she had used as a teacher of acting.

The twentieth-century musical had in some ways paved the way for this breakdown of roles. The writing of the *book* (or script) for such a complex production is completed only after a long process of consultation and collaboration within a group in which the composer, lyricist, choreographer, chief designer, director, and producer all have their parts to play, as well as the dramatist.

Plays wholly scripted by directors tend to take their final form during rehearsals and are literally inconceivable without the particular talents of the actors involved: the works of Robert Wilson and Richard Foreman are famous North American examples. Both these director-dramatists also function as designers, working as closely with technicians as they do with performers. Some directors, such as Tadeusz Kantor (1915-1990) in Poland, and Ariane Mnouchkine in France, have not so much written plays as developed them during rehearsals. In effect some companies of actors are joint authors with their directors, as are members of the Wooster Group in New York. Other directors work on established texts, both dramatic and otherwise; they cut up the original play, change scenes around, alter characters and settings, all the time refashioning, adding, repeating, until the finished work can almost be called a work in its own right: such are Jerzy Grotowski in Poland, Suzuki Tadashi in Japan (*A Tale of Lear* [1988] from Shakespeare's *King Lear*), and Anne Bogart in the United States (*Small Lives/Big Dreams* [1995] adapted from all of Chekhov's major plays).

In Italy Eduardo de Filippo and Dario Fo have been as active as actors as they have been as directors, and at the same time they have written their own plays in which they themselves perform. In Japan Noda Hideki served as managing director, sole play director, sole dramatist, and chief actor in his own theatre company. By 1992 he had written a play a year for ten years nonstop. His shows could be performed by no other company, so dependent are they on ensemble performance, local and topical events, and Noda's own personality. They also use time and place with great freedom, and each actor is seen to be playing many parts, not least Noda himself.

At a time when the forms of plays are less predictable than ever before, the opposite end of the spectrum is occupied by the solo performing artist, who is author, director, and performer of a script that presents and transforms his or her own experience or some other happening of actual life, often with only the simplest physical stage setting and minimal effects. Spalding Gray's *Swimming to Cambodia* (1985) is an autobiographical and opinionated monologue that displays what it is like for its author to be an actor, and vice versa. Anne Deavere Smith's *Fires in the Mirror* (1993) is a collage of extracts from interviews concerning riots and racial tension in a neighborhood of Brooklyn, New York, after the deaths of a black boy and a Jewish student. Onstage the compiler-author assumed in turn the voice and personal characteristics of each person she had interviewed.

Yet nothing is ever entirely new in theatre, except the technological means that continue to become available. Theatre historians can compare recent performance artists to the solo storytellers who were the precursors of more elaborate theatre forms in many lands, and who still thrive today in Africa and Asia, as well as in some special theatre companies in the Western world. Dramatist, director (or producer), and actor were all the same person a long time before the present century

Figure 2.2 *Small Lives/Big Dreams*: Anne Bogart's play devised in 1995 with the S.I.T.I. company based on the plays of Anton Chekhov. (Photograph © 1995 by Clemens Kalisher.)

in the small traveling companies of early modern Europe. Molière (the stage name of Jean-Baptiste Poquelin), whose fame today rests on his plays as preserved in text form, started in such a provincial troupe and then continued to carry out all three functions after he had left the provinces and become established in Paris in 1658. In still earlier times, plays drew on traditional material and were "developed" by the people who performed them, rather than being written by any one person. This practice is still common today in countries where folk traditions are strong and play making is traditionally a communal activity. In such cultures there is no scope for either a single author or a single director to impose a personal style and individual viewpoint on a production.

The modern stand-up comedian is also part of an old tradition, using much the same improvisational means as have the fools, jesters, mimes, and professional comics of many kinds who have worked all around the world in almost every age and society, as if no one could ever stop this simply staged and natural kind of entertainment. From the perspective of theatre history, many experiments that seem new and fashionable are really attempts to reclaim the improvised performances in simply-staged dramatic forms that are seldom to be enjoyed in our more elaborate theatres and word-based cultures.

> *In the preceding discussion, a lot of names were quoted to give an impression of the variety of work being done at the present time, and little information was given about any individual playwrights. Choose one or two of the playwrights to look up in journals or reference books (see "Suggestions for Further Reading") and discover more about their contributions to theatre.*

Plays exist in more kinds than one account can easily keep track of. Some have educational purposes and mix together instruction and information with the more usual excitements of theatre. Plays with a political purpose include factual information, address the audience directly, and call for positive action: this kind of theatre is sometimes called *agitprop*. Other plays reenact historical events in the locations where they actually occurred. Soviet Russia spent huge sums on such works; for instance Evreinov's *The Storming of the Winter Palace* (1920) was a mass spectacle employing many thousands of performers and reenacting this revolutionary event of three years previously. Less extravagantly, the same form is found in pageants and light-and-sound shows at country fairs and historical sites, places where no other theatre experience is available. Multimedia productions in huge arenas or public places have somewhat similar spectacular intentions, but they involve high-tech devices and supporting music and sound; these plays may use no actors at all, relying on recorded voices, puppets, or projected images to give some impression of actual lived experience.

Plays may even be said to exist without the aid of theatre. Drama and the imitation of specific human or supernatural events are enacted in public ceremonies of worship, remembrance, judgment, sorrow, thanksgiving, and victory. In ordinary private life, we "act" the parts of generous host or dutiful student; we set scenes for homecomings or departures; we become aware that others are putting on acts for our benefit, and we enjoy being an audience for children's make-believe. Plays are found everywhere in embryo form and unrepeatable circumstances, and this is one reason why we enjoy seeing them in the theatre, where they can be rehearsed and repeated, becoming in this process more fully considered and possessing all the advantages of theatrical production, skilled actors, and eager audiences.

> *Consider any play you know that has not yet been discussed and then, using the various terms introduced here, try to describe its form and style. Does it relate to any one kind of play discussed here, or to several?*

The Quality of Play: A Question of Style

For football or tennis, seeing who wins is only one reason for watching a game or a match: *how* the players play decides whether the game is worthwhile or not. So it is with theatre. Story, characters, and theme provide the basis for almost every play (like the pursuit of victory in a game), but Aristotle had listed three other elements in a tragedy and these determine how any play is presented and performed onstage: these three other elements are spectacle, music, and diction. You might think of a play as a hand with six fingers, one of them, the story, being its thumb. Character and theme are the fingers closest to the thumb and are very strong. We have already considered how these elements make up the backbone of a play. That leaves spectacle, music, and speech as the three that determine *how* the play is played; that is, they control the quality of a play in performance. Together they are responsible for what is called *dramatic style* and have a great influence on the nature of an audience's response. They are also part of the hand and therefore affect story, characters, and theme. Studying them will provide further insight into how a dramatist has told the story (what secrets are kept, what crises arranged), how the characters come to life (with what motives and what instincts), and how themes are developed (how attention is focused, insights provided, and thought provoked in the audience).

To consider style is to ask "How does this play work?" which, put like that, is a hard question to answer. The best way to tackle it is in three stages and to start with the *diction* of a play, which can be studied one word at a time, like words in any other piece of writing.

Diction

To appreciate diction involves a close reading of a play, looking at what will be said onstage and considering what these words imply and how they may be spoken. Treat a play like a cake and cut one slice, or, better, several small slices from different parts, and then examine each sample, separating it into still smaller pieces until you can find out what is the nature of each crumb. As you then ask how these minute elements fit together and react to each other, you may begin to answer the larger question of how the play works. If the samples are well chosen, you gain a good indication of a play's quality. For example, you might take one passage of a hundred or so words from the first major scene and another from the play's last scene, if possible both spoken by the same leading character.

Literary and linguistic questions are the easiest to start with, because they are more familiar. So in regard to a single sample of text, ask what sort of vocabulary is used:

> What sort of things do *nouns* represent? These might be real and solid, or abstract and intellectual.
>
> What sort of actions do *verbs* relate to? These might be practical, involving doing, moving, giving, taking, and so forth. Or they might be concerned with perception, such as thinking, knowing, seeing, and so on.
>
> Are the verbs active or passive, indicative or imperative? What tenses are common: past, present, or future?
>
> Are there many adjectives, adverbs, personal or demonstrative pronouns?
>
> Are words simple and monosyllabic, or do some have many syllables?
>
> Are the words of Anglo-Saxon origin or from Latin, French, or other some other language?
>
> Are some words used in more than one sense, as in puns and other kinds of word-play? Are some used repeatedly, with or without a change in meaning?

These questions may seem boring and untheatrical, but as we have seen, one of the great powers of the theatre is that it can use verbal language. Studying diction is the way to take the measure of what a dramatist has done with words. Few theatre people will sit down and examine a text with such thoroughness and pedantry; they rely on instinct and experience, and their own quick minds, to sense the tone, rhythms, manners, and idiom of a script to their own satisfaction. The less experienced may, unfortunately, assume that choices of style are their own to make and try to deal with all scripts in the same way, or they may simply follow what other directors and actors have done before. For beginners and those who are not sure of their own genius, the slower and more meticulous approach is a certain way of discovering how the diction of each particular script can best work in performance. When you sample the diction of a play of proved excellence, you will find that the information you glean is surprisingly theatrical. (A not-so-good play will yield comparatively little of interest.)

Take *Hamlet*, for example, and the most famous of its soliloquies. This is a complex speech and one that is difficult to understand at first. I have chosen it for that very reason, so that you can see words working at their theatrical best. For the moment, do not try to fathom its many meanings, but read it through as best you can before asking technical questions about word choice.

> To be, or not to be, that is the question:
> Whether 'tis nobler in the mind to suffer
> The slings and arrows of outrageous fortune,
> Or to take arms against a sea of troubles,
> And by opposing, end them. To die, to sleep—
> No more, and by a sleep to say we end
> The heart-ache and the thousand natural shocks
> That flesh is heir to; 'tis a consummation
> Devoutly to be wish'd. To die, to sleep—
> To sleep, perchance to dream—ay, there's the rub,
> For in that sleep of death what dreams may come
> When we have shuffled off this mortal coil,
> Must give us pause; there's the respect
> That makes calamity of so long life:
> For who would bear the whips and scorns of time,
> Th' oppressor's wrong, the proud man's contumely,
> The pangs of despis'd love, the law's delay,
> The insolence of office, and the spurns
> That patient merit of th' unworthy takes,
> When he himself might his quietus make
> With a bare bodkin.
>
> *Hamlet*, III, i

Critics have always differed about what Hamlet means and the importance of this speech in the play as a whole, but *how* Hamlet speaks is an easier question, and that is what concerns us here.

If you underline the nouns in this text and then make a number of lists, sorting them into various kinds, you will find that many nouns have to do with how Hamlet thinks and how other people think. *Question* is the first noun and the first of a series of nouns about thought: then there are a few simple ones, *mind*, *pause*, *respect*, and others concerned with large abstract ideas, such as *fortune*, *troubles*, *consummation*, *calamity*, *life*, *time*. As the speech progresses, the nouns become more judgmental, identifying what is right and, mostly, what is wrong: *oppressor, wrong, contumely, delay, insolence, merit, unworthy, quietus.* That last word is different, seeming to come out of another box. It is obviously from Latin and is used punningly, because *quietus* means "the paying of a debt" and "departure from life"; it also has a quibbling association with *quiet.* This is not the end of the soliloquy, but it is the point at which certain ideas seem to be brought together for the first time. Some words with more general connotations have referred to the practical business of living in some of its major, unavoidable aspects: *sleep, heir, sleep* (again), *death, dream* (here grammatical structure buckles and breaks down, and repetitions huddle words together), *life, time, love, law, office.* The noun *love* is related to its companions, but is also connected with the first series of nouns about thinking and response; its association with *pang* also sets it apart from the others. This companion word, *pang,* belongs to a quite different sequence of nouns, all referring to solid objects and physical sensations: *sling, arrow, arm, sea, shock, flesh, rub, coil, whip, pang, spurn, bodkin.* Here it is *sea* that reaches outside the series, as *love* had done out of the other, having much wider associations with death and timelessness. Alliteration on the adjective *bare* draws particular attention to *bodkin.*

What can we make of these collections of nouns? First, the series relating to how one thinks, dominant at first, dries up toward the end of this passage as if Hamlet has become more engaged in firsthand thought than in thought about thought. Second, the nouns in this passage represent a mind that is attracted to generalized thought, but not given over to it entirely; it is also continuously alive to direct experience, responsive to bodily reactions and to solid and harsh objects. Third, this mind reaches out to large concepts and draws toward moral conclusions. Fourth, at the close of this passage the various series are drawn together, after clusters of nouns giving an impression of gathering impetus and after a few suggesting an overflow of meanings. At this point speech focuses on one small object: a *bodkin.* This noun does not simplify matters, for it refers both to a dagger and to an article used in cloth making or for the pinning on of hats; however death is no longer an abstract idea, but a practical possibility. Besides, the adjective *bare* signifies both "merely" and "naked," so it may qualify both the small instrument and, by association, the state of mind of the person who thinks of using it.

How do these nouns work? They present a restless mind, a mind that seeks after some kind of finality and also for peace, a peace that overcomes both "troubles" and "love," that involves a reckoning and not an escape: a mind that also faces death or, at least, is aware that death is an immediate and very real possibility. The actor has to have great mental energy and a strong grasp on thought to keep a steady foothold during such a speech, and he must remain in touch with ordinary felt experience. This speech must dazzle with movement and variable sound yet be grounded in simple monosyllables that are immediately recognizable and to which every hearer can respond; it writhes and hesitates yet seeks some conclusive force and precision.

Having studied the nouns, read the speech again. Does it make more sense now? Are some nouns obviously more important than others? Next read it aloud, at first only a few lines at a time. Do you begin to sense what it is like to be Hamlet, and on which words or lines an actor needs to devote special energy of thought?

The verbs in this passage can be considered more briefly, because the same contrasts are found among them. Look at the nine occurrences of the verb *to be*, in its various forms: this implies very active thought. "To be or not to be": these first two usages, held apart by a negative, turn the simple verb into a word of huge import; here *to be* implies to exist or not to exist, to live and breathe, or to die. Many more simple monosyllabic verbs in this passage have to do with activity of thought and body, and also with death: *take, end, die, sleep, say, end* (again), *wish, die* and *sleep* (again), *dream, come, give, make, bear, take* (again), *make* (again). There is a sprinkling of auxiliary verbs (which are used with other verbs to establish mood and tense): *may, must, would*, and a final *might*. A very few complicated verbs, with more than one syllable, suggest something of the physical involvement, which was also apparent among the nouns: *suffer, oppose, shuffle*.

The most insistent verbal activity comes from Hamlet's desire or instinct to identify: from the simple verb *to be*, occurring twice at first, and then *to take, end, die, make, bear, take, make*, all of which are evidence that Hamlet becomes increasingly involved with conclusive action. Hamlet is not content with thought; he is drawn toward action, or at least toward the idea of action. In performance, these two impulses must coexist and engage with one another. This is one of the reasons why this is such an amazing speech, demanding of the actor an imaginative and intellectual energy that can make what he says outreach his audience's ability to understand. The words would be more comprehensible if they were spoken very slowly, but that is an option that the rhythms of the speech seem to forbid.

> *Try reading the passage again, first slowly and quietly to yourself and then speak it aloud with more energy. You should probably take a few lines at a time before trying the whole speech. How would you describe this experience? Does it tell you anything more about Hamlet, the person in the play?*

A shorter passage from a less highly wrought play will show what verbal analysis can reveal when the material to work on is less dense and less unfamiliar. A speech for May in Sam Shepard's *Fool for Love* (1983) reads:

> I don't understand my feelings. I really don't. I don't understand how I could hate you so much after so much time. How, no matter how much I'd like to not hate you, I hate you even more. It grows. I can't even see you now. All I see is a picture of you. You and her. I don't even know if the picture's real anymore. I don't even care. It's a made-up picture. It invades my head. The two of you. And this picture stings even more than if I'd actually seen you with her. It cuts me. It cuts me so deep I'll never get over it. And I can't get rid of this picture either. It just comes. Uninvited. Kinda' like a little torture. And I blame you more for this little torture than I do for what you did.

Very different from Shakespeare's *Hamlet*, Shepard's play brings up other questions about diction. Pronouns are frequent and repetitive, taking a leading role in shaping the sentences: fourteen *I*s , nine *you*s, and two *her*s; there also six *it*s and these, like the personal pronouns, are often the subject of a sentence. Adverbs and adverbial phrases are also frequent, usually used as a way of underlining what is being said: *really, so much* (twice), *no matter how much, even more* (twice), *even* (three times), *anymore, actually, so deep, never, over, either, just, kinda', more*. The speaker is bound up and driven by her own thoughts and feelings, her feelings for Eddie and for the unnamed other person, and her feelings for *it* specified, rather obliquely, as a *picture*—a noun repeated five times, far more frequently than any other of the infrequent nouns. Here is a complete list of the other nouns: *feelings, time, head, torture*, the last occurring twice and linked, curiously, with the adjective *little*, as if it were not of great consequence compared with those insistent and piled up personal pronouns and the recurrent *picture*.

Verbs in this speech show the nature of the "feelings" and "torture." Besides numerous *don't*s and, at the end, the positive "I *do*" and "you *did*," the sequence of verbs is *understand* (twice), *could hate, like, hate* (twice), *grow, can* (twice), *see* (twice), *know, care, invade, sting, seen, cut* (twice), *get, get rid, come, blame.* Here simple verbs of knowing, perceiving, doing, and strong feeling predominate; the main activity of the speaker's mind is obvious. In contrast, *invade, sting,* and *cut* suggest warfare, aggression, and pain; here is the operation of the *torture* introduced after the first occurrence of *picture.*

The spare language, repetitions, and personal pronouns tell us that this speaker is involved directly in what she says: as she feels, so she speaks. The short utterances, several without verbs, the occasional sentence made longer with insistent subsidiary phrases, the negatives, the emphatic adverbs, and the strong beat (often two stresses in pairs, sometimes single stresses) all give the passage a headlong, impassioned quality. But there are two circumstances that modify this impression. First the speech is preceded by a stage direction from the author-director telling us that May is holding her feelings as much in reserve as possible: the actress is told to deliver the speech in a "*very cold, quick, almost monotone voice like she's writing him a letter.*" The second is that a great deal remains unspoken: what exactly does the picture show, and what is it that is held back to the end and, even then, not named? She ends with "And I blame you more for this little torture than I do for *what you did*?" Somewhere in this speech is May's fear of what could be spoken. Fear of contact with Eddie, who is onstage and silent, is visually apparent as May continues to change into new clothes while she is speaking.

The study of the diction in this passage tells us that in performance May's speech will establish strong and directly experienced feelings and also suggest the power of further thoughts and feelings that are not expressed directly in words or in overt actions. Something is withheld; everything is askew: the past and present are dangerous, in a way not spoken about and yet known by the speaker all too clearly. The verbal style of this one speech offers glimpses and suggestions of dramatic forces that are hidden within its speaker and yet range widely across the whole play.

> *Try reading the speech aloud, at first slowly and then in a "very cold, quick, almost monotone voice." What happens if you invent something that Eddie has done, so that you always know what you are talking about? Does the speech become easier or more difficult to understand and speak?*

Knowledge of why and how words are used must be part of any thorough assessment of a passage. By themselves, without repetitions or insistent rhythms, the pronouns and many of the nouns and verbs in this passage would be quite unremarkable. Through further questions we can better assess the effect of how words are used.

How long, simple, or complicated are the sentences?

Are there many repetitions of words or patterns of speech? If so, are changes made in how they are used when they are repeated, and to what effect?

Is there a basic rhythm that can be described? Is this developed further or broken?

Is speech controlled by rhetorical devices, such as comparisons, similes, interrogations, exclamations, and so forth? (In renaissance and earlier texts, and in sophisticated comedies, these devices can be complicated, and variations in pattern can be very effective.)

If the dialogue is in verse, the effects of meter must also be considered: how regular, how far from ordinary speech rhythms, how musically subtle are the lines of dialogue?

Consider for example, Sara speaking to her mother toward the end of Act 4 of Eugene O'Neill's *A Touch of the Poet* (1946, 1957):

> Then Simon said how poor he was, and he'd never accept a penny from his father, even if he offered it. And I told him never mind, that if we had to live in a hut, or sleep in the grass of a field without a roof to our heads, and work our hands to the bone, or starve itself, I'd be in heaven and sing with the joy of our love!

Punctuation indicates how this speech should be broken up, so that words come in waves, growing in power. Although "or starve itself" is much the shortest phrase, this does not prevent the following clause from seeming like an inevitable and sustained conclusion; the contrast between them gives an impression of the gathering of energy before a last utterance. After this, two simple verbs sustain the flow within a single extended clause, giving an impression of release and freedom: no comma interrupts movement into "and sing with the joy of our love!" The nouns in this conclusion, *heaven, joy, love*, are unlike all the others, and they arrive here with no fuss or sign of difficulty. The verb *sing* lifts the phrase by introducing references to impulse and grace that are entirely new. Their position and rhythm have empowered the simplest words: "I'd be in heaven and sing with the joy of our love!" In this play, so far as this passage suggests, the ordinary is transformed into light and joy, or, perhaps, seems to be.

The whole speech has not yet been quoted. It continues after a stage direction:

> *(She looks up at her mother.)* And I meant it, Mother! I meant every word of it from the bottom of my heart!

The repeated verb *meant*, the short address to *Mother*, the self-consciousness about what has been said, expressed in "every word," and the clichéd conclusion in "from the bottom of my heart"—all weaken the impression of confidence that had been gained at the end of the earlier part of this speech. Short, emphatic phrases, together with the physical movement required for Sara to look up at her mother, break the sustained and ecstatic mood. These words and action remind us that speech is not necessarily a direct or complete representation of thought: despite a show of spontaneity, Sara had not been altogether convinced in the earlier part of this speech. One of the more difficult but necessary questions to ask about the diction of any play is how truly it represents the consciousness of the speaker.

Choose a play and take two speeches of ten or twenty lines spoken by the same leading character, one from near the beginning and one from near the end, and then examine their diction to find what mental forces are at work in these speeches. What conflicts do you find? What contrasts are there between the two passages?

Because the speaking of words is only part of what happens onstage, and spoken words may only partially represent the thoughts of the speaker, the effect of diction cannot be assessed apart from other factors. To gain a wider understanding of what is happening in the play, we can ask specific questions about the interchange between characters:

> Does one character dominate the dialogue, or is the lead shared between several? Do short speeches interrupt longer ones, or the other way around?
>
> Does a change of topic or approach surprise a person who is listening onstage, or is a single development sustained between several speakers? What are the occasions for any breakdown or sudden switch in subject or in the person addressed?
>
> How often do the leading characters only pretend to mean what they say? Do they put on fronts, intentionally mislead other characters, or tell lies? (This happens frequently in all kinds of play; deception is, after all, a specialty of actors.)

Other questions are equally relevant when a single character is speaking:

> Are there unexpected silences or shifts of attention?
>
> Does a character say he or she will do something and then not do it, or do something different?
>
> Are some words repeated without apparent cause?
>
> Do words with double meanings interrupt or modify a line of thought in speech?

All these questions can be answered in the affirmative with regard to the speeches we have already examined. Sara's change of both attention and rhythm after "sing with the joy of our love!" suggest unspoken fear or disbelief. May's repeated attention to the "picture" indicates a concern with what it depicts; that she never names what is in the picture only accentuates the mystery. Hamlet's "quietus" and "bodkin," close together, indicate a more positive resolve than could be expressed in the form of the question with which he had started the passage six lines earlier. Underneath their words, the minds of these characters are working in their own fashion so that words express only a part of their thoughts.

As noted in Chapter 1, this unspoken activity is usually called a character's *subtext*. Konstantin Stanislavsky (1863-1938) is usually credited with inventing the term. At the Moscow Art Theatre, he was the first successful director of the plays of Anton Chekhov—a writer especially skilled at suggesting unspoken thoughts—and later Stanislavsky formulated a method of actor training that pays great attention to subtext (see Chapter 5, "Expressive Acting").

Some plays have almost no subtext; the dramatists have made their characters speak as they think, thus drawing attention to what happens between them rather than to what is happening inside their minds. Story and argument are then more important than how these characters function. Dialogue may still surprise, and characters may be of two minds, but the conflict is expressed directly and explicitly, not through suggestion. An audience is not invited to dwell on what is unspoken, and the actor is not called upon to sustain silences or suggest hidden energies. Bertolt Brecht's *epic plays* (discussed earlier in this chapter) are examples of this way of communicating ideas, but most of us can read these plays only in translation; texts written in English will be more useful. Here is a passage from near the beginning of Caryl Churchill's *Cloud Nine* (1979), in which a number of British colonials are discussing their situation in Africa in Victorian times:

BETTY: I don't think mother is on a visit. I think she lives with us.
CLIVE: I think she does.
BETTY: Clive you are so good.
CLIVE: But are you bored my love?
BETTY: It's just that I miss you when you're away. We're not in this country to enjoy ourselves. If I lack society that is my form of service.
CLIVE: That's a brave girl. So today has been all right? No fainting? No hysteria?
BETTY: I have been very tranquil.

Dramatists who wish to draw attention to the inner life of their characters are not so brisk as this in their dialogue, but fasten on particular words, curious allusions and puns, and uncertain flurries of verbal activity. They also leave silences unexplained, provide hesitations, and use words where they are quite obviously inadequate to their occasion. David Mamet's *American Buffalo* (1975, 1977) has many examples, for instance its opening moments:

DON: So?
Pause.
         So what, Bob?
Pause.
BOB: I'm sorry, Donny.
Pause.
DON: All right.
BOB: I'm sorry, Donny.
Pause.
DON: Yeah.
BOB: Maybe he's still in there.
DON: If you think that, Bob, how come you're here?
BOB: I came in.
Pause.
DON: You don't come in Bob. You don't come in until you do a thing.

These are people with secrets. To make sense of this exchange, the actors have to know what they are not saying. The audience, at this point in the play, can only sense the underlying pressures the characters are experiencing in gesture, movement, tension, and change of attention.

A similar impression of underlying meanings can be inferred when characters say too much, talking with disproportionate or seemingly unnecessary energy, or when they turn to new topics without explanation. For example, Paula Vogel's *The Baltimore Waltz* (1991) starts with a speech by Anna that can seem funny and wacky on a first reading:

I've never been abroad. It's not that I don't want to—but the language terrifies me. I was traumatized by a junior high school French teacher, and after that, it was a lost cause. I think that's the reason I went into elementary education. Words like bureau, bidet, bildungsroman raise a sweat.
Oh, I want to go. Carl—he's my brother, you'll meet him shortly—he desperately wants to go. But then, he can speak six languages. He's the head librarian of literature and languages at the San Francisco Public. It's a very important position.

The shift of attention to Carl and his linguistic abilities, the strange emphases in "terrifies . . . traumatized . . . lost cause . . . raise a sweat . . . desperately," and the apparently irrelevant "It's a very important position," all suggest that Anna's mind is fastened on something she is not mentioning. Only later does it become quite clear that Carl has contracted AIDS, and that, at some level, Anna's distress about her brother's illness is never out of her mind.

Sometimes a dramatist will insert speeches that draw attention quite explicitly to an ongoing subtextual activity. In his first scene, Hamlet speaks of "that within which passes show" (I, ii), and later he calls it "the heart of my mystery" (III, ii). He does not explain what he is referring to, although, at the beginning of the last scene, he tells Horatio "thou wouldst not think how ill all's here about my heart," he explains little more when he adds:

> It is but foolery, but it is such a kind of gain-giving, as would perhaps trouble a woman.
>
> *Hamlet*, V, ii

Hamlet makes it very clear that he never speaks his mind "freely," as he says a person in a play should (II, ii).

In Sam Shepard's *Fool for Love*, when Eddie hears May talk about "the man who's coming over here" to take her out for the evening, he pounces on a single word:

EDDIE: First off, it can't be very serious.
MAY: Oh, really? And why is that?
EDDIE: Because you call him a "man."
MAY: What am I supposed to call him?
EDDIE: A "guy" or something. If you called him a "guy," I'd be worried about it
          but since you call him a "man" you give yourself away. You're in a
          dumb situation with this guy by calling him a "man." You put yourself
          below him.

May did not intend to give away her inner thoughts. Nor does Eddie, although his possessiveness has almost surfaced in the changing rhythms, repetitions, and final shift of emphasis of this speech.

> *Take a play you know well and, paying particular attention to one of its main characters, look for signs of subtextual thoughts and feelings: are they ever expressed in words?*

Spectacle

After diction, the two other fingers on the hand that help to control how a play comes alive in performance are spectacle and music. The visual effect of spectacle is much easier to study than music, because a lot of easy questions immediately suggest themselves; for instance,

> How much detail about physical things is given by means of stage directions or
> implications of the dialogue? What kinds of things are these? Some plays
> emphasize dress, others furniture or properties (or props) held in the hand (such
> as swords or telephones), or the quality of light on the stage, or signs of rank,
> race, or family.

Hamlet, like most plays of its period, has little to say about visual effect, but for that reason what is mentioned becomes all the more significant: various weapons (finally a poisoned rapier), letters and documents, two books, the stage props belonging to the players who come to court, two portraits, various flowers and herbs, skulls, human bones and earth, a coffin and the sound of a bell, a cup for wine and a pearl; and then, after every word has been spoken, the canon that are heard firing off-stage. Costumes also add to spectacle and help to establish place, occasion, and function. Some are designed to keep off intense cold or the dust and dirt of travel; some display signs of power and wealth, for the players and for the characters in the main play. For Hamlet and Ophelia especially, costumes become signs of mourning and derangement. Through these visual devices a "world" is created onstage for the play's characters to inhabit, struggle against, or seek to escape.

Stage directions in Mamet's *American Buffalo* say little about what is seen onstage, but they still demand a great deal: the simple words *"Don's Resale Shop. A junkshop"* set the scene and imply a stage crowded with discarded items, all out of their proper place but available and at hand. The dramatist has asked for an entire stage set crowded with objects in intentional disarray. Through dialogue and stage directions the playwright specifies a few particular objects, for example the coffee and food that is brought in. In the last act Teach trashes the junkshop with a "dead-pig sticker" so that this disordered world becomes still further disordered in an eruption of violence. A further specified item is very small indeed, but the object of intense concern, even when it is offstage: a small American Buffalo coin that is believed to be of great value. By these means, spectacle makes undeniable effects, contributing to story, character, and theme, being continually present to the audience and communicating in ways that words alone would be unable to match in continuous and wide-ranging effect.

Other plays are very specific about what is placed onstage and the mood or atmosphere that these items cast over the whole action. Influenced by film, many dramatists—in America especially—have been very demanding of set designers, stage technicians, and stage managers. Tennessee Williams's *The Glass Menagerie* (1945) has the following opening stage direction:

> *At the rise of the curtain, the audience is faced with the dark, grim rear wall of the Wing-field tenement. This building, which runs parallel to the footlights, is flanked on both sides by dark, narrow alleys which run into murky canyons of tangled clothes-lines, garbage cans, and the sinister lattice-work of neighboring fire-escapes. It is up and down these side alleys that exterior entrances and exits are made, during the play. At the end of Tom's opening commentary, the dark tenement wall slowly reveals (by means of a transparency) the interior of the ground floor Wingfield apartment.*

Williams called this work a "memory play," explaining in an introductory note:

> *Memory takes a lot of poetic license. It omits some details; others are exaggerated, according to the emotional value of the articles it touches. . . . The interior is therefore rather dim and poetic.*

Toward the end, the interior of the apartment is transformed to welcome a guest and *"The results are astonishing"* (scene 6).

For such a play, spectacle is an ever-present statement, influencing what is said, the actors' performances, and the audience's reactions. So different is this kind of spectacle from what was possible on the open, unlit space of an Elizabethan stage or in the small studio theatres of today, that such a play would lose hugely by being performed in either of those conditions. An audience is meant to "take it all in," as if looking at some large picture that is strange, changing, and alluring. Sometimes spectators are drawn to concentrate on a single point in expectation of some crucial movement or in search of an explanation to some puzzle, but at other times they are invited to survey the wide expanse of a carefully arranged scene in which individual characters can either relate to each other or seem to exist independently. Through lighting effects, stage business, or dialogue, audience members are encouraged to look here *and* there, to appreciate the "whole picture."

In some plays, the spectacle required by the dramatist contains a single dominant feature that offers a continuous challenge to the characters who come in contact with it. An example of this is found in August Wilson's *The Piano Lesson* (1987-1990) where *"The Setting"* is described in a special note at the head of the play as the *"kitchen and parlor"* of a house that is *"sparsely furnished, and although there is evidence of a woman's touch, there is a lack of warmth and vigor."* In contrast:

> *Dominating the parlor is an old upright piano. On the legs of the piano, carved in the manner of African sculpture, are mask-like figures resembling totems. The carvings are rendered with a grace and power of invention that lifts them out of the real of craftsmanship and into the realm of art.*

When everyone else is in a state of panic at the end of the play, running around the room, throwing water about, and calling out to a Ghost, Berniece goes to the piano and begins to play singing a song *"intended as an exorcism and a dressing for battle."* The one spectacular piece of stage property is now playing a leading part in the drama with the result that the character in contact with it has far greater power and relevance than she could have had without it.

In all plays one element of spectacle is always present: the actors themselves. Onstage, the characters are visible to the audience whether they are standing, sitting, or moving around in varying combinations and oppositions, or in isolation from each other. They are seen as they engage in various activities, each of which involves a particular speed, rhythm, posture, and unanimity or independence of action. No matter what is said, what is *done* onstage can have equal, superior, or contrary effect, and the relationship between speech and action is a constant tool for any dramatist. To understand how a play works in performance, this twin and sometimes contrary "voice" of physical presence must be attended to, as well as what is being said.

Certain very simple questions can be asked in order to assess the effect of this continuous and living spectacle:

> How many people are onstage, and how does the number vary throughout the play?
>
> How do visual groupings change in the course of the play, scene by scene and episode by episode?
>
> What activities are prescribed by dialogue or stage directions?
>
> What costume changes are required? What props and furniture are used?

Surprisingly perhaps, lists of these physical details can reveal a great deal about the theme or characters of a play—and much more quickly and surely than the dialogue will. (Inanimate things cannot lie, and bodily presence, in its essentials, is unmistakable and unambiguous.)

One of the great advantages of actors being used to create spectacle is that a dramatist can use them to say two things at once. An example can be found toward the end of Shepard's *Fool for Love*:

> EDDIE *and* MAY *come together center stage. They embrace. They kiss each other tenderly. Headlights suddenly arc across stage again from up right, cutting across the stage through window then disappearing off left. Sound of loud collision, shattering glass, an explosion. Bright orange and blue light of a gasoline fire suddenly illuminates upstage window. Then sounds of horses screaming wildly, hooves galloping on pavement, fading, then total silence. Light of gas fire continues now to end of play.* EDDIE *and* MAY *never stop holding each other through all this. Long pause. No one moves.*

Here, as often, sound and light are part of the spectacle. The effect captures the eyes and ears of the audience and, during all of the other visual changes, the kiss and embrace grow more impressive in their stillness until, at last, the two silent figures are shown in *"total silence,"* irremovably and tenderly together. No quantity of sensitive diction could establish or contain such acceptance between two people.

In any consideration of spectacle, a play's theme, story, and characters are all inevitably involved, and this invites a more general question that can be applied to diction as well: How lifelike is what happens onstage? It is important to ask this question, not because a play is good or bad insofar as it is close in every detail to the life it mirrors, but because the ways in which the play departs from a depiction of life are a good indication of how it works upon an audience.

> *Take any play and make lists of the activities of two or three of the leading characters—whether they change their clothes (on- or offstage), sleep, eat, walk, run, sit, kneel, write or read letters, pick up telephones, or whatever—and compare all this with what you do in the course of a day or a week. Then consider, How exceptional are these people onstage? What does this tell you about the image of life that the play gives and the differing involvements of the leading characters?*

Music

Music that is played or sung is signaled by clear stage directions, and its contribution to how the play works is usually limited to particular moments: Ophelia's mad songs; the soft words of Merle Haggard's "I'm the One Who Loves You" (music by Stuart Hamblem: *"moderato, with expression"*), which is heard at the end of *Fool for Love* as the Old Man is left rocking slowly in his chair and the fire glows for a while; the Irish reel played in the bar at the end of *A Touch of the Poet*. Music sustains its effect over longer time spans than words do, and, when sung by a particular character, it holds back other dramatic development for its duration. Sometimes it can generalize emotional involvement, whether that is upbeat or downbeat, making it more easily shared between characters and between stage and audience; and, slowly and irresistibly, it can intensify feeling.

These effects are easily noted and seen to contribute to a play at specific times, but music has a subtler and more widespread power in the theatre because *all* sound can become musical. In a well-ordered performance, certain sounds recur and develop, climaxes arrive and then can be swept away until a new sound emerges; silences are established and sometimes these are linked mysteriously together. In a very surreptitious way, a whole play can be like a piece of music in performance, and when this happens an extra assurance is felt onstage and in the auditorium; everything seems intentional and to have power beyond the ordinary. Movements, then, become something like dance, seemingly inevitable and delicately meaningful.

Such total experiences are very rare in hard-pressed theatres that lack the time or talents to rehearse adequately, but, in some particular scenes or some fleeting moments, all really good performances have something of this extra power. During long and careful rehearsals, actors and director listen for this music, and try to help it come into being. It can scarcely be heard at all by studying a play's text, and it may be totally drowned out in a poor performance. For a student, the best course is to know that this eloquent harmony of effect, this "music of the spheres," is possible in the theatre and to be attentive whenever the faintest sound of it can be heard. It is perhaps the greatest and rarest glory of theatre.

In many ways what we find on the page can be denied on the stage. The actors can disregard the text and put little in its place beyond a projection of their own personalities and talents. Or they may be incapable of an adequate response or be determined to impose their own response to the situation set up by the script. Sometimes a director will create a production that is quite different from that envisioned by the dramatist. No one can gain a full idea of what a play may become onstage simply by studying its text.

Theatre lives in performance, and for that we must consider both how a play is performed and where and when it is produced. The next three chapters will therefore consider theatre spaces, audiences, and acting. Consideration of acting, which deals directly with play texts, is delayed for a while, so that performance may be seen in the theatre and before an audience which together provide the necessary support for its professional existence. Later chapters look at stage design, production, rehearsal, and training. Of course, plays will continue to be in our minds: this chapter, which is longer than any of the others, has been the beginning, not the end, of an exploration of how plays function in performance.

3
_____

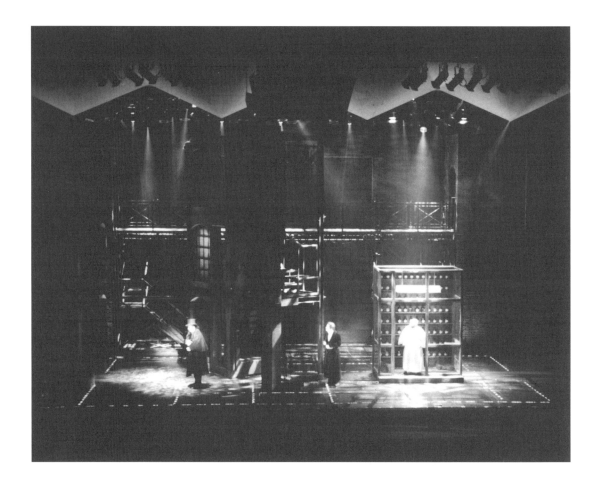

On Stage: *Jekyll and Hyde*, Leslie Bricusse (lyrics) and Greg Boyd (direction); set at the Houston Music Hall, by Vince Mountain. (Photo by Vince Mountain.)

Theatres

A theatre is composed of two basic parts: a place for the audience, and a place for the actors to perform. Optionally, it may also have space in which to provide a setting or "scene," a special environment within which the action of a play takes place. With these three elements we can describe any theatre building and begin to assess its usefulness.

Different Kinds of Theatres

Picture-frame Theatres

Most of the older theatres we visit today—and some of the newer ones—were built in a form that was considered very advanced and modern some seventy years ago (Figures 3.1 and 3.2).

In straight or slightly curved rows on one, two, or three levels, the audience sits facing a large hole in one of four walls. Rich decorations often surround this opening, and within it, as in a frame, the actors perform on a level platform extending a considerable distance back and away from the audience. Above, at the sides, and a little to the rear of this acting area, space and equipment are provided to support painted canvas and other kinds of scenery, and to store still more scenery that can rapidly take the place of that which has previously been on view. These surrounding spaces also conceal the various sources of artificial light and the means to create other stage effects, such as thunder, rain, snow, or an impression that the stage itself is moving. Another name for the picture-frame theatre, more commonly but, as we shall see, less accurately used, is *proscenium theatre*.

The picture-frame theatre became popular with the development of artificial lighting, first with gas and then with electricity. The theatre was designed so that playgoers sit in the dark with their attention drawn to the action taking place on a brightly or subtly lit stage seen behind a dividing arch or frame. The lighting and scenery in this theatre is capable of precise imitation of real-life conditions, with particular tones, shadows, and lights. Together with tricks of perspective, lighting can give an impression of great space or of a fantastic or opulent environment. Because every member of the audience sits facing in much the same direction,

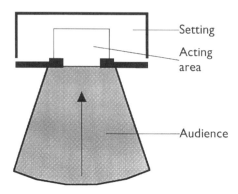

Setting

Acting
area

Audience

Figure 3.1
Ground plan of a picture-frame theatre.

groups of actors onstage can be deployed in complicated formations without obscuring anyone's view; and a single grouping may be held for some time with only slight variations, each one making maximum impact by reason of the surrounding stillness.

This theatre can present a carefully arranged image of individuals and their relationships, rather like an old-fashioned photograph of a family group set in a very noticeable frame. It can also be a lavish theatre, because lighting, scenery, and large-scale effects can represent conditions of life quite surpassing anything outside its frame, in brightness, luxury, mystery, or danger. The audience can watch another carefully and secretly organized world, set up before them for their pleasure, precise scrutiny, or wonder. Sitting comfortably in darkness, the audience submits to what is displayed.

At one time architects, technicians, actors, designers, and directors were all agreed that a picture-frame theatre was obviously the right one to build in a technological age. In such a space settings could become ever more marvelous or realistic, and actors could refine their performances with the knowledge that their smallest gesture would be visible. Directors working in these theatres could position and control their actors with great precision.

Since the Second World War, however, these excellent qualities of the picture-frame theatre have become less and less acceptable. Actors want more freedom. Some of them want to "get at" their audience, to "break out" of the "frame," and to experiment rather than assume studied postures. Dramatists and directors no longer want to compete with the cinema in providing an illusion of actual life or of luxurious and fabulously exotic worlds. Some want to simplify the background for dramatic action so that only the most significant details are shown, as if they were medieval icons or figures in a cartoon. Others want no setting at all so that they gain undeflected and intimate attention for what the actors are saying and doing. Some directors want to keep action moving incessantly so that they can challenge their audience to follow or to seek out for themselves where the center of interest lies. Others attempt to elicit the vocal or active response of their audiences, as if audience members were actually part of the action onstage.

All this is very difficult to achieve from within the closed "world" of the picture-frame stage. At one time, it was fashionable to provide brilliant lighting in only small areas within the frame so that a sequence of small scenes could be dominated by the actors, but this technique accentuated the actors' separation from the

Figure 3.2   The Mertz Theatre in the Asolo Center for the Performing Arts: built at the turn of the nineteenth and twentieth centuries at Dunfermline, Scotland, this five-hundred-seat picture-frame theatre was rebuilt in 1990 in Florida. (Photograph by Wayne Eastep, courtesy of the Asolo Center for the Performing Arts.)

audience sitting in its own darkness; it was also a style of production that looked very obviously manipulated. In an attempt to solve these problems architects and designers have invented other forms of theatre buildings or reinvented them from earlier models.

Another reason for the picture-frame falling out of fashion is its costliness: scenery has to be specially created for each new production and has to fill a large space; as labor costs have risen, this form of theatre has priced itself out of the running. An exception is its continued use for huge and sensational shows that can be expected to run unchanged for years and years: *Chorus Line*, *Phantom of the Opera*, *Miss Saigon*, and other well-financed and well-promoted investments.

Many of the theatres being built today are like those that were in common use before the invention of gas or electric light, and before cinema competed with theatre. These theatres have far more sophisticated equipment than their predecessors, but in effect their architects have been redesigning the wheel, rediscovering how to use some basic attractions of theatre that have been lost as a consequence of the scenic achievements of picture-frame theatres. Today theatres are being built with an *open* stage, *thrust* stage, *arena* stage, or *traverse* stage, and their auditoriums and accommodations for scenery are being reshaped to fit the stage design. As architects have become unsure of what form of theatre to build, all kinds of existing buildings have been brought into use and adapted in whatever form was practicable. Performances are also being given, once again, in public spaces such as streets, parks, halls of all sorts, and museums and churches.

Open-stage Theatres

The *open stage*, or *end stage*, is the simplest of the reinvented forms (Figure 3.3).

In an open-stage theatre the auditorium remains almost unchanged, but the frame has gone, and the only place to establish a setting is on the back wall and within the acting area itself. The Mermaid Theatre at Blackfriars in the City of London, which opened in 1959, helped to set an international trend. This open-stage theatre was simple to build, because it fitted into the main walls of an earlier building and was economical to run. As a result, open-stage theatres were soon to be found everywhere. Well-known examples are the small off-Broadway theatres that in postwar years were fitted into old buildings on Forty-second Street, west of Eighth Avenue in New York City. The simplicity of this arrangement is reminiscent of that used when plays were presented in banquet and assembly halls throughout Europe long before special theatre buildings became common.

The Mermaid and some larger theatres of the open-stage form have turntables in their stages to effect changes of location, but scenic illusion remains less than completely realized because the dramatic action does not become part of a picture. The division between stage and auditorium is not fixed and unassailable, because the frame has gone and light spills out from the stage. The audience feels closer to the actors, because the front of the stage is wider and more members of the audience sit within a few yards of the performers. In small off-Broadway theatres—*shoebox theatres*—actors can address their entire audience directly, or the whole interior can become a single site for performance, with entrances to the stage being made from the back of the audience, and sound and light enveloping everyone equally.

Thrust-stage Theatres

Because it is seen from three sides, a *thrust stage* brings its audience more fully into the action. Most spectators can see other members of the audience sitting opposite them who thus become part of the setting for the play (Figures 3.4 and 3.5).

In Spain and England at the end of the sixteenth century, the thrust stage was the usual form in which theatres were built. In the rectangular Spanish *corrales* or the circled Elizabethan public playhouses (Figures 3.6 and 3.7) audiences stood or sat around the stage, both below its level and in galleries or small rooms above. In our newly built thrust-stage theatres, such as the Festival Theatre at Stratford, Ontario, or the Tyrone Guthrie at Minneapolis, spectators are seated in rows raised one above the other and in a higher balcony. Elizabethan playhouses could accommodate two or three thousand, all seated within forty or fifty feet of the stage, and the Festival Theatre in Ontario seats nearly two thousand so that members of the audience seated the farthest away from the stage are only thirteen rows from the front. In a picture-frame theatre of similar capacity, many of the playgoers might be twice as far away from the stage.

With a thrust stage, contact between actors and members of the audience is still closer than with an open or end stage, but if actors wish to address the whole

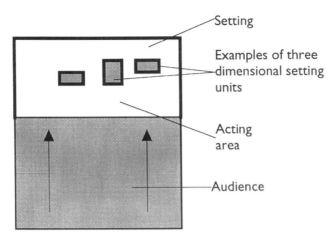

Figure 3.3 Ground plan of an open-stage theatre.

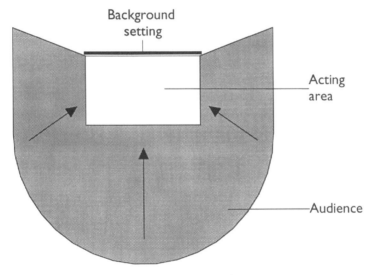

Figure 3.4 Ground plan of a thrust-stage theatre.

audience, they must either move to the back and center of the acting area, thus removing themselves from everyone by some twenty feet, or they must move around the stage so that they project some part of what they are saying to each of the three sides. Effort is needed for actors to project their voices strongly and clearly enough to be heard on all sides. The thrust-stage theatre is good for procession, choreographic movement, spirited comedy, and pageantry. Except in small scale, this theatre form is not very suitable for intimate drama or for drama involving intense feeling that has to be sustained or slowly developed.

Scenic settings can be used only when placed up against the fourth side of this stage. In renaissance Spain and England this background was almost unchanging from play to play, and some contemporary directors favor a similarly

Figure 3.5 A modern thrust-stage theatre: Marjorie Bradley Kellogg's set for George Bernard Shaw's *Heartbreak House* at Circle in the Square Theatre, New York. (Photograph of the set reproduced by permission of the designer.)

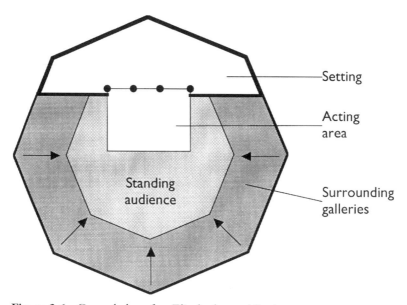

Figure 3.6 Ground plan of an Elizabethan public theatre.

neutral presentation. As a compromise, small pieces of scenery, such as a tree, fireplace, or the mast of a ship, and a few practicable objects, such as a throne, bed, or tombstone, can be brought center stage to indicate place or occasion, but these must not be so large or numerous that they obstruct the view of the audi-

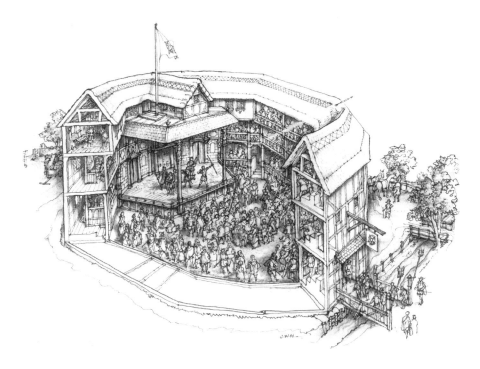

Figure 3.7 The Rose Theatre in Elizabethan London: a reconstruction, by scholar-artist Walter Hodges, depicts Shakespeare's *Titus Andronicus* in performance. (Reproduced by permission of the artist.)

ence across the acting area. The back wall of the stage contains entranceways for the actors, and here some small pieces of scenery may be introduced to show what lies behind, or whether the stage represents an interior or exterior location. But while these devices can indicate different places and times, they cannot re-create or give an illusion of real time and place. Basically the stage is always a stage on which the action of the play occurs, and the actors must define where they are by how they act and speak and by the clothes they wear or props they carry. Night scenes, for example, were indicated in Shakespeare's day by having actors carry lights, even though plays were presented in the daylight. These signs, together with how the actors behaved and what they said, were sufficient to establish a sense of darkness in the minds of the audience.

Modern thrust stages have light and sound to help set the scene, but for the most part with this form of theatre the audience's imagination has to fill out what is merely suggested onstage. For many members of the audience the background setting on the fourth side of the stage is within their line of vision only when an actor stands back close to it, or is making his entry from the backstage areas. For most of the audience, the main background for a play's action will always be the rest of the audience; this happened in earlier theatres and it continues to happen in modern theatres, because some light will always spill from this kind of stage into the auditorium. Actors have to dominate, and not only when they are speaking; in group scenes some of the audience will see only those characters who react to what is being said, and it is through their performances, with faces turned away, that the drama has to be communicated. An individual actor will dominate only when he or she is able to command attention from all sides by the dynamic qualities of performance, by expressive movement and speech, and by highly charged emotional excitement. The thrust-stage theatre is good for star actors, as well as for large-scale group activity.

Arena-stage Theatres

An *arena stage* completely eliminates the use of full-scale settings, except on the floor of the stage (Figure 3.8).

The audience sits on four sides of the acting area, as around a circus ring. The most carefully developed example of this form is Arena Stage in Washington, D.C. (Figure 3.9), but, because it is the cheapest type of space to build and to run, many small and temporary theatres have used the same layout. Entry to the stage is from its four corners or some other locations where seats have been removed; occasionally, entrances can be through a trapdoor. The actors' groupings and movements are viewed from all four sides, so that they lose the scenic support of the fourth side of a thrust stage. There are two important consequences. First, there is only one basic location for dramatic action at any one time; for example, it is difficult to suggest that some characters are within a house or prison while others are outside because any structure onstage has to be very small if it is not to obstruct some section of the audience's view. Second, an upstage, central position, from which an actor on a thrust stage can dominate the whole theatre without moving, does not exist here; even the protagonist at the end of a tragedy must move around to address all parts of the audience. In effect, this theatre tends to cut every performer down to the same potential effectiveness and to make all places on the stage of equal importance; it requires actors to maintain continuous movement throughout much of their performance.

To mitigate the disadvantages and to make the most of the advantages of this form, seating is often very steeply tiered, as in the arena stage of the Bingham Theatre at the Actors Theatre of Louisville, which opened in 1995 (Figure 3.10). By this means, an audience can more easily see across the stage and respond to the patterns of the actors' movements. Because the rows of seats are widest farthest from the stage, the disadvantage of this form is that a majority of the audience looks down on the actors, making face-to-face contact between actors and members of the audience more difficult. This is a considerable limitation. For comedy, an actor's eye level should be higher rather than lower than that of the majority of persons watching. When actors have to communicate deep feeling, they are also at a disadvantage in a small arena theatre because their faces must be tilted upward if they are to be seen and heard. A steeply tiered and encircling auditorium was provided in old-fashioned anatomy lecture theatres, where it was appropriate for the audience to have a clear and intimate view and yet remain at a distance from what was being displayed, and this is very much the effect that is created in smaller arena stages. A steeply tiered arena theatre is most suited to ensemble plays, where interactions between characters are especially significant and where perfect vision is a necessity.

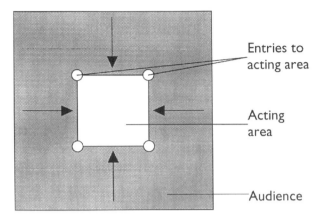

Figure 3.8 Ground plan of an arena-stage theatre.

Figure 3.9 The main theatre of Arena Stage, Washington, D.C. Note the "scenic" entranceways set up at two corners of the acting area. (Reproduced by permission of Arena Stage, Washington, D.C.)

Traverse-stage Theatres

The Sant' Erasmo Theatre in Milan and the Traverse Theatre in Edinburgh helped to pioneer a theatre form with a *traverse stage* (Figure 3.11).

Both theatre spaces are small with a stage running across the middle and the audience seating positioned on either side of the stage. Theatres in this form have

Figure 3.10   The Bingham Theatre of the Actors Theatre of Louisville. This 336-seat theatre, which opened in 1995, is half the capacity of the company's main house. Note the steeply tiered seats around its arena stage and the use of furniture and a "tree" to indicate location. (Photograph by Richard Trigg; courtesy of Actors Theatre of Louisville.)

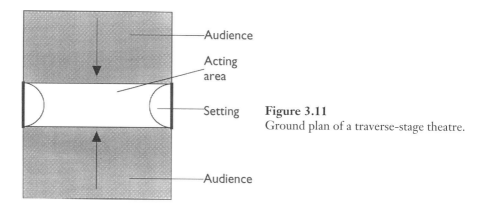

Figure 3.11
Ground plan of a traverse-stage theatre.

two scenic backgrounds, one at either end of a long and narrow acting area, which can be used to give fixed points of reference for a play's narrative. However, the audience sees both backgrounds at acute angles and therefore registers their scenery only when action is purposefully concentrated near them: in effect scenery can both dominate and seem to be nonexistent. Direct address to the audience is difficult because actors have to deliver their lines to two opposing sides, but dialogue shared between two or more characters can be played along the length of the stage so that the audience has a view of each individual or group taking part. In a small theatre, a traverse stage is preeminently suited to intense psychological encounter; in larger spaces, it is suited to plays showing journeys from one place to another or depicting conflict between opposing parties.

Other Types of Theatres

Many more variations of the three basic elements of a theatre building are possible. Some were once common but appropriate only to particular conditions that no longer exist. In the seventeenth and eighteenth centuries, a platform stage was used in conjunction with a deep background that accommodated changeable scenery behind a proscenium arch or frame; theatres in England during the Restoration period, from the 1660s onward, are good examples of this form (Figure 3.13).

Stage settings could not be brightly illuminated in the deep space behind the proscenium for fear of fire from naked flames, so the plays of this period often have stage directions such as this one from George Farquhar's *Recruiting Officer* (1706), act V, scene V: "*A Court of Justice.* Balance, Scale, Scruple *upon the bench* . . . Kite *and* Constable *advance to the front of the stage.*" Often the actors did not enter within the setting, but in front of it through one of the "proscenium" doors that opened directly on to the platform; there were two on each side. This is the essential difference between a "picture-frame theatre" and a proscenium one.

The proscenium theatre was suitable for very verbal and topical plays in which action was forwarded by talk between two, three, or four characters standing as close as possible to the audience and in relation to a background picturing an actual location. Asides, disguises, dance and song, and long complicated monologues were also well served.

In order to regain the advantages of this form of theatre today, some designers have built an additional platform out from the main stage of a picture-frame theatre which originally had no such provision. The added intimacy and directness of address to an audience are so attractive that a growing number of new proscenium theatres are being built with platform stages in the older manner; these also have old-fashioned galleries around the whole interior, embracing the platform and part of the auditorium and giving a greater sense of gathering together than is possible in a more confrontational open-stage theatre.

A special form of theatre was developed in ancient Greece between the fifth and third centuries B.C. (Figure 3.14). It served plays in which episodes of song, dance, and speech for members of a chorus alternated with encounters between single actors—*protagonists*—or between a protagonist and the chorus. To accommodate the chorus, a circular *orchestra*, or dancing area, was provided, and behind this was constructed a *scene* from which actors playing named roles could make their entries and exits. In time this smaller acting area was developed to become a much wider platform at a higher level than the orchestra. Around what was, in effect, a dual stage, a semicircle of seats was raised.

The scale of these open-air theatres in Greece was huge: the one surviving at Epidaurus can seat about twenty thousand spectators; its orchestra is some sixty feet in diameter. In this theatre space the patterned group movements of the chorus are impressive while, among the serried ranks of the audience sitting in the same light as the stage, a sense of common concern can arise with unequalled

Figure 3.12   The Shakespeare Memorial Theatre, Stratford-upon-Avon, 1930. Designed by Elisabeth Scott, this picture-frame theatre has been provided with a deep platform in front of its main curtain, but this part of the stage is not viewed from its sides as a true proscenium theatre would be. (Photograph by permission of the Shakespeare Centre Library, Stratford-upon-Avon.)

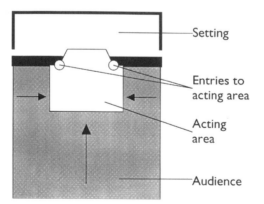

Figure 3.13   Ground plan of an English Restoration theatre.

force; terror or pity seems to have no bounds, so widely and obviously is it shared. For the actors, set apart from the chorus, grandly dressed, masked, and often alone, vocal power and clarity were absolute requirements for projecting the sustained speeches that the dramatists of the time supplied in full measure.

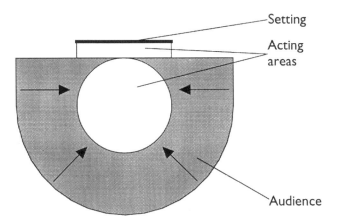

Figure 3.14 The basic form of a Greek theatre.

Other forms developed from the Greek theatres during the Roman Empire (Figure 3.15). The orchestra shrunk in importance as the role of a chorus lessened, while, at the same time and perhaps in consequence, the scenic background became more dominant. Smaller auditoriums brought the audience closer to the acting area.

Some modern theatres are compromises between Greek and Elizabethan models. They are smaller than the Greek and are roofed over; and most of their auditoriums are reduced to a narrower sector of a circle. The thrust stage is not constructed against part of the encircling galleries as in Elizabethan theatres, but is reduced in size and placed as in the corner of a large hall, with the audience seating rising in tiers in the shape of a fan opened to little more than ninety degrees (Figure 3.16; and compare Figure 3.6). The Olivier Theatre at Britain's National Theatre in London is an example of one of these compromises.

The simplest of all theatres involves only a few planks raised above an audience or a space cleared in the center of a hall or room with an audience sitting or standing all around. For popular performances throughout history, such theatres have been contrived in streets and marketplaces, large houses, gardens, places of worship, unused factories, or empty warehouses. In medieval times, a platform stage was often fixed on a cart so that it could be moved around. On holy days, one *pageant* after another would be wheeled to a single place, and on each an episode from the Bible was acted by amateur actors. These *mystery* cycles, and other *miracle* or *saint plays* were to be seen in many towns across Europe, especially in the fourteenth to sixteenth centuries. Sometimes a curtain screened off a backstage area of the cart in which the actors could prepare, and then the small platform became a thrust stage extended into the audience gathered round. Several small stages of this type might be used side by side, so that a single play could show a complicated narrative moving from one location to another. Panoramic dramas could show events occurring simultaneously in palace, city, and hilltop, or in heaven, hell, and ordinary life.

In these simple theatres, the location of the play's action was identified by stage props and costumes, sometimes elaborate ones, but no illusion of a real world was attempted: the scale of the stage was too small and the standing audience, able to

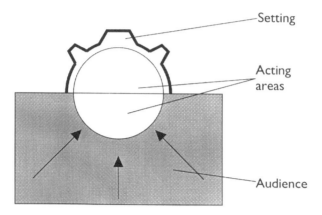

Figure 3.15   Ground plan of a theatre developed from the Greek theatre.

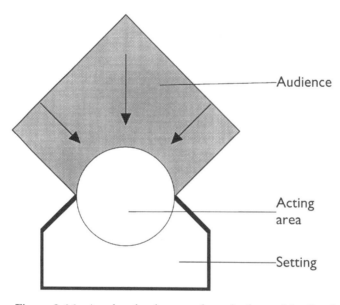

Figure 3.16   Another development from the form of the Greek theatre.

leave at any moment, could not be relied upon for patient attention. On the other hand, the actors' contact with their audience was easy and direct, so that verbal exchanges with spectators were common, and characters in the plays would sometimes leave the stage and continue the action among the audience.

In churches and churchyards, performances might be given at several places where a font, crib, choir, altar, image, gravestone, or door might serve to locate the drama. An actor representing Death could appear before a tomb where the devout were accustomed to meditating on death, or a mechanical dove could descend on a wire to represent the coming of the Holy Spirit at the place and time of year appropriate to the church's rituals and liturgical calendar. The church choir, vestments, visual symbolism, and holy writ all became part of the drama.

Variable Theatres

The conditions of medieval and popular theatres are very like those favored by some of the most innovative theatre companies working today. Given the increased cost involved in building special theatre spaces and elaborate scenic devices, improvised stages are returning to use. Plays are produced in what is often called a *black box*: a very simple theatre well-equipped with lighting and sound, but with no fixed staging or seating arrangements. The three basic elements—stage, auditorium, and scene—may be arranged in these laboratory or studio theatres in any shape or form, and so play directors are free to vary at will both the style of production and the relationship between actors and audience. Productions are not always equally simple, because the adaptability of a free-form studio theatre often gives rise to productions of the highest sophistication. Pioneering examples have included Jerzy Grotowski's Laboratory Theatre at Wroclaw in Poland in the 1960s, Ariane Mnouchkine's *Théâtre du Soleil* in Paris from 1964 onward, and Peter Stein's productions in the 1960s and 1970s for the Berlin Schaubühne when it was housed in a very large film studio.

As we have seen, theatres are built today in any of a number of forms, none of which is without serious limitations, so it is not surprising that companies dedicated to exploration and innovation should be drawn to buildings that allow complete flexibility in both form and scale; in such spaces they may develop a style of production that can reflect an unprecedented technological age.

> *Visit the local theatre you know best, if possible when no play is being performed, and make a very simple sketch of its three basic elements (like the line drawings in this chapter). Consider whether the theatre was built in any of the forms that have been described. Is it a compromise between two different forms?*

Spaces for Plays

Any one form of theatre will not be entirely suitable for all kinds of performance or all kinds of play. This would quickly become obvious if you could see the same play—ideally the same production—staged in two different theatres. Both scale and form will influence how you see and enjoy the play. How close are you to the actors? Do you look up at them or down on them? Are you seated comfortably, or do you have to stand? How visible and well lit is the setting? How aware are you of other members of the audience, those close to you or on the opposite side of the stage?

Today many theatres have two or more auditoriums. For example, the Playhouse in the Park at Cincinnati has two. Its large thrust stage, with steeply raked auditorium not quite on three sides of it, will stage Shakespeare, musicals, or large-cast realistic plays; it is not an easy theatre in which to perform quick comedies. Its small, Shelterhouse studio theatre houses new realistic plays and also the more intimate classics, such as Eugene O'Neill's *Long Day's Journey into Night*. Although Arena Stage in Washington, D.C., is known chiefly for the form of theatre from which it takes its name, numerous plays would not be well served by being performed there, so the company has two other stages that are not in any sense arenas.

Some plays seem to require two different kinds of theatre. Tennessee Williams's *Glass Menagerie*, for example, needs a very intimate theatre for its many quiet scenes between two characters; but its scenic demands, with several different acting areas and vistas extending beyond the central space, call for a large-scale picture-frame stage and complex technical equipment.

Restoration comedies, and plays by Molière and other seventeenth-century European writers, would be produced more often if a greater number of modern theatres had the platform stages that made possible the intimate audience-stage relationship for which the texts were written. To stage Restoration comedies on a picture-frame stage removed from the audience or on a large thrust stage with encircling and steeply tiered audience-seating entails a broad style of performance in which the subtlety and quickness of the dialogue tend to be lost—and these are among the plays' chief pleasures.

An English Restoration comedy might best be staged today in a restaurant, with the audience sitting around three sides of a stage and in the same light and on the same level as the actors; drinks and food could be served during the performance, and audience members be free to talk and comment amongst themselves. Modern dress for the play would lessen the visual gap between stage and audience. So a performance might become a lively and sometimes difficult game: characterizations would have to be strongly physical in order to register on all sides; dialogue, which can seem stubbornly wordy on the page, would have to be tossed and beaten around with a show of pleasure; the audience might call out in encouragement to the actors. Such plays were written to be shared with an audience in a manner that is impossible in too large a theatre or on a stage too removed from spectators.

Recent plays, such as Len Jenkin's *Poor Folk's Pleasure*, Anne Bogart's *Small Lives/Big Dreams*, and Paula Vogel's *Baltimore Waltz*, would seem either slight or laborious in too large a theatre, especially if that theatre had a picture-frame stage filled with a lot of scenery; large-scale projections or lighting effects could reduce the importance of the actors in a way that would be equally unfortunate. These plays require the attention of the audience to be concentrated on the actors and their movements, and for this to be possible productions need to be staged in an intimate and simple theatre. Action moves quickly from one location or one mood to another: lights and sound, a very few props, open space, and an audience close to the stage are all that is required. Paula Vogel has said that she has never written a play that needed to cost more than $100 to stage; she might have added that her works are at their best when staged in theatres seating little more than one hundred spectators.

In contrast, Sam Shepard imagined the main characters of his *Fool for Love* within the walls of a motel room. This play needs a setting like a box with three sides, against which its characters can press themselves and from which they finally escape. This, in turn, means that the theatre's auditorium must be shaped so that all the spectators can see clearly into the box; in a thrust-stage or arena-stage theatre this arrangement would not be possible. Nor must the theatre be too large or its auditorium too wide, because everyone must be able to see what is happening inside the box and must have a close encounter with the "relentless" playing that the author says his text requires.

Shakespeare's plays and ancient Greek tragedies fit most readily into theatres similar to those for which they were written. Yet this does not mean that they can be staged only in "replicas" of those theatres. If these physical forms were exactly reproduced in our own times, their use would raise other problems. Few contemporary actors would know how to project speech into a huge Greek amphitheatre or an open-air space such as the Globe Theatre. Yet adding sound amplification would immediately destroy the original audience/stage relationship. Moreover performances are no longer practicable for the public during daylight hours, so electric lighting would have to be introduced with the effect of still further altering the original conditions: the actors would no longer need to hold the audience's attention or set the mood of a scene by their own performances; their whole style would tend to be more subdued and less extroverted.

The audiences have also changed since those early times: modern safety regulations do not allow playgoers to stand and be free to move around during the course of a performance. Besides they are not so aware of class distinctions as were playgoers in Shakespeare's day, or so proud of their citizenship and direct political voice as those in the golden age of Athens. Changes in language, social habits, symbols, clichés, fashions, ways of looking and thinking further influence how performances are received.

The reproduction of a lost theatre can never be complete because later performances will always introduce many new elements—even if the building used the same materials and workmanship as the original. No production of any classic centuries after its first performance can achieve a museum-like fidelity, and no performance would benefit from an attempt to provide it. To bring these plays alive today, styles of production and theatre forms must be found that are appropriate both to the old texts and to our new actors and audience.

> *Consider any play you have already seen in performance or studied in the course of reading this book. Try to imagine how it might produce different effects in different forms of theatre. How important are intimate moments, or elaborate and realistic scenery? Must large-scale movements or crowd scenes be accommodated, and do these require a spacious stage? Was any of the text written to be spoken directly to an audience? What would be the best form of theatre for this play?*

Reducing any theatre to three basic elements involves sweeping simplifications. Many other factors influence how well the theatre operates, including size, equipment, front of house and backstage areas.

Size

Just as a large political rally is different in feeling and style from a small one of twenty or thirty committed members, and just as a lecture to three hundred students is different from a seminar for twelve, so a play will change as it moves from a large theatre to a small one, even if no word of its text is changed. Should the same number of people that filled a small theatre become the entire audience in a large one, the same production might look similar, but the actors would have to project more and, probably, play more slowly. The audience would not feel the same, either; playgoers would lack the reassurance of others sitting next to them and responding in the same way as they are. Anyone who has tried to raise a laugh in a big room with a few people scattered around will know how difficult comedy is without a close and contented audience: this is a measure of how a production will change if its chance of producing laughter is killed. When actors have to extend their movements to fill out wider spaces, their encounters with each other will be less intense and inevitable, and a crowded scene become less weighty and, perhaps, less believable. If what happens onstage has to be compressed into a smaller space, the acting may become more intense but not so open or so varied. But the greatest differences brought about by a change of scale in theatres cannot be measured by outward changes: there is the added exhilaration that comes from playing to a large audience; the sense of being totally exposed that can come when acting on a small stage and close to a quiet audience; the feeling of well-being when a company of actors senses that they are reaching every member of an audience without strain or uncertainty.

The size of a picture-frame opening, the number of seats in the rows and whether the rows are curved or not, the ceiling height of the auditorium: all these details matter very much, for reasons of acoustics, sight lines, and the audience-stage relationship. Actors playing to an audience seated far from the stage are inhibited from subtle playing, and their audiences seldom achieve any close empathy with the play's characters. An actor will seem short or tall according to the height of the frame within which the action takes place, or the thrust of a stage, or the height of the tiers of seating for an arena stage. The proportion of an audience that can be addressed directly at any one time will affect the spirit and openness of a production. Above all, if the players have to project strongly in order to be heard, a certain simplicity or crudeness is bound to intrude into their performances and thus into the production. The larger black-box theatres, which were built in the 1960s and 1970s, have become notorious for bad acoustics; they can be adapted to suit different theatre forms, but the cavernous spaces around and above the stage cause a great deal of the actors' energy to be absorbed in projecting sufficiently to be heard.

Equipment

The importance of technical resources is, to some degree, self-evident. How powerful and flexible is the light onstage, how precisely and swiftly can it be controlled? Does the theatre have a curtain that rises at the start of a performance and comes down at its close? Are there trapdoors, hydraulically operated lifts, sections of the stage that are movable on turntables or trucks? Is there a *fly-loft* above the stage from which pieces of scenery can be flown in? What provision is there for sound reproduction, or for an orchestra? Obviously all these factors will govern the extent to which an illusion of real life can be achieved, or a fantastic transformation of the ordinary. But even when a production has no illusionistic pretensions, the extent of these resources will decide the speed, neatness, magical surprise, completeness with which any visual or aural change can be effected.

Technical resources govern some of the most basic aspects of a production. If a theatre has little means with which to create what is often called the *atmosphere* or *tone* of a scene, the actors will have to do this work for themselves. That, however, is not always as bad as it may seem, if in consequence the audience's attention is directed more to the heart of the actors' performances and its imagination is set working to create the setting of a scene in their own minds. Many of the greatest theatres of the past had almost no technical support, and it was this kind of theatre for which Shakespeare and Æschylus wrote their great plays. Performing in such circumstances, actors can evoke the necessary atmosphere for each scene without the use of lights or stage machinery. The best of Molière's plays are not always reckoned to be those in which he used the elaborate scenic devices that had recently become available to him; some of the most frequently revived of his plays can be staged with very simple facilities.

On the other hand, some plays that have been devised in the closing decades of the twentieth-century would be impossible to perform without very elaborate technical assistance. Dozens of television monitors, huge video screens, banks of computerized projectors, laser beams, multiple-track sound recordings: these are some of the technical devices that have helped productions to "hold the mirror up" to present-day realities, or to bring a sense of nightmare compellingly on to a stage, or to activate the silent disappearance of huge scenic edifices.

Robert Wilson is a director who specializes in spectacle and creates dramas that are so elaborate and refined that he will spend whole weeks of rehearsal adjusting the lighting. Through the use of mechanical devices and remote control, he is able to make scenery or actors travel over long distances as if suspended in space. In the 1980s his productions became so technically complicated and, therefore, so very expensive that few theatres capable of staging his work could be found in the United States, and much of his work was seen only in Europe or in wealthy sections of Asia. For example, *Great Day in the Morning*, in which Jessye Norman sang spirituals, opened in Paris rather than at the Brooklyn Academy of Music for which it had been planned.

The technical resources of contemporary theatres will be considered again in a later chapter on stage design (Chapter 6). Equipment is being developed so rapidly that new methods and materials are coming into use every month, and no account could be fully up-to-date for very long. Gone are the days when a wardrobe, carpenter's shop, paint shop, electrics workshop, and various stores were the extent of backstage facilities. Metal workshops, a sound studio, a variety of computers and projectors, hydraulics, chemicals, plastics, radio and video equipment, television monitors with screens in various sizes—all have to be available, and for effective use each kind of equipment needs specialist knowledge backed by independent research.

Front of House

The decorations and fittings of entrance lobbies and auditoriums are significant parts of any theatre. The phrase *front of house*, which is used to describe all the resources that help in welcoming an audience, rightly suggests both a shopwindow and the front door of a home. A theatre may have a whole galaxy of facilities and concessions at its disposal: bars for serving drinks, snack bars, restaurants, trays for ice creams and chocolates, cloakrooms, public telephones, valet-parking, posters, art exhibits, bookstalls, souvenir shops, NO SMOKING signs, and so on. Although handling an audience can sometimes involve little more than a method of coping with unruly or weary lines of people waiting for admission—in the past this was commonly the case—for many of today's well established theatres it has become a specialized moneymaking enterprise. Either way, the reception a theatre gives an audience will affect the audience's response to a production.

Perhaps the most attractive and helpful front of house is the one at a Festival Theatre in a country park, where crowds come in the summertime to spend a day or days in picnicking, meeting friends, and enjoying many kinds of communal and family pleasures. Going to the theatre can then be a part of a holiday, happily enjoyed and long remembered. The creation of festivals has always been a part of theatre making around the world, even in places where little else is capable of drawing people away from the routines and responsibilities of their lives. In North America, the Shakespeare Festivals at Stratford, Ontario, Ashland, Oregon, or Montgomery, Alabama, or, way back during the 1930s at the World Fairs of Chicago and San Diego, have all shown that audience contentment will help a theatre to flourish when other companies are having to struggle merely to survive. Festivals of ancient Greek plays performed in the countryside at Epidaurus or the productions from many different countries presented at the Avignon Festival in the south of France are among the best known in Europe, and their success shows that theatre thrives when it serves an exceptional occasion, not a habit or routine, and when it offers communal enjoyment as well as private pleasure.

Packaging seldom sells a bad product twice, but it does help to sell a good one and to set up audience anticipation which will increase enjoyment and understanding. Imagine the different effect on an audience of the usual dusty gilt and faded hangings in the narrow foyer of an old Broadway theatre compared with that of the glass, chrome, and marble of many newer theatres. The spacious foyers of the Seattle Repertory Theatre draw a very different audience from that which assembles on the sidewalk outside a small theatre in a derelict and dangerous neighborhood of a down-at-heel city, even if the theatre has a guarded parking lot next door. Compare the physical front of house of any theatre you know with that offered by the first, precariously financed (but soon to become world-famous) Moscow Art Theatre when its interior had few comforts, and no luxury, having been hurriedly redecorated with white paint and its old woodwork left unpainted. Compare that with the Vienna State Theatre, which has a huge classical facade at its entrance and broad encircling foyers inside, along which wealthy patrons take gentle exercise during lengthy intermissions.

Some modern theatres keep their extensive foyers open all day, providing a place for people to meet and spend an hour or two of their leisure time. The National Theatre in London has eleven outlets for serving food or drink, three bookshops, three exhibition spaces, several locations where small-scale performances and live music are offered free or for a small charge before the main evening performance. Entrances are on two levels and give splendid views of the river Thames and St. Paul's Cathedral. Posters and photographs of many past productions hang on the walls, and racks offer pamphlets listing the theatre's current repertoire and that of other theatres, both large and small, all over London. An information desk is staffed to help make a visit more enjoyable. Many smaller theatres in Europe and America have followed this lead, as if they were trying to "change the image" of theatre and give it more prestige.

Salesmanship in the theatre is not essential, however. Theatres which have no time or money to enhance and glamorize the front of house, or where audiences have to stand in line for hours outside in the rain or cold, or go hungry after a long journey to a remote place, can also draw contented crowds and fill all their seats. In a scruffy old theatre you may sometimes find yourself, unexpectedly, in the presence of what seems to be the pure gold of theatre. Then you might wonder whether an expensive and reassuring welcome or luxurious foyers do not, sometimes, put to rest that sense of discovery and uncertainty that always accompanies the most overwhelming imaginative experiences.

Backstage

Careful planning of backstage accommodations is just as significant as arrangements onstage, in the auditorium, and front of house, and arguably more so. Will actors with large roles have separate dressing rooms or share space with the rest of the company? How comfortable is the green room (the communal waiting room and lounge for actors)? How spacious is the rehearsal room? How welcoming is the stage-door entrance for company members? How large, convenient, and well-equipped are all of the many workshops, stores, and offices? And so on. All these provisions affect the quality and nature of the plays that are presented in a theatre, especially in a theatre with a company that produces its own shows.

Backstage provisions also affect how a theatre is run. Is the theatre physically capable of presenting plays in repertoire (that is, several different plays within any one week), or must one play be taken off before another can be staged? Is the theatre suitable only for receiving and presenting touring productions that are cheaper versions of big-town successes or are intended to show off a star performer? Is the administrative office in the theatre itself or in some other building? (The latter is often the case in crowded inner cities, and this setup results in very different working conditions for actors, designers, and directors.) Is the theatre part of a larger organization with its own priorities and rhythms of work, perhaps sharing some of its facilities with an art gallery, concert hall, educational establishment, or sports facility? A theatre involves not only what is put on a stage: it is also an organization that serves the public and its own artists in ways that are dictated, in large part, by the facilities available.

> *Make a list of the more important resources belonging to any theatre—backstage, onstage, and front of house—and leave spaces for entering comments. Then, when you next go to a theatre, write down how your experience was influenced by each of them— so far as you can tell. Would you change any of the means used in order to provide better entertainment?*

4

Before the Play: At the Power Centre, Ann Arbor, Michigan. (Photo by David Smith Photography.)

Audiences

In the study of theatre, few topics are more important than this: without an audience, there can be no theatre of any sort. Besides the ability to draw many people together is one of theatre's most special and powerful attractions. In Chapter 1 we took a first look at theatre as a "social occasion" and observed how performances are able to "reflect" the interests of audiences. If you look back at those sections, you will recall why theatre's relationship to the public must be a major concern for any theatre and for anyone who wants to argue that theatre should have a special and thriving place in our society. To understand the role of the audience in theatre, we must try to be more particular and ask who goes to a theatre and what function theatre serves in society.

Who Is in an Audience?

There are a number of factors that determine the nature of an audience. The price of seats plays a part, but not so much or not so straightforwardly as one might think. In its early days, the Potomac Theatre Project had to struggle in order to survive. Then one day somebody calculated the actual cost of organizing, printing, and selling tickets and realized that after paying for this there was so little money left from the proceeds of ticket sales that it was not a significant part of the company's income. The company concluded that time and effort might be better spent on improving productions, so they decided to offer free admission and simply ask for donations as the audience left the theatre. Once this policy was put into effect, many earlier difficulties disappeared: more people came, and they left more money behind than had ever been received from the sale of reasonably priced tickets.

However steep or cheap the cost of tickets, this is not the only expense for theatregoers. They need to be able to afford transportation and parking, and to have the luxury of taking time off from other pressing activities; they must also find out what plays are being performed at which theatres, make a choice, organize the visit, line up a baby-sitter perhaps, and decide when and where to meet friends and when and where to eat, and who is paying, and so on. On top of that, members of the public must be willing to risk paying for a show that may prove unable to please them—knowing that there is no recourse for disappointment beyond a decision not to return to that theatre again or, perhaps, to any other theatre.

Most theatres producing their own shows at the present time in the United States or Europe have comparatively small and regular audiences. Theatregoing has become a habit, or an occasional diversion, for a few small sectors of society, many of whom are well established in life, read the same newspapers and journals, earn a similar income, and have a common level of education. Theatre patrons tend to be one of two types. Either they are in late middle age or older, with no children to look after and no job making urgent claims on their time, or else they are young people not yet tied down by family duties of their own or taking advantage of cheap tickets offered for educational reasons. This, however, was not always the case: it seems totally improbable today, but there was a time when all work would stop in a busy city so that everyone could go to the theatre. This happened among the citizens of ancient Athens and among all classes of people in medieval Europe; it still happens today in the so-called underdeveloped parts of Asia, Africa, and South and Central America.

Attracting Audiences

Most theatres in the European tradition are in search of new audiences and make every effort to broaden their regular audience. Those presenting touring productions in large theatres offer a very varied season in the hope that the people who come to see a show they know they will like, may then come back to swell the audience for a less popular offering that may well be cheaper for the theatre to book. This policy appears to be common, but it is doubtful whether it has the desired effect. It seems, rather, that there is a direct relationship between the size of an audience for a touring show and the amount of publicity that is manufactured to boost its star actor or its music, or some other newsworthy aspect of the production.

Theatres presenting a season of their own productions have a still more difficult task in reaching out to new audiences. Purchasers of season tickets become patrons who hold the same seats for each play on the same night of certain predetermined weeks during the year. Sitting among people whom they know or at least recognize, and seeing plays that have been selected for them, these theatregoers attend the theatre as a matter of more or less comfortable habit. For theatres, the sale of season tickets has the great advantage of bringing in money before production expenses call for it to be spent, but there are great disadvantages as well. By settling its repertoire in advance, a company forfeits the freedom to change the program when things go badly or when a new or topical opportunity arises; when a production proves good enough to run for longer than the regular number of weeks, the company cannot extend the run and so find a new audience for the theatre and make extra money. If a play fails to get a favorable reception, some patrons may not turn up for the seats they have paid for and, in this way, express their disapproval; then the actors are left the unenviable task of playing to empty seats, which can be sold to no one else. A desire to maximize the sale of subscriptions will lead theatres to make safe choices when deciding a season's repertoire, but this strategy can backfire when it discourages new theatregoers.

In an effort to make productions more accessible and audiences more mixed, some theatres price all seats equally. Unfortunately, in hard financial times, prices are usually levelled *up*, rather than down, and this reduces the range and number of people who are likely to buy tickets. Such a policy is particularly hard to make effective when some seats are situated high up or far away from the stage, or very much to one side with an obstructed view. Then all the good seats go to subscribers, leaving only the unsatisfactory ones for members of the public who come to the theatre because, by word of mouth, they have heard strongly favorable reports about a particular production—and these are the very people a theatre needs to attract.

The idea that everyone should pay the same amount to see the same show and have equally good seats is comparatively new. Divisions among an audience used to be very clearly marked. Theatres were built with a separate entrance to the cheaper seats, around the corner from the main one and lacking its opulence. Other theatres had a few, very favorably placed seats in private enclosures, which cost far more than any others. In royal courts, the whole entertainment would be paid for by the monarch through appropriate officials, and this single patron took pride of place in the auditorium. In Elizabethan public theatres and the proscenium theatres of the seventeenth through nineteenth centuries in Europe, seats were placed onstage alongside the actors for those members of the audience who could afford high prices. In all these cases money and privilege had great effect on how any production was seen. Members of the audience who crowded together in *the pit* at the back of a large public theatre or in *the gods* (as the uppermost level of uncomfortable seats was called) would often become impatient and noisy; they might rapturously shout out approval or let their dissatisfaction be known by drowning out performances with catcalls and pelting the actors with vegetables and other convenient missiles. It became a practice to station two armed soldiers at either side of the stage to discourage violence and riots. In comparison, the regular theatregoers of today, all sitting comfortably with a relatively good view of the stage, are staid and unresponsive.

The next time you go to the theatre, make a note of six to eight people sitting in front or to the side of you, and try to decide where and how they live. Are they very different from you? If the answer is yes, try to imagine what they would enjoy in the show you have seen. Can you think of another play that would have pleased them more, or of anything that might have made the evening more enjoyable for them? If they seem to have lives very similar to your own, consider whether the show could have been sold successfully to particular people you know who are very unlike yourself. These inquiries should make you more aware of the difficulty of increasing and broadening theatre audiences.

Public Relations

A theatre's location and times of performance also affect audiences. In Elizabethan days, theatres were not permitted in the City of London, so they were built in the suburbs, which did not fall under the jurisdiction of the city fathers. Because performances were held in daylight and in the early afternoon, merchants and

Figure 4.1   The Cincinnati Playhouse in the Park, designed by Hugh Hardy. This superbly sited theatre, which opened in 1969, commands a wide view of downtown and the tristate area. (Photograph by Sandy Underwood; courtesy of the Cincinnati Playhouse.)

other employers complained that their young apprentices took unofficial leave from work to waste their master's time watching the players. Preachers complained that theatres were the resorts of the idle, immoral, and criminal elements of society. But still the public continued to attend the theatre in large numbers. Later, the King's Men who occupied the Globe on the south bank of the river Thames, opened a second, indoor theatre, situated within the city but on a specially protected piece of ground exempt from the city's control. This was the Blackfriars Theatre, and here the players encountered different opposition: now the neighbors complained that they could not get to their own front doors because of the great number of coaches bringing wealthy people to the theatre. In both cases, theatregoing involved taking a lot of trouble and breaking the routines of everyday life; at the same time, however, many in these audiences were also enjoying unusual liberties and having a holiday from work and supervision.

Today theatres are often built in parks or other open spaces with convenient parking. These environments encourage a kind of audience that is prepared and able to go out of its way to visit a theatre set peacefully apart from life's ordinary activities; the average theatregoer is likely to be more leisured than hardworking, more at ease than enthusiastic. Other theatres are located on college campuses, and the convenience of such sites, together with special price reductions and organized study trips, can attract young playgoers, some of them attending under the eye of a careful mentor. Either way, going to a theatre means entering a special enclosure away from the mainstream of life; it is a protected and often subsidized experience.

Most theatre performances start between 7:00 and 8:00 P.M., later rather than earlier in the United States. This means that audiences have usually eaten *before* going to the theatre and are therefore not the liveliest people for whom to perform. The playwright/director Bertolt Brecht used to say that no play should start after the audience has had its evening meal, but some people today take the opposite view and support *dinner theatres*, which serve meals in the auditorium, perhaps the first course before the play and dessert at intermission. Theatre is often part of a night out, rather than an occasion that draws all sorts of people together and then dominates, for a time, every other concern.

Small theatres with ambitiously experimental productions and little financial overhead might seem the best able to offer an alternative to conservative or fashionable theatregoing, but these companies always have difficulty advertising their shows, because the proceeds from a full house of some hundred seats will not justify the costs of even the most modest advertisement in the daily press—and advertisements are seldom effective when they are modest. Word of mouth can provide free advertisement for a good show, but such news takes time to reach people, and a production may have to end its run before word starts to have much effect. Good press reviews appearing immediately after opening night offer a more effective free advertisement, but if a crowd should clamor to see a show in a small theatre, only a few of those customers can be satisfied at one time. Great pressure on the box office can quickly discourage potential theatregoers. The short time during which a good review is an effective advertisement may well have passed before seats can be placed on offer in sufficient numbers for potential theatregoers to take advantage of them.

The most convincing appearance of thriving audiences for innovative theatre in the Western world today are those attending touring productions that have had a great deal of publicity in the better newspapers and on television, or have been praised lavishly in theatre journals. In these cases tickets often have to be fought for or scrounged. But internationally famous productions go to only a few theatres and seldom stay in any one place for very long; the numbers seeing them remain tiny when compared with the population of the cities in which they perform.

The truly popular shows of our times are those that create huge spectacles on large stages in a few large theatres for years at a time. These productions can afford effective publicity at their openings and for a long time afterward; they are designed so that they can run almost endlessly, and tickets are sold far in advance. For the crowds wishing to see *Cats*, *The Phantom of the Opera*, *Les Misérables*—we all know their names—the expense of the tickets seems to be no drawback; once the momentum of demand has built up, ever more people will struggle to buy them. These huge and durable productions have caused the number of tickets sold and the amount of money taken to break all records, so that theatre, in general, can be said to be more successful today than ever before. The snag is, unfortunately, that the triumph of spectacular musicals does not help smaller productions that are being staged in the same cities—in fact, quite the reverse: they make such shows seem impoverished and unconvincing, at best minority pleasures rather than something on which it is safe to spend one's money. Companies starting out to woo an audience suffer still more in comparison.

Large-scale musicals provide theatre for a mass market, and it is very hard to break into that market; they do not encourage grass-root initiatives by young directors, dramatists, or companies. When young artists join the big musical theatre companies, they are expected to accept and conform to what is being done onstage, so they have very little scope for making their own mark.

Also, almost all spectacular musicals are about people living in worlds that have long since disappeared or are entirely fanciful, and the characters have little connection to everyday realities. At best—and that is when very efficient—they are dream machines that encourage escape and indulgence in whatever ways their producers have found to be widely acceptable. There seems to be no place for plays depicting life as it is now. The people associated with these shows exhibit a high level of professionalism and originality, but their talent does not create productions responsive to the changing circumstances of our lives or make theatre any more accessible than a very expensive night out in a big metropolis.

Almost everyone working in theatre today in North America or Europe is looking for ways to restore theatre's popularity and vitality, to make good productions and, at the same time, to create good audiences. The ideal audience for theatre would be lively, adventurous, thoughtful, and passionate, and it would be drawn from all the different kinds of people that live in the communities among which each theatre is sited; the playgoers would be fans and critical enthusiasts, wanting and, perhaps, needing to see what theatre can achieve. All sorts of new schedules, pricings, and presentations have been tried to attract better audiences, but these tactics do not go to the roots of the problem; at best, they are window dressing and salesmanship. Creating an audience may sound like a job for public relations specialists, but this task cannot be separated from that of making good productions that use all of the available powers of theatre. Finding an audience is best considered as an extension of that basic concern: theatre needs to change the way in which everything it does relates to its true public—which is nothing smaller than the entire society in which it lives and that it should serve.

Some observers are despondent: "Theatre is in crisis!" "Theatre cannot pay!" "A life in theatre is a waste of time!" These cries are heard on all sides, but few people seem to believe them because theatre goes on, in much the same way, from year to year, even if this means that companies have to survive from one crisis to another: a lot of effort and many dreams have been invested, and no one wishes to lose all hope. Other observers will say that theatre at the present time is more wonderful, certainly more brilliant and effective, than ever before; but that cry rings a little hollow, since even the strongest productions do not attract strong and varied audiences. Theatregoers remain unrepresentative of society as a whole: many people go only occasionally; most people never go.

Lack of confidence may be part of the trouble: lack of belief in the necessity of theatre and in its ability to renew itself by facing the world and reflecting the needs and desires that are very much alive out there. Small theatres that pay particular attention to their audience by staging plays for special groups of people—feminist theatres, American-Asian theatres, theatres for the deaf, and so on—are among the most productive and best attended in the United States at the present time, and there may be a lesson here for more established theatres. These smaller companies know what they want to stage and the people they wish to attract: they listen to their public, as well as to financial advisors and publicists; their artistic concerns touch life outside the theatre, the ongoing concerns of the public as well as those of the theatre.

Distant countries can also provide ideas and inspiration. In Tokyo in 1983, a young man who had done many student shows while attending university, started a professional company, and within ten years he had written, produced, directed, and starred in ten productions, and for none of them was there ever an empty seat. In all this time he received no public subsidy, except for the purpose of international touring, and no private patronage beyond that of his audience. Noda Hideki had found a recipe for making theatre, one that is not used in the West: his small company works for only six months a year, after which its members get on with the rest of their lives; it hires a theatre to perform in, and does not own or run one; it rehearses for two months and then performs for four; it stages only Noda's plays and keeps many of the same actors from year to year; it produces one new play every year and may revive one as well. All the shows are about what life is like in Japan at this particular time, and they explore ideas that are in common circulation about what that life might be or what it has been in earlier times. Energy, variety, great physical and verbal skills, self-criticism, fashion, topicality, and shared pleasure are all obvious ingredients in his work. Selling six hundred tickets for each and every performance never seems to have been a problem; for the public, the only difficulty is how to get a ticket.

Like the theatres in North America and Europe, many theatres around the world are struggling simply to survive, but there are exceptions. Many successful theatres stage shows that do not cost many millions of dollars to produce. Audiences in India crowd to Jatra and Marathi theatres to see new plays boldly and simply staged, and old plays brought unexpectedly and glamorously to life on a bare stage before thousands of people. Theatres like these are breaking many of the guidelines that restrain established theatre producers as they try to keep in business and look after their existing patrons. Perhaps more theatres would thrive in the West if they tossed out of the window all the accepted wisdoms of an earlier generation, the existing rules, regulations, and restrictions, even the safety nets and support systems. That is not a wild prescription, because good work in theatre always needs careful planning and will therefore develop very quickly its own strict disciplines.

By starting over again and taking nothing for granted, a theatre might learn how to touch an audience drawn from all parts of society, as theatres commonly did in earlier days. That is not to say that theatre should be old-fashioned. Quite the reverse: it should look to past example only to find new ways of working for a new age and a new audience. It does exactly this in some places that have other traditions and theatre organizations different from our own.

Be as honest as you can in making a list of the reasons why you go to any one theatre. Then make a list of the reasons why you would not wish to go.
Would any change in the policy of this theatre, no matter how difficult to bring about, have any impact on your eagerness or reluctance to go?

Serving the Public

Like any other business, theatre needs an appropriate organization. A popular misconception is that theatre people are "arty" and, therefore, more than usually inefficient and impractical. In fact, no one can survive in theatre for very long without being a lot more than merely efficient. When some public watchdog investigates a theatre's work, the business consultants and accountants hired for the job usually come back after long deliberation and say that the organization is already cut to the bone, the workforce is exceptionally well motivated, and the output is extraordinarily high. The common criticism is that too many people in the organization are overworking. Few critics outside the theatre realize that staging a production is such a complex job that no one can succeed in the task without being an expert and thrifty organizer. Choosing and mounting a whole season of productions, whether the shows are home produced or not, is a job in which one learns very quickly a number of essential business and public relations skills.

The first necessity is a workable and sustainable policy; the next is an appropriate chain of command. Attempting to do too much is a constant danger. Smaller companies can get into difficulties by trying to keep the flow of work going over too long a period or by making extended tours that overstretch the stamina of both actors and administrators. At the other extreme, larger companies that struggle to maintain a full season are liable to pare the size of productions down to a point where they look thin and lacking in confidence on their large stages, thus losing audiences even for their few major efforts.

To deal with these problems and most others, a theatre needs to be sure that decisions are made by someone, or possibly some group of people, who will take into account the nature of the work done onstage and in the workshops and offices, and also the reasons why all this is being done. Unfortunately the people ultimately in charge of larger theatres are often very much like business executives and have no practical experience of theatre making themselves, yet, being personally responsible for the company's financial viability, they have a say in everything else the company does. Financial success and efficient trading can become the objectives controlling all their decisions, both to good effect on the productions and to bad: good for stressing conservative values and using well-tested techniques, but bad for encouraging innovation and individual initiatives.

In nonprofit theatres, a board of trustees is responsible in the last resort, but their principal task is to hire a theatre administrator or director, to whom they leave the running of the theatre. The trustees then approve each season's program when it is submitted to them and take ultimate responsibility for decision making only in an emergency. When a theatre is in financial difficulties, the trustees are likely to choose an administrator to take executive charge; when the quality or success of the productions has slipped, they will seek an artistic director who will usually be a director of plays, or occasionally an experienced actor or designer. A formidable range of talents is required to provide both artistic and business leadership for operating a theatre, so trustees will sometimes decide that responsibility should be shared between two differently qualified persons, a choice that can lead to wasteful arguments and a company divided in loyalties. All too often a compromise appointment is made of someone with experience in both directions, but with skill in neither. This tactic can lead to unsteady leadership and short tenures. As a result of these challenges, publicly funded theatres tend either to play safely within recognized limits or to be driven, for however long this can last, by one person's individual vision or ambitions.

Figure 4.2 A training program alongside a theatre company: a commedia class at the Dell'Arte School of Physical Theatre, Blue Lake, California. The instructor, Joan Schirle, is a founder-member of the Dell'Arte Players Company. (Photograph courtesy of the Dell'Arte School of Physical Theatre.)

While these are the common patterns of organization, others also exist. Some companies combine theatre work with education and their leadership reflects this twin purpose. A professionally equipped theatre building may belong to a university that subsidizes a company to work in it; then a producer must ensure that students and faculty can use the professional theatre as a support for teaching and research. Another pattern develops when a small group of actors with specially developed skills starts a company and offers classes to the public in order to support themselves financially and pass on those skills; such a theatre needs to be run more like a school than a theatre, with someone to organize both teaching and productions.

Small companies may offer training classes more for their own members than for students from outside; in such cases one particular teacher-director is usually in

Figure 4.3 A masked actor from Creche, a production by Trestle, a company founded in 1981 by three students Toby Wilsher, Alan Riley, Sally Cook and their teacher John Wright. This show toured internationally for several years. The actor shown here is Sally Cook. (Photograph by John Morgan.)

charge and gives artistic development first priority, even before that of securing audiences for the company's productions.

Other theatres have been formed in order to make a political or social impact and their leadership and organization reflect this. One of the best known examples was the Group Theatre in New York in the 1930s. This company had twin aspirations: to show that theatre could function as a collective and to stage plays that had social significance. Since the 1970s, many small theatres have sprung up with political purposes that are far more clearly stated; for example, feminist theatres use productions to scrutinize women's role in society, or to advocate specific political action, or to build up audiences composed largely of women. Theatres have been formed solely to promote a wide range of political ideas and to raise public consciousness about inequalities and injustices in society; here the choice of plays and membership are often the first priorities, and quality takes second place. Some companies are organized as communes, more rigorously than the Group Theatre ever was. These organizations need a very open form of leadership under which to debate ideology and agree upon a common purpose, and also to keep up-to-date with a changing political situation and changing membership of the company.

A few companies have organizations that reflect a particular theatrical purpose. Some have been founded to give actors, and not play directors, the controlling voice in the hope that actors will gain greater independence as artists, and productions focus attention on the achievement of the performers rather than on directorial concepts. Others serve new writing or multimedia productions and give the controlling voice to dramatists, designers, or specialist directors. There are also mime theatres, puppet theatres, clown theatres, poets' theatres, and so on. Often, however, a company comes into being without any special objective beyond the desire of students who have worked together at school or university to continue doing so after they have graduated. These organizations may be short-lived, but, as with many new pop-music groups, they can provide the seedbed where a dramatist finds a distinctive voice, or a new director develops strong enough powers to work in more established companies and start an independent career.

The St. Nicholas Theatre of Chicago is an example of a student theatre that grew into a professional one and then disbanded. David Mamet worked there as author, play director, and one of three company directors, the others being fellow ex-students. *American Buffalo* (1975) had a first "showcase" at Stage Two of the Goodman Theatre, but it was able to have a sustained run at St. Nick's where it built an audience and was soon followed by *The Woods* (1977). Soon Mamet's plays were being staged regularly in New York and across the country and his career was independent and prosperous.

Many small theatres come into existence every year because a writer or director and a group of actors, with perhaps a designer, composer, or stage technician, have done a number of plays together and want to continue that relationship and those successes. Many such groups do not survive for long because of the hazardous and demanding nature of such work, yet the tide of new arrivals continues, a sign that theatre is constantly renewing itself.

Theatre organization is not easy to study from the outside, but it is sometimes useful to ask whether a production you have seen owes its success or failure to reasons other than the quality of the script and the artists involved, or the suitability of the theatre building and equipment.

Think about a production you have seen. Would another company, whose work you have seen, have had more or less success with this play? Was the production adequately financed, or (it can happen) overfinanced?

5

Head Shots: Actors' photographs gathered for auditions.

Actors and Acting

Very occasionally an actor onstage appears to be exactly the same as somebody off-stage, in ordinary life. But the actor never is, because performing before an audience in a carefully prepared production is *not* the same as existing in real life. Before long we come to realize that this person can do almost anything, no matter how simple, in such a way that we pay a special kind of attention. We also see that he or she can do some very unlikely things: be ignorant of what is going to happen and yet be ready for it; find the right word or action to solve a daunting puzzle, or be lucky, happy, or stupid beyond ordinary degrees. The actor can appear to receive appalling physical punishment and then recover from what looked like certain death, or can suddenly give a great cry of astonishment and leap ludicrously up in the air. Sometimes these impossible actions are done night after night, for a year or more. After a little reflection one soon sees how difficult acting is. Even appearing to do nothing onstage in the sight of many people is not easy. If you doubt this, try it yourself and you will soon discover some of the problems.

Somehow a skilled actor both astonishes and reassures us. We see this person do the impossible, yet we realize that he or she is one of us. We tend to forget all the difficulties involved and, encouraged by the fact that acting sometimes looks very easy, we even imagine that it would be sheer pleasure to perform in this way. We envision ourselves being actors and, in our own view, improving on the most amazing performance. These are seductive thoughts and one of the reasons why such large numbers of young people go onstage and seek the enjoyment of acting.

Acting is, indeed, an instinctive art. As children we all imitated others and, in our make-believe, we would become our heroes and betters. We all practice acting throughout our lives, whenever we pretend to be better, wiser, braver, or more amusing than we actually are, or, in some other way, different. We know enough about acting ourselves that when watching good actors, we can, as it were, share in their triumphs.

What Is an Actor?

Although acting is an instinct, known to us all, it is also one of the most demanding of arts. Constant training is necessary, for unless the voice and body are kept fit and under precise control, the actor will not be able to realize what he or she wishes to do in a role or supply the energy necessary to sustain an emotionally draining role over a period of two or three hours. During a single performance, the character performed by the actor may have to go through great tortures or great happiness and be ready for the opposite only minutes later, and this impersonation may have to be sustained as though the character is living over the course of ten or twenty arduous years. None of this actually happens, but it must seem to do so within the space of a few hours, one night after another. Those who have never acted a large role onstage can only guess at the physical, emotional, and mental strains that acting places on the performer. All an actor's life and being is drawn into this art; between the actor's self and the character there is no boundary, no holding back. The artist's material is the self, every part of it, used in every possible way.

Acting is a profession as well as an art, and managing a career as an actor is so complicated that relatively few are able to earn a good livelihood from it. Only those who are highly gifted, lucky, *and* tenacious can succeed, and no one could guess what proportions of each of these gifts are going to be necessary for success in any individual career. Perhaps the most daunting fact is that a good measure of professional success is absolutely necessary for full artistic achievement: the right role must be found for each stage of an actor's development; spending too long in one role or with any one company can hinder growth; working with the wrong actors or in the wrong play, or with inadequate rehearsals or unsuitable performance conditions can be seriously harmful. Actors have to learn when to say no as well as yes, and to know when and where to seek new work. These professional difficulties are some of the reasons why there are so many ex-actors.

Being an actor in the theatre can be a glamorous life, and it should look easy, but it is also a full-time occupation with strict and contrary demands. First of all, this art is collaborative—you cannot do it alone—and yet it is highly individual. It is instinctive and imaginative, and yet, at the same time, it is technically complicated, calculated, and repetitive. Besides the actor is driven by a need to find an audience: for personal and often unknown reasons, he or she *needs* to feed on a very public form of approval and acceptance that only comes with success.

Acting in a theatre is not the same as acting for film or television. Neither of these "lens media" involves performance in front of an audience that has come together to witness everything that happens. Even a TV "sitcom" with a live audience can be edited before transmission and the director always has a choice of several images for any particular moment according to how the cameras have been focused. For a feature film, part of an actor's performance can be perfected, in whatever time is available; anything that goes wrong can be repeated until it is right. When a performance is complete and each phase has been captured by the camera, one step at a time, a selection of those two-dimensional images is made and edited, and also supplied with whatever sound support the director thinks will provide the desired effect. By these means, film acting can be both subtle and overwhelming at the very same time, but the effect is largely the work of the camera operator, director, and editor. By the time an audience sees what the actor has done, his or her performance never has to stand alone. Never do the last moments of a drama have to be created according to whatever has happened to happen during a single continuous performance leading up to this crisis and in response to a live audience. A film is viewed when the actors are, perhaps, thousands of miles away and unable to add or subtract anything.

Only in the theatre is an actor in live contact with an audience and able to communicate directly a sense of risk, play, conflict, amazement, and exposure; only here is the actor's creativity at work so that it is present for all to see and share, in all its openness and freshness.

The Actor as Instrument

Anyone trying to work professionally as an actor in the theatre must be high-powered, with many natural gifts that are well developed and under strict control.

Voice and Speech

The voice must be trained so that it is worth listening to, and such attainment is not so easy as it sounds. It depends on correct breathing and correct use of all the physical means of producing sound in the throat and head. It also depends on making myriad choices that vary the quality of sound for each moment of speech. In early training, an actor is often encouraged to consider voice as a separate organ, and is taught how to make the sounds of the various consonants and vowels with absolute clarity, as well as how to breathe. An aspiring actor needs to have a good ear, and must put in plenty of intelligent practice. The student will learn how to create and control varieties of volume, pitch, tone, and texture, and how to sustain speech for long periods and project the voice so that it carries a great distance without strain.

Learning to time speech is a part of this training which is surprisingly effective to someone unfamiliar with it. The actor should be able to manage tempo, rhythm, phrasing, and cadence so that everything spoken has a musical quality, an authority and finesse. Whatever is being said, the sound alone should be able to hold attention and give pleasure. Additional skills are needed for texts written in verse, and these, of course, include Shakespeare's plays, a challenge that almost every actor in the world confronts at some time or other, answering the demands of meter, rhyme, and the many other complexities of this writing so that speech is both natural and assured.

Like a musician, an actor can caress and inspire an audience by the very sound of speech, or can use that sound to disturb and alert the audience. The power of voice and the harm that can come from incorrect voice production are reasons why some actors speak of their "voice" as if it were a special gift or attainment, and why acting schools have voice teachers who become revered and sought after as permanent members of the larger theatre companies.

Onstage, however, speech never exists alone, and it is dangerous for an actor to concentrate for too long on developing the voice as a separate element in performance. Speech must also be attuned to the inherent values of the character and play as they come alive on the stage. Finding this balance is an absolute requirement, because it is quite possible to destroy or obscure the meaning of words, and their allusiveness, force, or ambiguity, simply by speaking too well. An actor must not become carried away by the effectiveness of the sounds that he or she makes and, as it were, listen to them being spoken in order to produce them the better.

Speech is most effective when it is impossible to consider it as a separate part of performance. The more demanding the text to be spoken, the more imperative is this warning: the bad Shakespearean actor is one who relies on good verse speaking to do far too much of the work. Cicely Berry, voice director of the Royal Shakespeare Company in England, warns students against this in her book, *The Actor and His Voice* (1988), in which she insists on an "organic" connection between speech and the actor's total response to the text:

> When the voice is not interesting enough, it is rarely to do with it not being good enough, but simply that it is not being given the right stimulus. . . .

> Freedom with the text comes from knowing what you are saying—i.e., knowing well the character, motive, and action.

Physical Demands of Acting

Like the voice, an actor's body needs to be developed and disciplined. More than physical fitness, in the usual sense of that phrase, is involved, although that is part of it. Economy of effort and efficiency of movement are prime requirements, because an actor may well be called upon to do a considerable physical feat without contortion or without any sign of stress, either during this particular moment or immediately afterwards. For dramatic reasons a long play may be most physically demanding in its very last scene, when the leading actor must seem fresh and eager, not at all tired from a long performance. Sometimes very small movements have to be made with special clarity and timing, so that no one in the audience will fail to see them; only perfect physical control will ensure that no unwanted movements draw attention away from the simple gesture that is all important.

Timing, again, has to be subtle and perfect: if speech is music, movement on stage is dance. Some actors train themselves to maintain a regular inner pulse or beat throughout a performance, so that slight variations from a regular tempo can make a strong impression. A basic physical rhythm can be established for a character and subtly varied for each phase of the drama.

In many ways an actor's performance should be like a dance. The actor's whole body should be expressive in posture and gesture; and it is equally important that the actor use the fixed space of the stage choreographically, so that his or her movement across the space has the meaning and economy of a skilled visual artist drawing on a sheet of paper. At every moment, where and how an actor is placed onstage and where and how any movement is made should all speak for the character being portrayed, even though only the actor, and not the character, will be conscious of this, and even if the actor is at the same time creating an immediately recognizable picture of a very ordinary life. Such dancelike elements of performance affect an audience independently of words, and, therefore, the great majority of its members have no clue as to why they sense a change of dramatic intensity or why they pay attention to one small gesture or cannot take their eyes off one of the characters, or why they laugh more and more freely or are suddenly arrested by doubt or insecurity.

Full physical control gives an actor more than aptness for the play and the ability to catch the audience's attention: it also provides a constant opportunity for the actor to exercise imagination and inventiveness. Movement is a second language, powerfully expressive in its own right, so that when an actor is in full control of his or her body in time and space, a gesture, movement, or posture can have the freshness of an entirely original creation. In making any movement, the actor can be like a poet inventing new words or a musician drawing new tunes, rhythms, and sounds out of the air. This is why a great actor can walk onstage and astonish thousands before he or she has said a word. The effect of this apparently inexplicable power can seem so simple that the actor is said to be a "star," as if he or she has come from another more amazing and confident world.

In the 1960s, when the French actor and director Michel Saint-Denis came to New York to join with John Houseman in setting up the Juilliard School for actor training, he insisted that all students should work on technique everyday. He outlined his scheme in *Training for the Theatre* (1982). For the first term, work on the body starts as follows:

> Emphasize full awareness of body. Just as a musician has complete control of his instrument, an actor must have coordinated control of his body. Focus on releasing tension through relaxation and developing muscular strength and flexibility.

Term after term, the list of tasks begins with phrases such as "Continue general body training" or "Continue movement classes with a new teacher. Make class more demanding." Twice the students are to have a new teacher, as if any one mentor would be insufficient or too reassuring. By the third term of the fourth year comes the directive: "Continue to build energy and stamina. . . . Experiment with more subtle movements."

Control of body and voice also serves the actor's need to imitate. Someone who has learned how to use his or her body is well trained to observe another person objectively and to recognize the points of tension within that person's body and its habitual posture and movements. With this knowledge, the actor can be more accurate in reproducing behavior so that he or she can take on the very form and functioning of the other person and not merely hit off a few immediately effective tricks of outward behavior. When assuming another person's voice, the same opportunities are open, so that the impersonation is not merely the reproduction of a few special vowel sounds or other dialect variations, but the use of what can be called a different voice, its sounds made according to how the other person takes in breath and uses the mouth and tongue.

The Actor as an Individual

Good training of voice and body must develop in conjunction with the powers of imagination and temperament, so that the actor can realize the full force of an individual personality in performance. Imaginative reach must be extended, so that whatever a play demands can take lively form in the actor's conscious and unconscious mind and so move toward a fitting expression. Performance in good and varied plays, together with constant self-criticism, will improve the quality of an actor's imaginative input, but study of life outside the theatre is also required—and this should include all kinds of life, not only those met in ordinary and daily circumstances. Wider experience must be sought out, and this means that the actor needs to read books, especially poetry, fiction, and histories, and look at paintings, photographs, and films, and, if possible, travel. In all this the actor must be observant and active in mind, so that he or she discovers new modes of being and the means to achieve them, noting and storing them away for use at some later date. When preparing for a particular role, an actor's exploration may be narrowly directed, but at other times, to stock the memory and quicken the imagination, he or she should follow instinct and natural curiosity at least as much as paying attention to the particular demands of a text or any advice that teachers or directors may give. An actor should always be, in part, self-directed, and very seldom off-duty.

To encourage the use of whatever experience or observation has been gathered and now lies hidden within the actor, no training helps so directly as the use of masks. Putting on a "neutral" mask—that is, one without any distinct characteristics—can free the wearer from customary reactions and habitual inhibitions and encourage originality and largeness in physical expression. It is rather like becoming a child again and exploring afresh how one might move and what one might feel. A character mask—one that makes very clear demands on the wearer because of its exaggerated features—can draw forth movements and sounds that the wearer has never made before in response to the mask's depiction of age or childhood, nobility or senility, happiness or grief. The mask must be put on with great care, and at first it may feel like a restraint, but with practice a new freedom comes as the actor's imagination seeks expression suitable to this new, and often shockingly new, facial presence. With this means of physical expression, the actor can become more resourceful and remarkable, more assured and more open to an audience's appreciation.

Quite naturally every actor is impatient with training that often concentrates first on this technicality and then on that, while the opportunity to perform is delayed. The old proverb about learning to walk before one can run is particularly apt for describing the development of an actor, because too many stage performances in large roles too early in a career can encourage clichéd performances and quick solutions rather than that deeply centered truth and versatility that distinguish good actors from the not so good. But although the actor needs basic technical training quite as much as any other kind of artist or athlete, and more than some, the need to perform in a sequence of demanding and varied roles is equally important: only when an actor performs before an audience will everything fall into its proper place and individual talent mature. An actor needs to find and trust himself or herself in performance, and this can happen only onstage where no instructor can be present, and no course of study can be followed.

If actors are impatient, so are their teachers. Gordon Craig (1872-1966) was a theatre director and theoretician who worked and taught all over Europe, yet at the height of his career, when he considered what he wanted an actor to be, he concluded that he could not rely on any human being of any sort; he would prefer to use a superefficient marionette. For him, the technical challenge of acting was so complicated and huge, and the need for self-discipline so continuous, that an inhuman second best seemed preferable to the third-rate, all-too-human actors he was accustomed to seeing and hearing, and with whom he had attempted to work. This taunting overstatement contains an important core of truth, and Craig's words are remembered by many to this day: acting is easy for no one, and training alone cannot solve any of the most important problems.

When you next go to the theatre, make a note soon afterward of whom you think was the most remarkable actor and the reasons for this opinion in terms of what was done

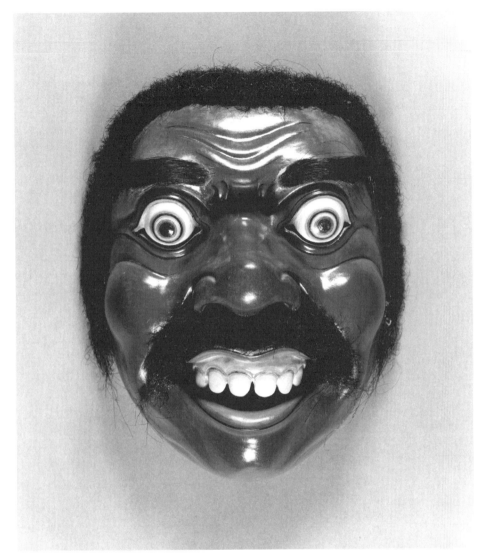

Figure 5.1 A mask from Bali. The maker, I. B. Alit, supplies both Western theatre companies and local dance-drama groups. (From the original in the author's collection; photograph courtesy of Oxford University Press.)

onstage, not in terms of personal appearance or characteristics, very noticeable though those will have been. Would any of these actions and their effects be impossible in real life?

Different Styles of Acting

Although the basic resources of an actor are constant, the uses to which they are put are infinitely varied. This could hardly be otherwise, for not only should theatre "hold the mirror up to nature" (see Chapter 1) and therefore be able to show characters onstage who are as varied as human beings are in real life, but the mirror should also be capable of presenting those characters from different viewpoints and with differing emphases.

Sometimes an actor must create only outward behavior, showing no sign of the inner hesitations or confusions that obscure most of what we do in ordinary life. At other times an actor needs to accentuate inner tensions, prolonging moments of indecision and giving exceptional clarity to half-formed thoughts that usually drift helplessly in semiconsciousness. Sometimes one emotional response must be emphasized, forgetting all others, so that the actor becomes a representative of all the hate, envy, joy, or grief that the audience has ever felt or imagined to be possible. In farces, an actor must simplify reactions and at the same time speed them up, so that their animation and oddity become almost, but not quite, incredible. In a documentary play, an actor may have to become an impersonal "official voice" or thirty-six different characters in turn, varying in an instant age, sex, opinions, and intelligence. Some comedies require a very limited range of physical mannerisms, and others will require that the actor has an ability to improvise and to be open to whatever happens among the audience or fellow actors. According to the kind of performance that is required, a special process of work will be developed, leading from first rehearsal to first performance, and beyond.

Some theorists say that an actor does one of two things: either presents the self onstage in various thin disguises according to the role played, or hides the self totally in a sequence of impenetrable disguises. This implies that an actor is either a *personality* and always recognizable, or an *impersonator* and always amazing an audience by the latest transformation: either a *virtuoso performer* or a *character actor*. There is some truth in this, but it is too simple a division, actors being more various and more variable than any two categories would suggest.

> *Make a short list of actors whom you have seen in at least three different roles, noting down the plays they were in. Can you divide these actors into "personalities" and "impersonators," or do some of them belong to both types?*
>
> *If you do not know more than two or three stage actors this well, try the same exercise with film actors.*

Other theorists would say that actors can be divided between those who work *externally* and those who work *internally*. The former create the outward signs of a character's individuality in action and speech, relying on a deeper truth to emerge during this process; *internal* actors concentrate on creating the inner mood and ways of thinking and feeling, trusting that outward signs of the inner character will gradually become manifest. In practice, however, most actors seem to use both methods, in differing and ever-changing proportions.

Finding names for each and every species of actor would be a lengthy and cumbersome business and probably inconclusive. Besides, acting style depends on the play text since an actor changes method with each new script and, to some extent, with each new director. For a less confusing means of defining types of actors, we can turn to history and describe the dominant styles of actors *and* plays in each of the main periods of European or Western theatre. This method will suggest the wide range of styles that is still available today.

You will not always recognize one of these styles in the performances you see. This is partly because the four types of acting that this historical approach will distinguish are not mutually exclusive. The following pages should therefore be understood as defining four traditions in theatre and four extremes of acting styles rather than giving a name for each possible kind of actor. Most actors will take something from each in developing their individual art and craft. Although most plays are written so that one style should predominate, many call for a blend or a mixture of styles, or for movement from one to another. A crucial decision for any director or leader of a company of actors is to define exactly the style or mixture of styles that is going to be used for a given play.

Classical Acting

The plays of Æschylus and Sophocles, together with the physical form of Greek and Roman theatre buildings, encouraged what is called today the *classical* style of acting. The neoclassical tragedies of Jean Racine (1639-1699), Friedrich Schiller (1759-1805), and other writers throughout Europe in the seventeenth and eighteenth centuries called for many of the same characteristics, and their works have helped to ensure the continuance of classical acting to the present day.

The classical actor seeks to give a clear and unified impression and to exploit himself or herself as an instrument. The aim is neither to imitate human nature in all its variety nor to distort it. Without doing violence to what is natural, the actor seeks, rather, to transfigure, enlarge, and illuminate what is found in life. This type of theatre is used to show a marvelous world, peopled with extraordinary and superbly gifted beings. The heroes of history and the present time are carefully studied and their behavior imitated onstage in so simplified, purified, and universalized a way that as characters they are strengthened and enlarged and—classicists are not afraid of this word—made more beautiful.

In ancient Greece, the actor wore masks to help fix the dominant impression of character and, although later classical actors dispensed with masks, they continued to simplify and strengthen the actor's appearance with the use of makeup and stately costumes. Classical actors were always highly conscious of voice, bearing, and movement, and have prided themselves on clarity, economy, and decorum.

The preferred plays of classicists had only a few major roles, sometimes with only one part making exceptional demands and the others being comparatively unimportant except to provide support or contrast. A conscious artistry was required for shaping the very long speeches that were common in these plays, and also for maintaining a careful balance and contrast between three to five separate acts. Other features to be served were strong themes elaborated and explicitly treated and a progressive build up toward a culminating crisis involving difficult choices and intense emotions.

Each major role was prepared over a long period of time—in Greece performances were held at first at yearly intervals—and, when possible, they would then be played and perfected over many years. Every detail of a characterization would be worked up thoroughly and then fixed, leaving only the smallest scope for improvisation during performance. Thomas Betterton (1630-1710), the classical English actor, continued to play the thirty-year-old Hamlet until he was seventy years of age.

Colley Cibber (1671-1757), theatre manager, actor, and playwright, wrote in praise of Thomas Betterton as if he were superhuman. His descriptions of the actor, especially in his *An Apology for the Life of Colley Cibber* (1740), are probably the best introduction to classical acting in English. Here are some selections:

> Betterton never wanted fire and force, . . . yet where it was not demanded, he never prostituted his power to the low ambition of a false applause. . . .

> In all his soliloquies of moment, the strong intelligence of his attitude and aspect drew you into such an impatient gaze and eager expectation that you almost imbibed the sentiment with your eye, before the ear could reach it. . . .

> In the just delivery of poetical numbers, particularly where the sentiments are pathetic, it is scarce credible upon how minute an article of sound depends their greatest beauty or inaffection. The voice of a singer is not more strictly tied to time and tune than that of an actor in theatrical elocution: the least syllable too long, or too slightly dwelt upon, in a period [sentence] depreciates it to nothing: which very syllable if rightly touched, shall, like the heightening stroke of light from a master's pencil, give life and spirit to the whole.

The dangers of this kind of playing are that a leading actor can become too selfishly the star, not interacting with the rest of the cast, and that his or her performance becomes too contrived and stiff, too settled in technical accomplishment and too remote from observed behavior. The great excitements of classical acting are amazing range and precision, made possible by finely developed voice and physique, together with emotional intensity, made possible by a technical control which is able to hold back reserves of power for an overwhelming climax.

Most actors we see today make an individual impression through easily recognizable traits, mannerisms of speech or movement, or even affectations, but when an actor has eradicated such obvious signals as imperfections and has heightened the impression of great emotional involvement, the deeper secrets of personality can surface, to be developed and then displayed for an audience; among these usually hidden resources are the indelible roots of individuality within the actor from which the strongest feelings of all kinds find their nourishment.

At the end of the twentieth century, few English-speaking actors work in the classical tradition. Sir John Gielgud is probably the best known and most skilled, although his technical accomplishment has been more evident in voice than in physical action. In small parts in films he is instantly recognizable, whether he plays a butler or an aristocrat. In the theatre, his greatest roles have been Shakespeare's Hamlet and King Richard II, parts that make huge vocal demands, and his various recordings of these roles give some impression of the intensity and shapeliness of his portrayal of both. Sir John's account of Richard II in his book, *Stage Directions*, emphasizes the pattern, symmetry, line, grace, beauty, and "musical intention" of the text. He wrote that the inner character of the king is developed in a "series of exquisite cadenzas and variations," and that the overall aim of a production should be to present the dramatic action and verbal music so that they "create a complete harmony of effect."

Perhaps the classical tradition of acting is most alive today among opera singers, the stars of old-fashioned musicals, and the most accomplished and consistent in style of comedians. As performers these artists can hold the attention of a huge theatre audience by creating an outsized impression of temperament and personality. They exercise their technical skills in a comparatively narrow range of parts and are highly calculating artists who know the value of simplicity, strict timing, and musical control. In Asia, where ancient traditions of theatre are protected with far more zeal than in the West, classical finesse and power are more often to be seen today. Ellen Lauren is an American who has trained and acted in Japan with the Suzuki Company of Toga, where techniques are based in Noh drama and ancient ceremonies. Her performances back in the United States show that the values of classical acting are still achievable and very much alive in the present time.

Demonstrative or Epic Acting

During the later centuries of the Roman Empire, theatre performances were largely confined to farces, spectacles, and light entertainments. Barbarian invaders and church fathers were able, in their different ways, to suppress drama for about five hundred years afterward. But suppression was not destruction, and in the later Middle Ages drama emerged again, largely as a folk activity, in both pagan and Christian forms. The actors could get help from the clergy who knew a great deal about music and Latin play texts (which were studied as examples of good writing); and through the churches actors had access to costumes, props, and playing spaces. In general, however, the new theatre produced at this time was an amateur movement. It also belonged to festival days: the actors lived ordinary lives, but on annual occasions they took upon themselves such roles as Jesus or Herod in a miracle play showing episodes from the Bible, or as the King of May or King of Fools in festivities and dramas celebrating seasonal change or social events. The plays presented, not a crisis or a single situation, but a long and varied narrative in a wide panorama.

We know that a basically new style of acting developed with the emergence of these mystery or miracle plays, because at first there were no star actors as in the former classical manner, no full-time acting companies, little training, and little criticism. As in ancient Athens, the actors, with very few exceptions, were all male, but they did not wear masks. No one performer had to draw all the attention to himself, but it would be an actor's job to mark, sharply and forcefully, a certain part of an emblematic picture, or stand for one figure in a narrative. The audience observed what was happening, rather than experienced sympathy for an individual faced with a personal dilemma. The directly affective language used for moments of great feeling in many of the medieval miracle plays shows that these actors were capable of emotional performances and could evoke sympathy, but the brevity of these incidents and the simplicity of their verbal expression also show that these potentially intense moments were not dwelt upon or developed so that they provided occasions for overwhelming expression of deep-seated emotion or individual perception.

In a new way the actor created his part in the play. Assuming a few clear indications of his role and its relation to other characters in the drama, he allowed these signs to speak for his character, to "demonstrate" the character's part in the scheme of the whole drama: Herod had a loud voice and raged; devils were made to look ugly and often had tails and carried pitchforks; the "souls" of the blessed in heaven had pure white skintight coverings to represent their unblemished natures; and so on. Actors depicted what these characters were and what they did, without ambiguity or self-questioning. Frequently, in pauses in the dramatic action, the characters spoke aside, addressing explanatory comments to the audience or asking for specific responses; whether instructional, satirical, or broadly and racily comic, this direct address encouraged the audience to respond actively to what was happening onstage, and it became an essential part of the dramatic experience.

When, during the fifteenth and sixteenth centuries, professional troupes of actors began to be formed, they at first kept to the same style of acting. We can observe a highly developed vehicle for such performances in the plays of Christopher Marlowe, Shakespeare's exact contemporary whose career was cut short by a violent death in 1593. Speeches in his plays are often elaborate, but seldom subtle or apparently spontaneous as Shakespeare's so often are: the colors of speech are primary, and its statements bold, so that finer distinctions derive from the bringing together of a number of different responses one after another, each in itself simple, hard, and direct. Visually Marlowe's style had emblematic clarity rather than a Shakespearean suggestion or atmosphere: Marlowe's Tambulaine is dressed in black and stands with drawn sword beside the golden hearse of Zenocrate, his dead wife, rather than striving, like Macbeth, to make sense of his immediate experience in the darkness of his castle, as an owl hoots and someone unseen knocks at the gates. Marlowe's plays are dominated by their heroes, but the sequence of events and variety of their reactions have meanings that none of the characters can fully understand: the audience must witness and consider a process or picture, rather than share with the principal character in a quest that progressively reveals the nature of self. Only at the end of *Dr. Faustus*, Marlowe's last play, and for a few moments in *Edward II*, did Marlowe use a more expressive, Shakespearean style.

During the twentieth century in the West, important elements of this demonstrative style were rediscovered, almost single-handedly, by Bertolt Brecht (1898-1956), the German director and playwright. (Marlowe's *Edward II* was one of Brecht's earliest productions and was influential in shaping his style.) For his own company in Berlin after the Second World War, Brecht assembled actors who had not yet completed their studies at conventional acting schools, so that he could train them while working on his own productions. He called his style *epic theatre*, in opposition to a then prevalent and greatly debased classical tradition, which he called "Aristotelian." (An epic poem is usually taken to imply long and detailed stories told against a background involving the fate of nations.) Brecht insisted that a production must encourage its audience to observe a picture of the world, to "face something," rather than draw it into sharing in some exceptional experience of an exceptional man. Brecht did not want his actors to "cook up" emotions—his words—so that they would "carry away" the imagination of their audience; they should rather represent or retell events accurately one after another, and so, from the juxtaposition of almost independent episodes, create a considered and challenging imitation of life. He did not want to mix laughter and tears, or to hide a character's basic nature until the end of a play at which time all would be revealed.

Brecht wanted full, bright, and even stage lighting, with no half lights or obvious mystery. In rehearsal, he sought economical gestures that would signal a character's involvement in each action with great clarity and economy. As a dramatist, he created strong story lines, sudden changes of fortune, an elaborate and provocative succession of different viewpoints, and what he called *Spass*—which might be translated as "sport, fun, energy, vitality."

With Brecht and with medieval and early Renaissance drama to help us, we can define the demonstrative or epic actor: clear and vigorous, "standing for" a character rather than "being" one; instantly recognizable and efficient as one part of a wider picture or narrative. Each episode is acted so that it speaks for itself, neither laying subtle traps for the audience nor leading them by the ears and eyes to share a single and irresistible emotional experience. The actor appears much less special than a classical actor does, but he or she is keen-minded, observant of human behavior, and able to choose and reproduce, one after another, the salient features of what has been seen and studied. This actor is strong and challenging: more like a cartoonist than a painter of noble and sensitive portraits.

The kind of acting Brecht admired can be seen today, not only in the Berliner Ensemble in Berlin, which consciously continues his tradition, but also in companies that share his ambition that theatre should make its audience think about the world they live in. But his example has not proved easy to follow in detail, because he developed very lengthy—and therefore very expensive—rehearsal processes that involve actors in serious-minded research and debate about the social and political issues involved in each play. This has meant that theatres in North America, which are without the large public subsidies of the state theatres of Europe, do not often take up the challenge. In England, where there is some subsidy, Brecht's influence has broadened—some critics would say, weakened—into many different styles of drama and acting. Although Edward Bond and Howard Barker have both carefully distanced themselves from Brecht, among plays written in English, theirs are perhaps the ones that show most effectively what epic acting can achieve today.

Another way of becoming acquainted with the epic style would be to look at good puppet theatre: there each "actor" is clearly recognizable at all times, his or her reactions are simple and strong, and what is said is usually clear and immediately to the point. When watching this type of acting the audience knows that it is not witnessing enormously gifted human beings and that the world of the play is not a replica of life outside the theatre, but something obviously calculated and manipulated for effect.

In North America demonstrative or epic acting is not often one of the styles noted in books about acting, but it is well known in history and in theatres in Europe, Asia, and Africa, and from time to time it can make an appearance anywhere: it is one of the basic resources of all actors.

Expressive Acting

Other names have been used to describe expressive acting—realistic, natural, naturalistic, psychologically truthful, internal, Stanislavskian—but viewed historically and with a reference to expressionist art in general, *Expressive* may be the most generally valid and least confusing term.

Shakespeare made new demands on actors by asking for idiosyncratic characters who are self-questioning and involved with conflicting emotions. For his plays, neither truth to nature in general terms nor a buildup of emotional power is sufficient; speech and action must become expressive and suggestive of individual feeling and imaginative experience. Shakespeare's writing was probably well in advance of his actors' abilities, because no criticism of performance written before the eighteenth century gives any indication of the subtle psychological interest that has been discovered in the acting of these plays during the last two centuries.

In England, Charles Macklin (1699-1797), David Garrick (1717-1779), Edmund Kean (1789-1833), William Macready (1793-1873), and Henry Irving (1838-1905) were the principal actors who sought out in their rehearsals and performances the means to display an astonishing depth and subtlety of feeling. Among those who followed and challenged their lead in the United States were Junius Brutus Booth and Edwin Booth (1796-1852 and 1833-1893) and Edwin Forrest (1806-1872). During the eighteenth and nineteenth centuries Shakespeare's tragedies were used as vehicles for a new psychological realism in acting; at the same time melodramas and comedies with extraordinary and yet recognizable characters provided roles in which these actors had freer scope to display their originality and create broader effects.

The new actors were highly individual, no longer seeking the polish and all-around accomplishment of the classical ideal. Each discovered his own novel interpretation of well-worn roles: Garrick's Hamlet was active, Edwin Booth's thoughtful; Kean's Macbeth was fiery, Macready's agonized, Irving's fearful and haunted, Forrest's strenuous and commanding; Irving's Lear was ancient and pathetic, Forrest's noble, even in madness. According to Macready, the chief task of an actor was to:

> fathom the depths of character, to trace its latent motives, to feel its finest quiverings of emotion, to comprehend the thoughts that are hidden under words, and thus possess one's self of the actual mind of the individual man.
>
> Quoted in H. Irving, *The Drama*

Both Garrick and Irving were criticized for faulty verse-speaking, but their defenders argued that these two actors alone among their contemporaries spoke as if they had felt the need to speak the words they uttered. They were so concerned with motivation that moments of conflicting thoughts and emotions—known for a time as *points*—became more important than the slow building up of sensations or the clarity of the whole stage picture:

> Where Hamlet says to his interposing friends: "I say, away,"—then turning to the ghost, "Go on, I'll follow," Garrick's variation from extreme passion to reverential awe is so forcibly expressed in eyes, features, attitude, and voice, that every heart must feel. Where the Queen says the Ghost is but the "coinage of your brain," his turning short from looking after the apparition with wildness of terror, and viewing his mother with pathetic concern, is most happily executed.
>
> Francis Gentleman, *Dramatic Censor*

Actors began to look for occasions to "play against the text," to suggest an "inner action" or "subtext" that could not be expressed through words alone. Irving's scene with Ellen Terry playing Ophelia was a notorious example of this: it was played as a love scene with a tenderness that Hamlet dared not make explicit in words or any other direct sign.

As a consequence of this psychological expressiveness, actors became more interested in apparently unconsidered details of behavior that might betray otherwise hidden concerns and compel belief. Records of Garrick's performances are the

Figure 5.2 Henry Irving as Macbeth. (Watercolor by J. Bernard
Partridge; reproduced from the souvenir program of the Lyceum
Theatre, London, 1888, in the author's collection.)

earliest to show this kind of calculation. For example, when the Ghost reappears to
Hamlet in his mother's closet:

> Hamlet immediately rises from his seat affrighted; at the same time he contrives to
> kick down his chair, which, by making a sudden noise, it was imagined would con-
> tribute to the perturbation and terror of the incident.
>
> Thomas Davies, *Dramatic Miscellanies*

It was soon found that details of this sort could support both the star performance
and the general impression of a whole scene, and, by the end of the nineteenth
century, the actors' concern with expression of complex motivation became part of
a new "realistic" movement in playwriting and scene design. Throughout Europe

Figure 5.3   Edwin Forrest as King Lear: "Ay, every inch a
King!" (act 4, scene 6). (Photograph by Gabriel Harrison; repro-
duced from Gabriel Harrison, *Edwin Forrest: the Actor and the Man*
[Brooklyn, N.Y.; privately printed, 1889].)

and America, theatres competed with each other in giving an impression of real life
on the stage while, in Moscow at about the same time, Konstantin Stanislavsky,
dissatisfied with a debased classical tradition, began to describe the various ways by
which an actor could train himself to present both "inner truth" and outward "realism" of behavior.

Stanislavsky's influence has been so widespread that most present-day actors
have, in their training, studied his books and followed the exercises they suggest.
Like the classicists, Stanislavsky was concerned with voice, movement, tempo,
physical efficiency, and so forth, and recommended the daily practice of singing,
dancing, fencing, acrobatics, and other physical skills. But he was an innovator in
that he wanted an actor to be trained in feeling as much as in the means to express
it, and it is for this that he is chiefly remembered today. The actor's mind, will, and
emotions had to come under control, just as much as the voice and body. Stanislavsky devised exercises to strengthen the actor's ability to *imagine* in rehearsal that
what is meant to be happening onstage actually *is* happening, and thereby to realize

Figure 5.4 David Garrick as Hamlet. From a contemporary painting. (Photograph from the Shakespeare Centre Library, Stratford-upon-Avon.)

in performance all the implications in body and in mind. The actor must not only be able to say, convincingly, "I have just escaped death at the hands of my brother," but should also be able to reproduce in his or her mind—and thus in behavior—all the effects of such a thought.

Stanislavsky taught actors to consider the "*magic If*": to imagine and react to a dramatic situation by considering a close analogy to it. Few actors have, for example, escaped death at the hands of their brothers, but many might get close to the appropriate reactions by considering the situation *as if* it were made up of one or more less extraordinary events: *as if* the character had escaped death in a road accident, or, because imagination can change the scale, location, and occasion of an event, *as if* he or she had nearly been pushed over a precipice, or *as if* the brother, as a child, had stolen a cherished toy.

In drawing up his exercises, Stanislavsky was influenced by the psychological investigations and theories of Ivan Pavlov (1849-1936), especially with regard to

Figure 5.5   Edwin Booth as Hamlet. Portrait by W. W. Scott, from the artotype by E. Bierstadt. (Reproduced from William Winter, *Life and Art of Edwin Booth* [New York and London: Macmillan, 1893].)

the use of mental associations to train emotional memory. When an actor had to feel a certain way, Stanislavksy would encourage him or her to remember an incident from past experience that had aroused similar responses. The actor's task was not to re-create a certain feeling, but to remember the circumstances that gave rise to it. Becoming quiet and relaxed, he or she would be directed to rethink where the incident took place, what clothes he or she was wearing, who else was there, the time of year and day, the colors of the objects involved, their shape and size. Thus, by consciously becoming aware of the context in which a particular feeling had occurred, that feeling might again be released. After repeating this exercise many times, an actor should be able to simplify the process so that remembering only

Figure 5.6 Richard Thomas as Hamlet, at Hartford Stage, 1988-1989. (Photograph © T. Charles Ericson; courtesy of Hartford Stage.)

one apparently trivial part of an experience would do the trick: so, for instance, by thinking of the pattern of a wallpaper, or of the sun striking a chair at a certain angle, or of the smell of an apple, an actor could re-create a highly charged feeling of desperation, because this perception and this feeling were at one time accidentally coexistent.

Stanislavsky also devised exercises for concentrating an actor's attention and for strengthening belief in stage fictions—for instance, for giving an impression that cold tea is whisky or a deadly poison, or that the stage floor is the top of a mountain. He taught actors to become more conscious of their own temperamental equipment, how to retain control in emotional crises, how to "act with others" onstage, how to maintain contrary emotions—in this instance, to effect what Brecht was soon to despise, the mingling of tears and laughter.

With Stanislavsky's help, a long line of psychologically expressive actors reached a new consciousness of ends and means. His kind of actor could reveal the usually hidden battleground of human consciousness, in its subtleties and large exaggerations, its power and helplessness, blindness and momentary clarity, isolation and openness, and even in its boredom and irrationality. In order to achieve all this, the actor first had to discover and then master his or her own inward nature. Instead of showing classic strength and shapeliness, an actor would sometimes have to appear weak and imprecise; instead of depicting epic objectivity and firmness, he or she would often have to be sensitive and apparently uncertain.

In the United States, Stanislavsky's influence was strangely subverted because for some years only his first book, *An Actor Prepares* (tr. 1937) was available in translation, and that work emphasizes inner training. However, Stanislavsky would often change his mind about what others called his "system," and his later books emphasize other concerns. *Building a Character* (tr. 1949) and *Creating a Role* (tr. 1961) argue for the importance of "physical actions" and show the actor how to work toward a performance that carries conviction by considering what precisely the character *does*—how he or she functions physically—and then doing the appropriate actions. This was a very different route toward performance than that of thinking about motivation and building up a stock of related memories from one's own real-life experiences.

Stanislavsky's early teaching, not the teaching of the later books, led to "the Method," as taught by Lee Strasberg (1901-1981) and others at the Actors Studio in New York. With great zeal and by expending a great deal of time, these second-generation teachers insisted that each actor find his or her own "inner truth" in a role. Their creed was in tune with the times, in which originality was greatly prized, and actors, along with other artists, often felt estranged from society and, consequently, misunderstood. The Actors Studio gave all its members a license to be themselves, and the Method soon became enormously popular and influential. Its teaching was especially suited to film acting, in which the smallest reaction can be sought out, recorded, and enlarged by the camera, and in which editing can speed up or clarify what in the theatre would be ineffectual. New film stars came out of Actors Studio, and established ones went there from Hollywood to improve their skills. Among its alumni have been Marlon Brando, Montgomery Clift, Paul Newman, Joanne Woodward, and Marilyn Monroe. The Method soon began to be taught throughout the United States, and beyond.

In the theatre, the effect of the Method has been to encourage actors to be introspective and stubborn, to neglect vitality in performance in favor of deep-seated expressiveness and, sometimes, inaudibility. In the years after the Second World War, when stage sets also tended to copy film in being highly realistic in imitation of offstage conditions, actors became more and more concerned with reproducing reality in performance, so that they wanted to "live" their roles—or very nearly so. They would go and find out, among real people and in real circumstances, what it is like to starve oneself, or to climb a mountain, or to be a taxi driver—if that was what their character did—in the hope that they could then make themselves entirely credible in performance and do nothing to break the illusion of real life and real thought and feeling.

Expressive acting in its most highly developed form is most suited to plays that, in important though different senses, we may call realistic. Shakespeare's plays are suited to highly expressive acting, but they demand many other virtues as well, those of both classical and epic acting. Chekhov's plays, most of which were premiered by Stanislavsky while he was evolving his teachings, are among the most consistently rewarding for this kind of acting. Plays by Harold Pinter and David Mamet have dialogue with strong theatricality, but they also have nuances that suggest motivations and drives that operate at a largely unspoken level deep within the characters and call for subtly expressive performances. Some dramatists, writing for both film and stage, have discovered how to write dialogue that maintains an appearance of the ordinary processes of living as if it were written for a film script, while gearing up both action and speech for the more openly expressive and less protected conditions of stage performance.

Ensemble Acting

Today a fourth kind of acting is becoming increasingly common, and there is no question about how to name it. Working together for many months or even years, and usually guided by a single director, a number of like-minded actors will learn how to work with each other in an *ensemble* and thereby develop a common style based on a common trust of their own impulses. Rather than selecting a play script ahead of rehearsal or having a preconceived notion of what their play will be like in performance and what its effect will be on an audience, these actors are likely to work together in improvisations, exploring situations through physical movement and seeking an imaginatively conceived means of expression and interaction. As a basis for this work, they may choose a theme or a piece of nondramatic writing, or some specialized physical activity, some music, or a group of visual images.

Ensemble acting is usually dynamic, seemingly extroverted, capable of depicting extremes of feeling, but at the same time carefully orchestrated and unified in effect. An actor's individuality may well be enhanced by the confidence arising from working as part of a group, but this is no style for an ambitious and self-aware star or anyone unwilling to spend a great deal of time learning the group's style or what is often called its *common physical language*.

Ensemble acting has become common for numerous reasons:

A company that concentrates its efforts on developing and coordinating the work of its actors is playing theatre's strongest card against competition from film and television: its productions hold an audience by offering a close encounter with actors of uncommon skills and high energy.

At a time when elaborate sets and costumes have become prohibitively expensive, an ensemble can use a bare stage to great visual effect by having actors working together in a physically active style.

Directors of an ensemble of actors are sure of the human material they are working with and are able to initiate an entire production themselves, creating their own actions and dialogue. By avoiding the complications of working with a large company that employs specialists for each part of a production, directors themselves are able to control the comparatively simple arrangements for lighting, sound, and other staging effects required by a traveling ensemble company. They can make sure that every detail is exactly responsive to the acting that is always at the heart of an ensemble production.

Fresh impulses, free of theatrical clichés, can originate in group exercises and explorations, especially when the actors are using music or masks to stimulate performance, and these impulses can be developed to greatest effect among actors who share the same processes of discovery.

An ensemble provides a small, enclosed world in which to work; in contrast with the uncertain conditions of most acting engagements, this set-up is protective and reassuring.

Work can start without having to lay out a great deal of money, since only space, for exercise and rehearsal, and a common purpose are required. Later expenses for set design and building, stage management, and running crew can be, and usually are, kept very low. Often there is no dramatist to take a cut of the proceeds.

Ensemble acting seems to offer a completely open road to actors, to which they can bring whatever they have previously experienced.

In an ensemble, actors find both self-definition and common loyalties. This can give high voltage to their productions and lend pride to their professional lives, and, in turn, it can create fans.

Ensemble acting serves a comparatively new kind of theatre and is therefore hard to describe. Achievement varies widely from group to group, because companies are easier to form than to hold together in truly developmental work. Great success can have its dangers too, because extreme discipline under a strong director can stifle individuality or encourage performers to become obsessed with technique, like some acrobats or specialty dancers. The work of a group can become very uniform—it is as if a huge trademark has been stamped on everything it does; the work is instantly recognizable and, consequently, boring.

One way to understand ensemble acting would be to study one particular group by reading through a number of reviews of its different productions until the dominant characteristics become clear. Of course, it would be much better to see a production and then go to one of the ensemble's "open workshops," in which groups demonstrate their way of working when visiting a town or setting up residency at a college or community center. This sort of research often leads one to become a fan of that particular group, because knowledge of what the actors are trying to do enhances enjoyment of their productions and appreciation of their skills and personalities. For a more critical understanding, it is necessary to compare the work of two groups that are performing at about the same time as each other.

Ensembles are distinctive even in their names. Culture Clash is a Los Angeles-based Chicano comedy theatre consisting of only three members. The San Francisco Mime Troupe and the Dell'Arte Players Company of Blue Lake, California, have developed very different styles, by working with masks to wordless performances. (*Dell'Arte* is an abbreviation for *commedia dell'arte*, a term that describes small companies that stage improvised comedies with recurrent characters; this form of theatre is part of a tradition reaching back to sixteenth-century Italy.) The Saratoga International Theatre Institute (SITI) works exclusively with the director Anne Bogart in a style based on her "viewpoints" methodology and using choreographic "compositions" as source material for staging and performance. SITI usually develops scripts in rehearsal and goes on emending them as knowledge of the work grows with successive performances.

Some ensembles have worked together for many years and become famous around the world. In the decades after the Second World War, Living Theatre and Open Theatre both started in New York as protests against the limitations placed on acting opportunities in established and commercial theatres. From 1965 to 1973 Jerzy Grotowski's Theatre Laboratory in Wrolac, Poland, trained a small ensemble of actors so that they could achieve an unprecedented expression of corporate determination and extremes of feeling (often involving suffering and endurance). Tadeusz Kantor's Cricot II Theatre, also in Poland, developed a style during the 1970s in which actors were used almost as puppets manipulated by the director who appeared onstage with them; trained as a visual artist and scene designer, Kantor used his actors and simple stage props to create images that were immediately striking and also evocative and memorable, notably in *Dead Class* (1975).

Figure 5.7 Demonstrative acting in *Juan Darien*, a "Carnival Mass" by Julie Taymor and Elliot Goldenthal, directed by Ms. Taymor. Sets and costumes by G. W. Mercier and Ms. Taymor. (Photograph © Donna Gray; courtesy of G. W. Mercier.)

Ensemble acting defies a single definition, beyond that implied by its name and the means it uses. It consists of a permanent group of actors, without stars; simple staging; group rehearsals and development; directorial control; self-generated play scripts exactly matched to the performers' talents and aspirations. The acting is usually very active physically, moving away from the imitation of lifelike behavior and toward musicality, extension or exaggeration, and dynamic theatricality.

Consult newspapers and journals and find some interviews of two or more actors, preferably belonging to companies you have seen in performance. Ask yourself whether what they say about their ways of working aligns them with one or several of the four styles of acting that have been described here.

6

Lucifer's Child, Acts I and II: Designed by Marjorie Bradley Kellogg. (Photo by T. Charles Erickson.)

Stage Design

In a theatre we are sometimes conscious only of the actor, perhaps only of eyes or voice, or hands; and then we can lose all distinction between the play and reality, seeming to live, in our own minds, in the action that is taking place onstage: we think and feel for a character, as if he or she had no separate existence apart from us. On such occasions, we ourselves seem to create what we see and hear; we *are* the drama, and it exists for us. Thinking about such moments afterward, it is tempting to believe that nothing counts in the theatre except the dramatist, the actor, and us, and that good theatre should provide a direct and unimpeded interplay of consciousness between all three. But this view is too simple: our ability to focus so entirely on eyes or words comes only after we have been aware of a much wider context that has already aroused many different reactions. In our minds we have previously registered the space in which we sit or stand and everything onstage around those eyes: our senses have been aroused in particular ways, and our thoughts have been prepared for what is to come, which may, in itself, seem very simple. Theatre is always complicated: it speaks to all our senses; everything counts, and nothing is wholly neutral. To get a sense of how settings affect our involvement in a play, it is necessary to talk about stage design.

What Is Stage Design?

It should be clear already that more is involved in deciding what to place on a stage than what is usually called "a set design"—that is, a small illustration stripped of many essential details. Such a "rendering" indicates choice of a historical period and color scheme for the scenery, its proportions and visual style, the background for performance, and the specifics for whatever is needed to build or supply all the doors, staircases, windows, and furniture that are required to accommodate the action of the play. The set design may also include a more distant view suggesting a whole environment of roadway, grass, desert, mountains, industrial plants, or a populous city, as appropriate. From this set design, working drawings can be prepared for building the set and stage props.

What is placed onstage is, however, only part of stage design. In recent years a new word, *scenography*, has been used to indicate that design in the theatre must also take into account the placement and surroundings of the stage, and ensure that all the physical elements of a production give a unified impression. Yet even this new word is not entirely satisfactory, because by itself it does little to indicate that the "design" of a production must also encompass the contribution of every individual actor and the total impact of the play upon the senses of an audience.

A stage designer or scenographer has an enormous task, one that is crucial in many small ways. Usually a number of designers work together, separate individuals being responsible for scenery and stage props, for lights, costumes, and sound; and sometimes for special effects. They must all work together with the director of the play because what they all do affects every part of a production. Change the clothes that the leading actor wears, and *Hamlet* becomes a different play. A costume that helps one actor to become more formal or more careful could have an opposite effect when worn by another, perhaps being unsuitable in color or cut for the person who wears it and so making him or her look clumsy and ill at ease. Give Hamlet long hair or the white face of a clown, and every moment of the play changes. Keep Hamlet close to the other characters by restricting the effective floor area of the stage and the emotional pressures will be different from those on a spacious stage where the hero's isolation can be effected more completely, and moments of close encounter can seem more of the character's own choosing. Move the action further upstage—that is, further from the audience—and any actor will have more difficulty in drawing all attention to himself or herself.

A set designer and his other design colleagues needs to get to know, very completely, the play, the stage, the auditorium, and the theatre company that is producing the play, especially its actors and director. Usually, the first step is to read the text of the play and then to imagine it in action and begin to form some idea of how it should look and feel onstage. Next each designer does a number of very quick sketches, as well as a good deal of research about materials, colors, sounds, music, photographs of people and places, reproductions of works of art. Eventually images of actors in action begin to form in the designers' minds, along with a sense of space and confinement, energies and rhythms.

At this time the designers and the director should be working together very closely as a plan for the whole production begins to emerge. They must also work out, at least in basic terms, what is needed onstage to accommodate the physical activities that will be required for the production. Then design decisions start to be made, with all the designers contributing drawings of a set, a simple model, costume designs, and lighting and sound plots.

The imaginative thinking and the consultation and development required for stage design make the whole process very time consuming. Unfortunately theatre works for much of the time in overdrive and no one is paid overtime, so a designer may be engaged on two or three projects at once, each one on a strict timetable for construction. Under these conditions, a lot of stage design involves little more than drawing up workable plans for variations of more or less standard ways of coping with one kind of play or another. True scenographic originality does not come easily and takes far more time and effort than is usually available. At the end of the twentieth century, huge advances in technology have made it possible for theatres to produce more amazing effects than ever before, but unfortunately there is all too often a chronic shortage of funds, so that, rather paradoxically, designers are at this time a particularly overworked and overstretched sector of the theatre profession.

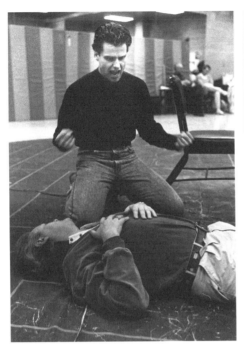

Figure 6.1A and B   Julius Caesar in early rehearsal and in performance at the Alabama Shakespeare Festival. (Photographs courtesy of the Alabama Shakespeare Festival.)

Advances in technology should save time, but they don't; more can be done, but the time to get everything working and coordinated takes longer and longer, leaving no time for adequate consultation and development. Almost endless time can be taken on refinement and a great deal of money goes into securing the up-to-date equipment.

When the visual staging of a play is the product of the imagination and considered judgment of a single mind, working in skilled collaboration with the director of a play and with everyone else in the workshops and on the stage, a complex and unexpected experience can be created, one that, without muddle or imprecision, engages and saturates the minds of an audience. Designers can create a production that is like a brilliantly orchestrated symphony, and can inspire as inevitably and movingly as great music.

> *Think of the last time you went to the theatre and write down the predominant colors of the stage set and a description of the clothes worn by two leading actors. What difference would it make to the play if the colors of the set were changed, or the style and colors of the clothes? Why did the designer make the decisions he or she made in these matters?*

Varieties of Stage Design

When starting on a new project, a designer must first decide *how* to work, what kind of scenography is appropriate to the job at hand. This is not fundamentally a question of fashion or historical accuracy, and not only a matter of personal taste. Rather it involves basic decisions about how to stage a particular play and how to use the theatre and actors. Many names have been used to describe the styles of stage design, none of them very precise. However, if we consider their effect on audiences and their historical development, five main styles may be distinguished.

Minimalist

Sometimes a designer has only a platform to work with. In early times, the layout of theatre buildings restricted what could be brought onto the open stage, so very little designing was possible, and no such person as a stage designer existed. During the renaissance, as described in Chapter 3 ("Thrust-stage Theatres"), a thrust stage was backed only by a permanent facade, through which actors would make their entries and exits. It was the actors who created a sense of place onstage, by what they said and what they wore or carried with them, and, perhaps above all, by their physical bearing and activities. For some scenes, large props would be brought onto the stage to accommodate and give significance to the action, and to give a point of focus for the audience's attention. This minimal kind of staging encouraged the variety of scene and action that is characteristic of Shakespeare's plays. In the present day, stage designers must struggle to retain these features in theatres that have been built and equipped for visual presentation that is very different in style and in which staging a production is more cumbersome and expensive.

Even with small resources, the look of what was put on the Shakespearean stage was of crucial importance, though what the effect would be was for the most part decided by the leading actors, who chose among racks of costumes, and by the bookkeeper, who drew upon the theatre's stock of props. Costumes were especially important because they could send very precise messages about the class or function of a character, the time of day, the weather, the location of a scene, whether interior or exterior, the political realities of battle or debate, and so on. Types of swords and other weapons would denote rank, allegiance, class, or race. Thrones, beds, various kinds of tables and chairs, tombs, arbors, trees, town or prison gates would change the center of action onstage and give vital information about what was happening. For some productions special costumes or props would be commissioned, and someone, whether actor, dramatist, or manager, would give instructions about what was required.

In many respects the dramatist was the stage designer, because he chose the characters, location, and action, indicating what he wanted in his stage directions and dialogue. The various stage directions were enough to create within a single play a great variety of *shows* (the term used at this time), from a crowd of people onstage involved in solemn pageantry or active warfare, to a few actors isolated on stage with nothing but what they stood up in to help them maintain dramatic impetus. Introducing scenes of dressing up and undressing, embracing, kneeling, feasting, dancing, fighting with fists or weapons, rites of wedding, funeral, or homage could make major visual impact, and all of this was at the dramatist's discretion. Many theatres had an upper level to the stage, so the visual effect could be varied further by introducing a split focus and vertical relationships.

Figure B.1 A festival theatre. The parklike setting of the Carolyn Blount Theatre in Montgomery, Alabama. (Photograph courtesy of the Alabama Shakespeare Festival.)

Figure B.2 A festival theatre. The "Grand Lobby" of the Carolyn Blount Theatre in Montgomery, Alabama. (Photograph courtesy of the Alabama Shakespeare Festival.)

Figures B.3 and B.4 The Festival Stage of the Alabama Shakespeare Festival. (Photographs courtesy of the Alabama Shakespeare Festival.)

Figures B.5 and B.6 Model and stage set for *The Playboy of the Western World*, designed by Marjorie Bradley Kellogg for the Seattle Repertory Theatre. (Photographs courtesy of the artist.)

Figures B.7 and B.8 Lighting effects: two contrasting views of the set for *Yerma* at Arena Stage, Washington, D.C. (Photographs by Joan Marcus; courtesy of Arena Stage.)

In Greek and Roman times, stage design also depended largely on what the actors wore and on a dramatist's use of space. Greek theatres had large stage areas, known as orchestras, on which the entire audience looked down, so that the deployment of choruses in varying groupings, processions, and dances across this space played an eloquent part in performance. Even the movement of a single actor, across the large circular space and separated from a huddled or formally grouped chorus, could have large visual effect. The meeting of Orestes and Electra, the surviving children of Agamemnon, the taking of Iphigenia to be killed at the altar, the entry of an old nurse or armed warrior through palace doors to tell horrifying news, the return of Oedipus alone after a rending scream, his eye sockets bleeding, are all crucial moments in ancient tragedies which would have registered with great visual power as single figures faced members of the chorus and they scattered or regrouped, terror or pity expressed and amplified by their gestures and movement across a large area.

The early Greek dramatists and choreographers had a degree of control over visual staging that our designers today no longer have in less spacious but better equipped theatres. But the Greeks did develop and use some painted scenery and also machines for displaying tableaux and for flying characters onto and away from the stage. It would seem that they were not entirely satisfied with their choreographic use of a vast space, and they also took pleasure in creating innovative spectacles for specific climactic actions. Masks, too, added to the effect of costume, and their design was of crucial importance to the performance.

The advantages of such minimalism in stage design were rediscovered long after classical and renaissance theatres had disappeared or fallen into disuse, and a revival followed, especially on the new thrust stages and arena stages that have been built in the second half of the twentieth century and are well served by this kind of presentation. In other forms of theatre a simple and unchanging background together with carefully focused and varied stage lighting have sometimes been used to make the actor once again the chief center of attention. The fact that simple staging costs less in time and money has much to do with its renewed popularity, but it is also used because of the powerful effect that can be derived from a few well-chosen props and costumes.

Samuel Beckett's plays are a case in point. *Waiting for Godot* (1953) calls for no more by way of stage design than: *"A country road. A Tree. Evening."* A "road" sounds a difficult matter to bring onto a stage, but productions in which Beckett himself was closely involved did not represent the road by any cumbersome stage setting: bare boards and a plain backcloth often sufficed. The tree was usually rudimentary in form, and beyond that only a *"low mound"* is required. (See first stage direction, act 1.) Such economy does not imply that stage design is of negligible importance: the single tree is repeatedly the object of the characters' attention and so gains an iconographic or symbolic importance, like the large props in earlier plays: Agamemnon's tomb in the *Oresteia*, the manger of the stable in which Christ is born in the medieval miracle plays, the throne on which sit successive kings in Shakespeare's history plays, and so forth. In minimalist stage design, a few objects can stand out strongly and grow in significance as the action of the play is continually redefined by contact with them; such staging might also be termed *symbolic* or *iconographic*, so much meaning can be conveyed by particular physical elements placed onstage.

Minimalism is also the choice of most of the small touring ensembles (see Chapter 5, "Ensemble Acting"). For them stage settings must not compete with the expressive power of performers, supported by music, costumes, and hand props; besides, they need settings that are easily transportable and readily adaptable to all shapes and sizes of playing spaces.

> *If you have studied a Shakespeare play, make a list of the objects that its dialogue and stage directions require to be brought onstage by actors or stage hands, and then consider how they contribute visually to what is being said and done. Do any of the characters react to them in significantly different ways?*

Pictorial

A play can be staged on a simple platform, with the actors performing in front of a picture of the place where the action is meant to be taking place. In the seventeenth and eighteenth centuries, proscenium theatres were built and equipped especially for this kind of staging (see Chapter 3). On removable cloths and sliding panels, a battlefield, garden, public street, or domestic interior would be depicted according to the demands of the drama from scene to scene; and on the platform in front of these pictures, characters of the play would engage with each other and also with the audience with whom they were in close contact. The job of the *scene painters*, as they were rightly called, was to locate the scene and give a series of eye-catching vistas that would enlarge the audience's view of the setting of the action but not compete with the moment-by-moment vivacity of the characters in the play. What the leading actors wore was their own affair, and the stars would often commission special costumes to please themselves and flatter their own looks.

This kind of background scenery went out of general use when electricity transformed the lighting of the stage and the auditorium was darkened, but the desire to set the characters of a play over against an extensive and detailed background has survived for some purposes. For old plays, which were written to be performed in front of a pictorial set, some designers will reproduce and adapt the old style for new theatres, believing this to be the most appropriate way to give life to the texts. For some new plays a different kind of pictorial design has been developed: instead of painted pictures employing illusionistic perspective, designers now use projected images, taken from photographs of real places and real events, and the actors perform in front of a cinema-like screen or curtain. Sometimes clips from films are used, so that the pictorial representation of place can include moving figures, crowd scenes in small scale, or enormous blown-up images of individual people in close and revealing contact with each other. These pictorial settings, back-projected onto a screen or curtain, may differ entirely in proportion, tempo, rhythm, and location, from the situation and movements of the characters in the play that is being acted in front them. As in the old proscenium theatres, the audience has a double view, seeing both the personal drama and its larger context. For political, documentary, or sociohistorical dramas, this device can be used to relate the personal choices of a play's characters to their wider implications, thus raising moral and political questions. Some designers working in an eclectic manner (see below), introduce projected pictures into a setting that is representational and not at all pictorial.

Illusionistic Realism

As we have seen earlier, the invention of gas and electric light in the second half of the nineteenth century changed theatre buildings and the relation of stage to audience in unprecedented ways. A new kind of set design was developed that could reproduce real interiors and indicate outdoor locations with much greater credibility. Authors began to write plays in which the actual conditions of life had to be copied meticulously onstage, and actors quickly had to learn a realism to match (see Chapter 5). It was not long before authors called for more than the reproduction of ordinary circumstances; their stage directions specified effects that had previously been unthinkable. Stage machinery also developed technically, and soon the stage became a three-dimensional mimic world that could change in front of the audience's eyes, and almost any natural or man-made phenomenon could be brought into the theatre.

By the end of the nineteenth century, productions presented waterfalls, express trains, shipwrecks, snowstorms, and macabre haunted castles that, at first, compelled belief because the devices that created them were so new. Ballets, pantomimes, melodramas, and what were known as *extravaganzas* eagerly exploited this new capacity, but even playwrights who usually asked for a sober, everyday reality onstage would occasionally also call for that illusion to be broken by something far grander, involving amazing vistas and cataclysmic events. The last act of Ibsen's *When We Dead Awaken* (1897-1898) has this stage direction:

> *The mists settle thick over the landscape.* PROFESSOR RUBEK, *holding* IRENE *by the hand, climbs up over the snowfield, right, and soon disappears into the low cloud. Biting winds rage and whine. . . . Suddenly there is a roar as of thunder from high up on the snowfield, which begins to slide and tumble down at terrifying speed.* RUBEK *and* IRENE *can be glimpsed indistinctly as they are caught up and buried by the mass of snow.*
>
> The Oxford Ibsen

Other plays called for stage design that was less sensationally illusionistic, but no less ambitious. An historical occasion or notable piece of architecture would be meticulously re-created, so that audiences were given the impression of actually "being there" and were no longer looking at a distant picture. Audiences were also invited to view worlds that were unfamiliar and inaccessible except in a theatre. Here, for example, is part of the opening stage direction in Maxim Gorki's *The Lower Depths*, which was first performed at the Moscow Art Theatre in 1902, with Stanislavsky in the leading role of Satin:

> *A cellar, which looks like a cave. The ceiling consists of heavy stone arches, black with smoke and with the plaster falling. The light comes in from the audience, and downwards from a square window on the right. The right-hand corner is taken up by* PEPEL's *room, separated from the rest by a thin partition, close to the door of which is* BUBNOV's *plank bed. In the left-hand corner is a large Russian stove. . . . In the foreground by the left wall stands a block of wood with a vice and a small anvil fixed to it; in front of it is another, slightly smaller, block, on which* KLESHCH *is sitting, trying keys in old locks. At his feet lie two large bunches of keys of different sizes, held together by rings made of bent wire; a battered tin samovar; a hammer; files.*
>
> trans. Kitty Hunter-Blair and J. Brooks

Figure 6.2   Victorian spectacular staging. Large crowds were deployed against painted "flats" in Beerbohm Tree's 1898 production of *Julius Caesar* at Her Majesty's Theatre, London. The settings were supervised by the painter Alma Tadema. (Reproduced from a photograph in the author's collection.)

It is not surprising to read in Stanislavsky's autobiography that he had gone, together with the play's director and scene designers, to crowded tenements in the poorest and most dangerous section of Moscow so that they could stock their memories with appropriate images and make sketches of objects needed for the stage. Nevertheless, this and other stage directions show that lighting had as much to do with the illusion of real life as did scene construction and painting or the collection of used objects found at appropriate locales.

From the introduction of electricity onwards towards the end of the nineteenth century, lighting proved to be the most powerful means of creating illusion. The stage would be filled with a near replica of an actual offstage location and then lit, by what seemed like magic, to enhance its verisimilitude and control the mood of each scene. Between them the set designer and lighting designer could provide a mimic reality and then suggest whatever gloss the dramatist chose to place on it. We have already seen how Tennessee Williams's *Glass Menagerie* calls for a whole neighborhood to be shown onstage, as well as the interior of an apartment (see Chapter 2, "Spectacle"). According to its first stage direction, David Belasco's *The Girl of the Golden West* (1905) opens with a spectacle on which an illusion of sunlight casts a romantic glow and then magically, before a word has been spoken, the scene changes to a second setting, lit in quite a different way:

> *The curtain rises to a glimpse of Cloudy Mountain, in the Sierras. The peak is white, the sky above very blue, and the moon, which seems strangely near, shines on the steep trail leading up to the cabin of the Girl. A lamp, placed in the cabin window by Wowkle, the squaw, shows that the Girl has not yet come home from her place of business, the Polka Saloon.*
>
> *This scene shifts to an exterior view of the Polka Saloon and the miners' cabins at the foot of Cloudy Mountain. The cheerful glow of kerosene lamps, the rattle of poker chips, and an occasional "whoop" show that life in the Polka is in full swing.*

In many recent plays, lighting effects are a major resource for the dramatist. Lanford Wilson's *Burn This* (1987) requires a very particular and fashionable setting that has ample scope for special lighting effects through large windows and a skylight, and also a mirrored wall:

> *The setting is a huge loft in a converted cast-iron building in lower Manhattan, New York City. Factory windows, a very large sloping skylight, a kitchen area, a sleeping loft, a hall to the bathroom and Larry's bedroom, and another door to Anna's bedroom. The place is sparsely furnished. . . .*
>
> *The time is the present. It is six o'clock in the evening, mid-October. The sky has the least color left, one lamp has been turned on.*

Physically the set remains the same throughout the play, but the effect of the setting is changed by the stage lighting, as the action passes from day to evening to nighttime. The last moments are lit only by the distant light of uptown high-rises seen through all that glass and, very briefly, by the less permanent light of a match and a piece of burning paper placed very close to the only two characters onstage. Variations of light have given the set an important role in the drama, and in this last change the use of light is able to show how precariously the issues between the two leading characters have been resolved; if they have found an intimate security, it is in near darkness and over against the lights of the great city.

> *When you next go to the theatre, ask yourself whether you are meant to believe that what you see is* really *happening. If the answer is yes, try to remember if lighting changes helped in achieving this impression and so added to your understanding of the story or characters.*
>
> *If the answer is no, try to remember if any part of what you saw gave some limited illusion of reality: if so, consider how this was brought about — by stage effects or by lighting changes, or by the actors — and whether such a moment affected your enjoyment of the play.*

Fluid

Another name for fluid stage design would be *plastic*, but a word is needed that implies more than changing shapes. Whereas illusionistic sets were built and engineered out of solid materials and were intended to look solidly real, the sets in fluid stage design can give the impression that nothing onstage has a specific or limited reality. In recent years, lighting has become still more important to this style, and, thanks to microtechnology, any effect can flow into another. With sophisticated stage equipment, even solid-looking objects are made to move and change their shapes.

Most of the devices that created stage realism at the close of the nineteenth century would seem ludicrously inefficient today. Theatre technology has made huge advances, and, still more significantly, film and television have led audiences to expect a far more effective evocation of actuality and specific locales. As early as the 1890s a Swiss stage designer, Adolphe Appia (1862-1928), called for the abandonment of illusionistic realism, which he decried as clumsy and never totally convincing. He wanted stage design to give the *sensation* of a man walking in a great forest, not to place him among inadequate imitations of growing trees.

Appia had a special interest in music (and in Wagner's operas in particular) and he believed that light should be used as if it were music, forever changing, positively and "vividly." The task of lighting was not to be confined to illuminating the acting area or reproducing the light effects of the real world; rather it should accentuate or transfigure chosen *aspects* of the stage action and should evoke emotional responses directly by means of its color, intensity, movement, and points of focus. With Appia, darkness became a positive instrument, as well as light: the stage might be crossed by long shadows, and its dimensions seem endless. The audience's attention could be held and developed without a single actor being onstage. Appia believed that by means of light the stage could express an "inner reality" and could become its own world, like the worlds of dream and imaginative thought. The movement of human figures was, however, a significant element of Appia's infinitely variable stage, and since he wanted to coordinate everything onstage, Appia worked closely with Emile Jaques Dalcroze (1865-1950), a teacher of physical movement according to a method called *eurythmics*.

Appia designed very little that was actually produced, but the revolutionary effect of his theories and drawings became widely recognized through his books, especially *La Musique et la Mise en Scène* (*Music and Stage Design*) written in 1892 and published in 1899.

At about the same time, Gordon Craig was formulating similar ideas in England and Germany, and later in Italy. In *Towards a New Theatre* (1913), he reproduced four drawings of a flight of steps that showed the effect of the new fluidity of light (Figure 6.4). The form and proportions of the steps do not change from one picture to another, but the light playing on them does, helped by the placing of a few figures. By these means, and without making exact reference to real conditions of life, the emotional effect of each design is distinct: light and airy, or substantial, or mysterious, or weighty and tragic.

In the United States, Robert Edmond Jones (1887-1954) became the champion of the new stage design. His *The Dramatic Imagination*, published in 1941, was an attack on cumbersome, confining, and incomplete realism. His designs gave to the stage a glowing spaciousness that allowed plays to become real in the imagination of their audiences; he did not attempt an illusion of actuality onstage as if the world of the play were in competition with life outside the theatre. Jones's stage designs were found to be especially successful for plays by Shakespeare and O'Neill, wherein the visual imagery created onstage could work in the audience's minds in combination with the imagery of the poetic texts.

Figure 6.3   Appia's design for act 3 of Wagner's *Tristan and Isolde*, 1923. (Photograph courtesy of Richard C. Beacham, from the Schweizerische Theatersammlung, Bern, Switzerland.)

Fluidity in design has not entirely displaced the solidity of illusionistic realism; the popularity of film and the prevalence of "lifelike" acting styles have done much to ensure its continuance. Compromises between the fluid and the illusionistic are sometimes attempted, when the innovative freedom of Appia, Craig, and Jones is introduced in an otherwise realistic set design. In a prefatory note for *Glass Menagerie*, to return to our earlier example, Williams asks for the new kind of unrealistic stage lighting:

> *Shafts of light are focused on selected areas or actors, sometimes in contradistinction to what is the apparent centre. . . . A free, imaginative use of light can be of enormous value in giving a mobile, plastic quality to plays of a more or less static nature.*

Tennessee Williams called this a "memory play" and relied a great deal on light and music to establish an appropriate unreality.

In the last decades of the twentieth century, the masters of stage design—the new style gave a masterful power to the designer—have used movable scenery as well as fluid lighting. For *King Lear* at Stratford-upon-Avon in 1955, the American-Japanese sculptor Isamu Noguchi brought a succession of sharply colored shapes onto the stage as a mobile support for the action: red diamonds, three times a man's height, came forward together as conflict increased; and a huge black belly-shaped cutout dropped down for the storm, oppressing the stage.

Figure 6.4A-D   Gordon Craig's four drawings of The Steps, from *Towards a New Theatre*, 1923. (Reproduced from a copy in the author's collection.)

In Brussels in 1958, Czech designer Josef Svoboda staged *Hamlet* with a great mirror hung across the stage at an angle forty-five degrees to the perpendicular. The set had numerous rectangular units that were capable of moving backward and forward to provide stairways, rooms, platforms, and even a bed, and everything was reflected in the giant mirror. So Elsinore, the world of the play, could be a compact rectangular structure at the back of the stage, above which the isolated figure of the Ghost was reflected, or, as various elements moved forward silently, it was a complex three-dimensional jigsaw with dark shadows, sometimes made oppressive by a further perspective reflected in the suspended mirror.

Numerous actors with no named parts, like those who had served in the nineteenth century to fill out realistic crowd scenes, have also been used, when finance

Figure 6.5 Setting for Shakespeare's *Macbeth* by Gordon Craig. (Reproduced from a copy of *Towards a New Theatre* in the author's collection.)

allowed, to contribute to the plasticity and expressiveness of stage design. Austrian director Max Reinhardt (1873-1943) was a master of these effects, combining huge realistic sets with a well-drilled crowd, fluid lighting, and music, so that his productions had an expressive eloquence beyond the reach of any earlier realism.

Reinhardt's greatest success was a mime-drama, *The Miracle* (1911), which was staged in large arenas in Europe and North America. His actors had to sing, dance, and speak in unison, and they were trained in the eurythmics of Dalcroze, Appia's collaborator. In this staging Reinhardt used crowds of people as a living element of stage design to evoke a sense of wonder and emotional intensity. Similar orchestrated effects were needed to sustain the expressionist plays written in the first decades of the nineteenth century in Germany and elsewhere (see Chapter 2, "Expressionist Plays"). The last scene of Georg Kaiser's *From Morn till Midnight* (1912), with its Salvation Army songs and anonymous speeches, will not respond to a realistic enactment but depends on rhythmic climaxes and the powerful ebb and flow of its large crowd.

Eugene O'Neill's *The Emperor Jones* (1920) and *The Hairy Ape* (1921) are the most memorable plays written in English in the expressionist manner. The original stage designer for both was Robert Edmond Jones. Stage directions from *The Emperor Jones* indicate how light, space, and crowds of actors in unnamed roles combined to give a poetic fluency and expressiveness to the action:

> *A cleared space in the forest. The limbs of the trees meet over it forming a low ceiling about five feet from the ground. The interlocked ropes of creepers reaching upward to entwine the tree trunks gives an arched appearance to the sides. The space thus enclosed is like the dark,*

Figure 6.6   The setting for Shakespeare's *Hamlet* by Robert Edmund Jones, at the Haymarket Theatre, London, 1925. (Photograph courtesy of the Raymond Mander and Joe Mitchenson Theatre Collection.)

noisome hold of some ancient vessel. The moonlight is almost completely shut out and only a vague, wan light filters through. There is the noise of someone approaching from the left, stumbling and crawling through the undergrowth. JONES' *voice is heard between chattering moans. . . .*

Gradually it seems to grow lighter in the enclosed space and two rows of seated figures can be seen behind JONES. *They are sitting in crumpled, despairing attitudes, hunched, fac-*

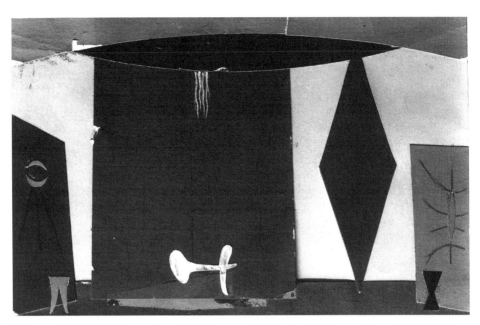

Figure 6.7 Model of a setting for Shakespeare's *King Lear* by Isamu Noguchi (1955) for the Royal Shakespeare Company. (Photograph courtesy of the Shakespeare Centre Library, Stratford-upon-Avon.)

ing one another with their backs touching the forest walls as if they were shackled to them. All are negroes, naked save for loin cloths. At first they are silent and motionless. Then they begin to sway slowly forward toward each other and back again in unison, as if they were laxly letting themselves follow the long roll of a ship at sea. At the same time, a low, melancholy murmur rises among them, increasing gradually by rhythmic degrees which seem to be directed and controlled by the throb of the tom-tom in the distance, to a long, tremulous wail of despair that reaches a certain pitch, unbearably acute, then falls by slow graduations of tone into silence and is taken up again.

With a specially constructed domed background for the stage, light seemed to envelop the action and was imperceptibly graded in intensity.

Choose a play with at least five scenes and, assuming you are in charge of the color and intensity of lights for a production, list the colors for each scene and describe how bright and dark the stage should be. Can you think how these changes in lighting would contribute to the effect of acting the play and to its meaning?

Presentational (or Eclectic)

The expansive possibilities of fluid stage design are not within every company's financial means, nor do they serve every author's purpose. Similarly the up-front directness of minimalist design does not serve the vision of all plays or satisfy the expectations of all audiences. During the second half of the twentieth century a "postmodern" kind of stage design has developed, and it is likely to become the most commonly used.

Figure 6.8 Max Reinhardt's production of *The Miracle* at Olympia, London, 1911, show-ing his use of huge crowds and dramatic lighting in a large arena. (Photograph courtesy of the Raymond Mander and Joe Mitchenson Theatre Collection.)

In creating this new style, it is hard to know whether the designers have responded to dramatists, or the dramatists to designers. Perhaps writers are copy-ing the fluidity of film or the contrasts between scenes that are so common in Shakespeare. Perhaps they are reflecting the multiple influences to which we are all subjected in an age of television and instant access. Whatever the reasons, new plays often have many short scenes, each requiring different locations and some-times different styles of presentation. For these texts, thoroughgoing illusionistic design would be out of the question, yet a wholly fluid design would not reflect the specific reality needed to match the realism of the dialogue. Most designers have responded by choosing and clearly defining a few realistic elements for each scene, and presenting them boldly, using high-tech lighting and complex sound tracks to give a sense of shock or surprise that was not possible in earlier minimalist design. Self-contained illusions of specific interiors or locations are not attempted, and, unless broad, empty spaces are required, little attempt is made to fill the whole stage area for each new scene.

The "Note about the Staging" in Tony Kushner's *Angels in America* (1992) describes this presentational style of design and suggests its attractions for a dramatist:

> The play benefits from a pared-down style of presentation, with minimal scenery and scene shifts done rapidly (no blackouts!), employing the cast as well as stage hands—which makes for an actor-driven event, as this must be. The moments of magic—the appearance and disappearance of Mr. Lies and the ghosts, the Book hallucination, and the ending—are to be fully realized, as bits of wonderful *theatri-cal* illusion—which means it's OK if the wires show, and may[be] it's good that they do, but the magic should at the same time be thoroughly amazing.

This kind of stage design probably originates in productions by Bertolt Brecht for the Berliner Ensemble after the Second World War (see Chapter 2 "Expressionist

Plays"). With Brecht, a selective and somewhat sober realism was used in a presentational manner. Instead of making many complete scenes appear as real as possible, Brecht and his designer, Caspar Neher (1897-1962), would import real, carefully chosen objects that spoke for a wider reality, including objects that showed long years of use or represented personal decisions made in the past by a given character in the play. Illusionistic stage devices were of little interest to them and the means by which the stage was lit or the scene changed were often clearly visible to the audience. Above all there was no attempt to evoke simple and strong emotion through dreamlike atmosphere and variations in lighting. For Brecht a presentational style of design was intended to make his audience think clearly about issues and persons taken from real life. His style was, of course, entirely suited to the epic style of acting (see Chapter 5, "Demonstrative or Epic Acting") which he sought for his productions.

Contemporary practice of the presentational style is often more vibrant and eye-catching, and ear-catching as well. Providing contact with reality is a matter of sending rapid signals, as in a couple of stage directions from Eric Overmyer's *On the Verge* (1986):

> Lights! A flashy sign, neon: NICKY's. Some palm trees and streamers: A gaudy, prerevolutionary Havana-style nightclub.

> MARY *saddles up and comes downstage. . . . The stars come out. . . . She surveys the horizon and her prospects. . . . She disappears in a blaze of light—End of play.*

When playwrights are aware of the possibilities of stage design, they often call for effects that can only be achieved in a presentational manner. Paula Vogel's *The Baltimore Waltz* requires thirty scenes to be played in fluent sequence. Different locations are identified by the actors, costumes, stage props, and furniture, but some illusion of a wider context is given through the use of sound and music, which the author suggests should be an almost continuous accompaniment to the action right up to the last scene. The effect is presentational and eclectic, rather than minimalist. Scene-opening directions include:

> Scene VIII *Anna enters the empty hotel room. On the bed, propped up on pillows, lies the stuffed rabbit.*

> Scene XIX *German band music swells as Anna and Carl sit in their railroad compartment, side by side. Anna, pale, holds the stuffed rabbit in her lap.*

> Scene XXIII *Music: Kurt Weill. Anna goes over to a small cabaret table. There is a telephone on the table. The Radical Student Activist sits at another identical table, smoking, watching her.*

At the opening and close of this play, several locations are presented simultaneously.

> *Choose a play you know well and argue in favor of a stage design from among the five kinds described here. Might elements of another kind of stage design be included?*

Processes of Stage Design

Between the idea for a stage design and its realization, many people must work together, and first notions will have to be modified to fit the actual circumstances of production. No designer, however practiced, can foresee all the problems involved; no design, however simple, can reach its final form without unexpected variations of material being taken into account.

The greatest variables are, of course, the actors and what they are going to do onstage during the show. A costume designer needs to know the actors who will wear the costumes and will discuss designs with them. It helps to sketch them in action in specific scenes of the play. (A set of good costume designs can be one of the best visual illustrations of any staging of a play, showing how character relates to character, and scene to scene.) The fitting of costumes—not only in cut and size, but also in color and texture—is also vital, because it can enhance or ruin both costume and performance. The designer will take part in shopping expeditions for fabrics, attend fittings in the wardrobe, and will, perhaps, modify a costume design as late as dress rehearsal as new demands are made by what actors have discovered in rehearsals.

During production, a set designer is everywhere in a theatre: observing in all the workshops to see how scenery and props are being built, sitting in the sound studio to hear the recording of music and sound effects that will help to set the scenes, and working in the offices to organize work around rehearsals and pre-views. He or she visits merchants' yards, junk shops, and gift boutiques, helping to look for props, door handles, furniture, drapes, and floor coverings.

Integration of the various aspects of design has to be watched continuously. In particular, lighting must be integrated with all the other aspects of design, because it can alter color, apparent shape, scale, atmosphere, and the entire look of scenery and costumes—whatever these may look like on the drawing board or in the work-shops. Alter the lighting, and a scene may be received in dead silence, when previously, played word for word and move by move in exactly the same way, it left an audience helpless with laughter. (If this seems hard to believe, try telling a good joke in near darkness.) The last adjustments to lights are made very late, during dress rehearsals and previews, as the actors' performances, and therefore the cues for light changes, begin to mature and become more or less fixed.

With the development of multitrack recording, sound has become a newly effective element in stage design, which tends to be the responsibility of a separate designer; this job requires extensive knowledge of music as well as specialized tech-nical proficiency. Sound is so intimately connected with performance, that creating and fine-tuning it requires work with the actors almost from the start of rehearsals.

In well-equipped modern theatres, stage design or scenography has become a huge task of planning, building, and coordination. A unified series of decisions has to be made, but seldom can one person do all the tasks, especially in the last days before opening night, when many different operations are proceeding at great speed in different workshops and onstage. In normal practice, except for very small productions, four designers join together with the director to create a single, uni-fied production, one designer each for set, costumes, lights, and sound, and each one of these may have one or more assistants. At dress rehearsals, the director and the three or four chief designers will sit in radio communication with each other, ready for consultation and effective action.

The designers' relationship with each other and with the play's director is cru-cial. They must know how each other works and foresee the tempo and shape of rehearsals, as well as the nature of the final production. Successful directors tend to

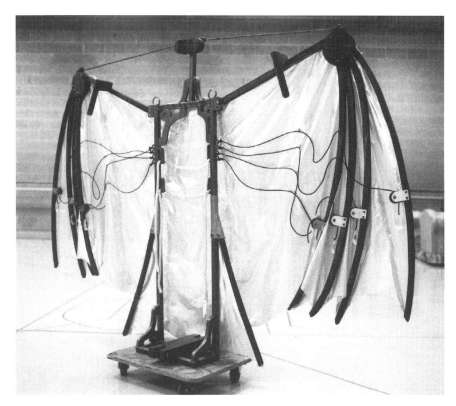

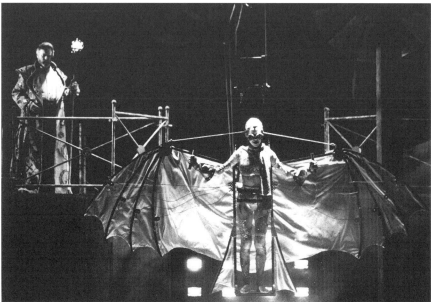

Figure 6.9A and B   Armature and finished costume for Ariel as a Harpy in Shakespeare's *The Tempest* at the Alabama Shakespeare Festival, 1994. The director was Kent Tompson; costumes were designed by Elizabeth Novak. (Photograph courtesy of the Alabama Shakespeare Festival.)

Figure 6.10A and B   Two designs for Chekhov's *Cherry Orchard*. a. Minimalist realism, with illusionistic lighting at Seattle Repertory Theatre. b. Presentational stage design at the American Repertory Theatre, Cambridge, Massachusetts. (Photographs © Chris Bennion, Seattle, Washington, and © Richard Feldman, Newton, Massachusetts.)

work with the same, equally successful designers, one play after another. In this way, they can be responsive and sensitive to new ideas, and the least possible time will be wasted on misunderstandings. Just as good performances are more likely when actors understand each other yet provide strong contrast to one another, so director and designers need not be entirely similar in outlook and temperament: for their team to work, stimulus and challenge, just as much as a good working relationship, are essential. Even conflict can be useful, so long as the partnership remains open and mutually supportive. With good collaboration, the work of physically staging a play is enspiriting and adventurous.

> *Choose any one moment in a production when you have been especially held by the play and try to figure out the separate contributions of its four designers. Imagine how the effect would have changed if one or two of those designers had made different choices of color, size, positioning, fashion, or style. Are there any changes you would have recommended?*

Day	Date	Function	Electrics	Scenery	Props	Costume	Make-up	Sound
Mon	Sep 23	ELECS/SOUND: Load in	1 to 5					
Tue	Sep 24	ELECS/SOUND: Load in cont.	1 to 5					
Wed	Sep 25	ELECS: Load in cont.	1 to 5					
		SCENERY: Load in		1 to 5				
Thu	Sep 26	SCENERY: Load in continue		1 to 5				
Fri	Sep 27	SCENERY: Load in continue		1 to 5				
		Props Load in time TBA						
Mon	Sep 30	SCENERY: Load In - finish		1 to 5				
		ELEC: Focus	1 to 5					
		Set Spike			1 to 3			
		Press photos, Actor call 5pm 6:00 shoot Location TBA						
Tue	Oct 1	ELEC: Focus	1 to 5					
Wed	Oct 2	SCENERY: misc notes		1 to 5				
		ELEC: Focus	1 to 5					
		Actors on Stage 7-11	7-11	no tech	no tech			
		Qing over						
Thu	Oct 3	ELEC. & SCENERY Notes	1 to 5	1 to 5				
		Actors on Stage 7-11 (7:30 Go)	7-11	7-11	7-11			
		Qing over						
Fri	Oct 4	SCENERY: Notes.		2 - 6				
		ELEC/ SOUND: Notes	2 - 6					
		Que Sound						1:30-5:30
		TECH PART 1 (7:30 GO)	7-11	7-11	7-11			7-11
Sat	Oct 5	DAY OFF ALL DEPARTMENTS	No Tech	No Tech	No Tech	No Tech	No Tech	No Tech
Sun	Oct 6	10 of 12						
		TECH REH	11 to 4	11 to 4	11 to 4	11 to 4		11 to 4
		DRESS REH #1 (7:30 Go)	6 to 11	6 to 11	6 to 11	6 to 11	no make-up	6 to 11
		NOTE: EDWINN DROOD - Load in Begins - Mendelssohn						
Mon	Oct 7	Misc Notes	9-6	9-6	9-6			
		Wardrobe in				2-6		
		DRESS REH #2 (7:30 Go)	7-11	7-11	7-11	6 - 11	6 - 11	6:30 to 11
Tue	Oct 8	Misc Notes	9-6	9-6	9-6	9-6		
		DRESS REH #3 (7:30 Go)	7-11	6:30 to 11	6 to 11	5 to 11	5 to 11	7-11
		Photo Call - Shoot performance						
Wed	Oct 9	PREVIEW (8:00 Go)	7-11	7-11	6:30 - 11	6:30 to 11	6:30 to 11	7-11
Thu	Oct 10	PERFORMANCE #1 (8:00)	7-11	7-11	6:30 - 11	6:30 to 11	6:30 to 11	7-11
Fri	Oct 11	PERFORMANCE #2 (8:00)	7-11	7-11	6:30 - 11	6:30 to 11	6:30 to 11	7-11
Sat	Oct 12	PERFORMANCE #3 (8:00)	7-11	7-11	6:30 - 11	6:30 to 11	6:30 to 11	7-11
Sun	Oct 13	PERFORMANCE #4 (2:00)	1-5	1-5	12:30 - 5	12:30 to 5	12:30 to 5	1-5
Wed	Oct 16	Brush-up Rehearsal 7-11	No Tech	No Tech	No Tech	No Tech	No Tech	No Tech
Thu	Oct 17	PERFORMANCE #5 (8:00)	7-11	7-11	6:30 - 11	6:30 to 11	6:30 to 11	7-11
		Note: EDWINN DROOD - Opens - Mendelssohn						
Fri	Oct 18	PERFORMANCE #6 (8:00)	7-11	7-11	6:30 - 11	6:30 to 11	6:30 to 11	7-11
Sat	Oct 19	PERFORMANCE #7 (8:00)	7-11	7-11	6:30 - 11	6:30 to 11	6:30 to 11	7-11
Sun	Oct 20	PERFORMANCE #8 (2:00)	1-5	1-5	12:30 - 5	12:30 to 5	12:30 to 5	1-5
		STRIKE	5-9	5-9	5-7	5-7	5-7	5-7

Technical Schedule: For Carlo Goldoni, *Pamela*.

Production

A good theatre production is made by many talented individuals working creatively and together. This cannot happen just by hoping that it will: it takes time to get it right, and that is helped by good planning and, usually, by one person being in overall control. In the ancient Greek theatre a dramatist-director would both write the play, and direct it, and also take a leading role in the performance; in effect, he was in charge of almost everything, except finance and administration. Molière in seventeenth-century France and Bertolt Brecht in twentieth-century Germany had much the same authority and ran their own companies. In the eighteenth and nineteenth centuries, the key person was usually an *actor-manager*, the chief actor of a company who was thereby in a position to choose plays for the repertoire that would flatter his particular talents. In Britain, David Garrick and Henry Irving (see Chapter 5, "Expressive Acting") had great success working in this capacity, and this tradition was continued until quite recently by Laurence Olivier (1907-1989). In the United States, actor-managers have included the Booths, father and son (see Chapter 5, "Expressive Acting"), and the comedian William Burton (1804-1860) who ran Burton's New Theatre on Broadway and starred in all the plays.

Today the business of setting up and running a theatre production has become so complicated that no actor who is rehearsing and performing could keep up with the continual stream of problems and decisions. Professional administrators are called in for many tasks, but the main decisions are made, in varied ways, by a producer or producers, a producing director or artistic director, or by the director of the play. Occasionally a dramatist or leading actor may be among those in charge of a theatre, but running a large company allows little time for any other profession.

Producers and Artistic Directors

In the theatres on Broadway or in the West End of London, or in the commercial theatres of any large city such as Tokyo or Sydney, effective power is concentrated in the hands of a producer, the person, or sometimes the syndicate, who owns or leases a theatre building, sets up a company to produce the play, and controls all finances. A production may start with a theatre building that is available at a certain time and for a certain period, with an actor or actors who are assured of audiences when playing a certain range of parts, or with an established author who has written a new play.

Until recently shows produced commercially would have a long out-of-town trial, touring from one theatre to another while perfecting, as far as possible, both script and production. Rising costs have meant that touring is often replaced by a prolonged run of previews in town, before the official first night. Still more often, the decision to produce a play commercially will follow a first production at a non-profit regional theatre or a small independent company; the commercial producer may make some financial contribution toward the costs of this preliminary testing, thereby registering an interest in the script, director, or leading actors, and starting on the rest of his work.

The producer or producers will provide the theatre, choose the play, and contract with the director, designers, and leading actors. Then in consultation with these principals, the play's actors will be hired, as well as its composer, musicians, choreographer, fight director, technical director, production manager, and so on as necessary, together with administrative, front-of-house, and publicity personnel. The producer is finally responsible for assembling a team that will work well together and for all the decisions and arrangements intended to ensure the production's success with an audience. Producing is more than a tough-minded business venture, because nowhere, not even in the most technical or financial details of a production plan, can the producer afford to forget how the show as a whole will work for an audience. Successful producing involves the exercise of a very keen theatrical imagination and good judgment about the varied artists and technicians involved. Business and art cannot be separated in the making of theatre.

Although producers tend to favor their own group of associates so that they can maintain some continuity in their work, most productions they oversee in commercial theatres are unique enterprises, each one mounted for its own sake and in its own appropriate way, with little thought of a sequel. Noncommercial theatres, with permanent companies of actors and technical and business staffs, have less ability to respond uniquely to each production, but they gain by having members who already know how best to work together and by having an audience who will pay in advance to see their work. It is an open question whether the strength that comes from long-term associations is preferable to the freshness and excitement of unique productions, or the other way around. Most critics prefer the seasoned and expert work of permanent companies, despite the obvious risks that such groups may fall into mere routine and be less able to respond to the special demands of a new script or an outstanding acting talent. Large audiences, on the other hand, generally prefer highly charged, all-star, and once-only productions. These shows will be more expensive to see and may well strive for immediate and surefire effects; their actors will lack the mutual understanding and common style that come only after years of working together.

Artistic directors or producing directors of nonprofit regional theatres have enormous tasks of day-to-day administration, since they often have more than one auditorium to fill as well as responsibilities to trustees and local educational and community authorities. They can never clear their desks and tackle a new production as if nothing else mattered: there is the "season" as a whole to think about, for this year and the next; one play's budget and its demands on the wardrobe and workshops have to fit in with the demands made by all the other plays. Artistic directors who are able to maintain a company of actors throughout the year are still more limited in how they can cast or stage any one play, but they can nurse new talent among actors, directors, and designers. At the same time they can develop an audience receptive to the way their theatre presents its shows and to its choice of shows. Yet most of the commercial problems of the producer of a single production are still theirs, not least of which are satisfying their audience and balancing the books. Financially there may be less risk from play to play, but, at the end of the twentieth century, the maintenance of a theatre company is so against the grain of other commercial enterprises, where output and profit are the main objectives, that to keep going at all, let alone to insist on the highest quality, calls for constant vigilance and a great deal of expertise, goodwill on all sides, and, at times, cunning. Only in a very limited sense is any production *not* a commercial enterprise and a major risk.

Paradoxically the problems facing the artistic director of a seasonal repertory theatre come into focus when one of its productions achieves a great box-office success. Although in most fields of commerce, success is at once bankable, in theatre it is not: neither output nor prices can suddenly be increased; sales capacity cannot be boosted or more outlets opened. Some advantage can be gained by selling this product to the commercial sector, but that takes the best artistic talent away from the theatre to Broadway or away on long tours, and their absence reduces the possibility of creating further successes.

When a regional theatre has more than one failure in a season, the problems are all too obvious: funds earmarked for other shows have to be drawn upon to keep paying salaries, while the rest of the season, and perhaps the one following, will suffer as a result. A snowball effect can quickly occur: for if standards decline, so do ticket sales, and so further economies become necessary. Besides, at such times everyone's efforts go into keeping the theatre afloat, rather than into discovering and developing new talent and new ideas.

In 1985 the Theatre Communications Group, concerned about how theatres were adapting to changing times, sponsored a series of discussions with the artistic directors of America's institutional theatres, and then published a record of these meetings in *The Artistic Home*, by Todd London. The new pressures facing the people who run these theatres are spelled out in this book, for example:

> If the "wish lists" artistic directors carried to TCG meetings in their heads had been written down, one word would have appeared almost everywhere: "flexibility." More flexible schedules, they wished for, and flexible rehearsal processes, flexible previews, flexible subscription series, flexible budgets and flexible programming.

> It is simpler to scale down production costs—by doing smaller cast shows, for example—than it is to cut full-time staff members, who are part of the daily life of the theatre and whose interests are, therefore, more regularly voiced. The duties of artistic directors have, likewise, grown more demanding and complex, but theatres have, on the whole, not allowed for equivalent artistic expansion, even though it is the artistic work which ultimately determines success or failure.

In Chapter 3 we have already considered different theatre organizations and the possibility of forming new policies and finding new audiences; in this chapter our concern is with how a new production comes into being and how well it is served. The main point is that every show needs to find its appropriate home where it can take root and grow strongly, without suffering from damaging restrictions brought about by the administrative and financial problems of producing. Again, it should be clear that business and organization cannot be separated from artistic work in the making of theatre; good ideas and talent are not enough.

The safest and most comfortable home for a production is often very small. It might be with a group of people starting to work together who are sure of a common purpose and therefore able to function as an efficient artistic commune. Another possibility might be a group of people working consistently with one director (who is also the producer and artistic director of their theatre), and doing no more plays in any one year than the group can manage on its own, without a large support system. In both cases, overhead and running expenses will be low, and through extensive touring a production can be kept playing for as long as an audience can be found to see it, or until the next show is ready or almost ready. In some ways, these companies are fly-by-nights, working in isolation and serving their own needs more than those of any community or permanent audience. They depend on consistently good reviews in local, national, and international journals to bring theatre enthusiasts to see their work wherever they travel. Although such companies can produce a small number of plays very well, they may be limited in their ability to develop a new show because of the narrow range of the acting and production teams. The artistic security of such companies is very enviable, but it can be a major danger unless a company maintains a strong and unsatisfied quest for good work and unless each play challenges its abilities.

In almost every case, an inexperienced author or director with his or her own view of what theatre can and should be is best advised to seek out a small, independent company, one whose productions appear to be in line with the same ideas and ideals. Commercial producers have too much money at risk in staging works to be able to work with beginning playwrights, and not for profit repertory theatres have too many ongoing company projects and problems to be able to give new work full attention. Many large regional theatres have a small studio theatre where untried talent can be given a showing, and those that do not will often run a series of workshops or play readings of new works. But these productions are, by definition, marginal to the management's main concerns, and everyone involved will be aware of the low priority of the work. Moreover, these *tryouts* have little chance of being promoted to *main-stage* productions. The best home for new talent will often be in the smallest of theatres, even if they have restricted budgets, few personnel onstage and offstage, and actors who are, possibly, less experienced. At least here, however, everyone will be fully committed to the production, and that is a basic necessity for innovative work.

Dramatists or directors starting their careers today need to be very patient and work as junior members of a large theatre or must be satisfied with the limited resources of a small company whose ideas and work methods are much like their own. Alternatively, and in my opinion most hopefully, they must start their own companies and work out their own means to achievement. Then, perhaps, the truly talented and original beginners will be able to present their work on their own terms without having to make damaging compromises. Once they have proven themselves, they may be sought out by larger and better equipped theatres with whom they can then start working at or near the top.

If you have seen the work of any one company over a whole season, try to figure out why the plays you saw were chosen for production. What do the selections tell you about the aims of the producer or artistic director? Alternatively, ask the same question about the plays offered by any repertory theatre, as listed, for example, in American Theatre *or other journals. See if you can check your findings by consulting a mission statement issued by the company or, perhaps, by asking the opinion of someone at the theatre.*

The Production Team

The sheer size of the team necessary to mount a full-scale production in a late twentieth-century theatre is evident if one looks at all the people listed in the credits of a theatre program. At the Huntington Theatre in Boston, for example, there is listed both a producing director and a managing director, and there are separate lists for officers in administration, marketing and public relations, development, department of education and outreach services, subscription and box office, production, building maintenance and security. Under administration the following positions are featured:

> business manager
> house/company manager
> executive secretary
> information systems manager
> accounts analyst
> literary associate

The functions of these persons are self-explanatory, except perhaps for the last named, who is responsible for the research used in repertoire planning and production, and will also provide material for programs, give talks to theatregoers, and support the education and outreach services.

Heading the production staff is the production manager and his assistant, both of whom share the task of coordinating the whole operation. Here we also find:

> technical director
> master carpenter, with two carpenters and a stage carpenter
> prop master and assistant
> scenic artist (responsible for painting what has been constructed)
> costumer, with an assistant and a costume design assistant
> head draper, draper, two first hands, two stitchers
> costume crafts/dyer (for various practical techniques used in costuming)
> wardrobe coordinator
> master electrician
> production electrician/electrics board operator
> sound engineer
> production office intern

Named on a separate page of the program and working entirely on the current production, in addition to the actors, author and, perhaps, composer, there will also be a director for the play, a music director, and perhaps a choreographer, together with designers for scenery, costumes, lighting, and sound, a casting consultant, possibly a dialect coach, a production stage manager and assistants to many of these principals. Also named for a production may be its original producers and others with a financial or copyright interest in the script or the production or any particular part of it. Usually a list of special sponsors will follow, in addition to the pages of patrons that are a permanent feature toward the back of every program published by the theatre.

Directors at Work

Once the organization is complete and a production schedule in place, the play's director has day-to-day charge of the work at hand. The first task is to meet with the various designers and agree on a common approach so that decisions can be made and construction started in the workshops to be completed in good time for the dress rehearsals. Ideally nothing should be decided until all the roles have been cast and rehearsals have begun, but only the very richest and the very smallest theatres can afford to work this way. With luck the main casting will be known early enough for costumes to be designed to suit those who will wear them. Among the other early jobs are discussions with the press and publicity departments, last-minute casting decisions, and the gathering of a stage manager and assistants who will organize rehearsals and keep the finished show running.

Once rehearsals start, the director has three major responsibilities: to unity, individual talents, and the script.

Unity

Everyone involved in a production should have a common vision of what the production is going to be and how to achieve this. It is not enough for the director to say what the "concept" will be, or why the play is being produced, or what "interpretation" is being given to the script. The production's unity will stem from the way all work is tackled in rehearsals.

Sometimes the director will require a certain style of acting, perhaps a particular kind of speech or sensitivity to language, perhaps physical movements that are apparently free or, quite the opposite, formally controlled. Actors may be required to pay attention to the music of a particular composer or period, or to the manners of a particular place or social grouping. Improvisations may be used to explore the characters and situations of the play. Sometimes the entire cast will join the designers in doing research about the historical, political, or moral issues raised by the play, and they will be encouraged to share with each other whatever they find most interesting in books or newspapers, or from expeditions to sites outside the theatre or interviews with people having particular views or memories. Sometimes all the actors will be asked to read a particular book, or visit an art gallery or museum, or view certain films together, so that they can share a discovery appropriate to the future production and fill their minds with the same visual images.

Individual Talents

A director must help the actors, and the designers, composer, technicians, and every other member of the team so that they work to the best of their own abilities for the production. Bullying, cajoling, inspiring, suggesting, asking questions, providing a lot of information—one technique may work for one person and the opposite for another. Some directors bend their own view of individual roles or of the meaning of a crucial speech—or even of the play itself—to accommodate the views and talents of leading actors. Others may appear to hold a very fixed or extreme view in order to awaken more lively responses from their actors, or they may cut short all argument, trusting the actors to find a personal commitment by at first submitting to direction and then slowly adapting what they have been given to their own instincts and abilities. Still other directors work with an almost military firmness, requiring exact and constant response to precise instructions so that they can achieve sharpness or intensity in the playing. Whatever tactic is used, the director's overall strategy should be the same: to use the assembled artists as well as possible for the particular task at hand.

The Script

A director is responsible to the author, whether he or she is dead or alive. The most obvious task is to ensure that the actors know what the words they are saying mean for their characters, but beyond that the director should seek out and use the innumerable clues in the script about how the words will work onstage. When the author was also the play's first director—as Athol Fugard, David Mamet, or Len Jenkin often are—the script will have been revised during rehearsals and cut very strictly until each word bears a full weight of dramatic purpose. In reviving these plays, a director should make use of this work that has already been done. Even when the author has not been present at rehearsals, he or she may have used similar considerations when writing and revising the text so that it will repay an equally careful attention. Samuel Beckett is perhaps the prime example of an author who wrote with great precision; experience has shown that the very shaping of his sentences carries messages that need to be present in performance. Attending rehearsals or not, dramatists are collaborators whom the director should not underestimate. Every script is not scrupulously written, but directors should not make assumptions about this too lightly, or too early in the process of rehearsal.

Sometimes a script has been punctuated with unusual care—and not only with commas, colons, dashes, ellipses, and so on. George Bernard Shaw (1856-1950), who had a particularly acute ear for cadences in speech, used to insist that some words be printed with extra space between each letter to show that they should be given more than usual weight; this device can be seen in the original published texts, alongside the usual italics and capitals. Harold Pinter is so fastidious in all such matters that in between two sentences he will sometimes write stage directions for either a *"Pause"* or a *"Silence."* Directors of his plays have been known to hold a "pause rehearsal" to take these notations fully into account, before they are lost to view in later stages of rehearsals when the actors' instinctive playing has become stronger and, rightly, more dominant.

The story goes that when a well-known dramatist sent the script of his new play to the National Theatre in London, its spare dialogue was typed out with a great deal of empty space on the pages. The Script Department of the theatre, following normal procedures, sent it out to be retyped in a more economical format, so that actors and stage managers would not have to turn over to a new page every minute or so. When the author received a copy for his own use when attending rehearsals, he was furious and demanded that the script as he had typed it himself should be the only one used. He had taken great care to reflect on the page the way he heard his words being spoken. So he sent back the theatre's version with a curt note: "Here is the offending article."

With Shakespeare's plays, and others in verse or heightened and elaborate prose, strict attention must also be given to meter, rhyme, phrasing, pointing, alliteration, and all the manifold ways in which a poetic text works on the mind. If a director decides that these concerns are too literary and fussy for the theatre and does not spend time on them, the dramatist's artifice will still be present in the dialogue, and the director will run the risk of the words being spoken without a sense of why they are what they are. In turn, this will mean that speech will be difficult for the audience to understand—sometimes it will quite literally become impossible to *hear*—and, worse still, the production will lose a built-in vitality and conviction. "What is wrong with most 'traditional' productions of Shakespeare," wrote the director, Harold Clurman, "is that they have little relation to the nature of Shakespeare's writing." (*On Directing*) Clurman made this criticism in 1972, but the same is sometimes true today of both traditional and nontraditional productions. Respect paid to the work and imagination that have gone into the writing of a script will always be repaid: as well as giving direction to actors, it can help to shape whole scenes, because the music of speech will supply rhythms and tempos that suggest or interact with the rhythms and tempos of the action.

Attention to the play text is also necessary when the director consults with designers before rehearsals begin; this is a continuous process, as rehearsal and design is all part of a single process of research, imaginative engagement, and realization. In most cases it is the script that has inspired the director's interest in the production in the first place, and he or she will have studied it over and over, while deciding on the principal aims for the production, developing its visual setting and style, inventing stage business, and guiding the actors. A director should quarry deep into the play's dialogue. In Chapter 2, we have considered how words express an author's purpose and define the nature of a play, its tone, tempo, atmosphere, theme, and the individuality of its characters—all matters of great importance to a director. Words repeated from scene to scene, often by different speakers and in different situations, are particularly useful guides when a director is developing a production along the lines of the author's imagination.

A director may decide to set aside an author's instructions with regard to the location or period of a play's action. For example, a production of Oscar Wilde's *The Importance of Being Earnest* or Shakespeare's *Romeo and Juliet* or *The Merchant of Venice*, may set the action in the present day or the 1920s or 1930s, in order to reflect more readily the lives and concerns of its audience. But this strategy will not work well if the elegant and sustained speeches of these plays, which were natural to the theatres of their times, are spoken as if they were the ordinary talk of the present day or of a time much later than that of the original production. A compromise will have to be reached between the director's scheme for the production and the author's use of words in the script, and the director can achieve this only by paying close attention to the smallest details of the dialogue as it was written.

Stage directions are a special case, since the playwright provides them to show how a scene should look and how the actors should move or behave within it, even though such directions will never become part of the actors' performances in the same intimate and inevitable ways as the words written to be spoken. Some directors ignore stage directions entirely, believing that by doing so they "free" the actors and encourage their own fresh invention. But it is foolhardy for a director to pass by the advice of an author, especially if he is experienced as a director or an actor, or if he has worked on the script during rehearsals of an earlier production—at least not without testing its validity in exploratory rehearsals or workshops.

> *Before you next go to the theatre, read the play you will be seeing and consider what you, as director, would have told the designers and actors before rehearsals began, about acting style, physical staging, and the meaning of the play. These are difficult questions, so concentrate at first on one scene only; after that it may be possible to tackle the whole play. Once you have seen the production, try to reconstruct what you think its director told the company about his or her intentions and consider whether you would change your intentions in the light of what you have seen.*

Two Styles of Directing

Some critics believe that bringing a "concept" to a production or an "interpretation" to the staging of a play is the most important contribution a director makes. Certainly having a clear idea of the purpose of a show from the very start of the design process and rehearsals can help in making a strong and lasting impression; it also makes clear to the audience what the director has contributed to the production. When time is short or the company is new and inexperienced, this "conceptual" approach may be the only way to get a production together on schedule. Yet a concept, being so much less complicated and variable than any script, will always tend to reduce a production to what is easily understandable and readily attainable. The director who relies on close adherence to a concept can also severely limit the use made of the individual talents of the actors in a company.

An alternative view of the director's job was bound to arise—the belief that he or she should bring together a cast, designers, musicians, and technicians to work on a particular script, at a particular time and place, and *then* discover what these people can make out of their work on the play that has been chosen. The whole enterprise thus becomes a process of discovery, and only toward the end will anyone—including the director—begin to know all that has happened, where the strengths of the show lie, what truths it affirms, and what it can do for an audience. This way of working can empower everyone in the company to contribute to their full abilities, until the time comes to select and develop the best that has been done. Then the director intervenes to shape and firm up the production so that its various discoveries can draw and hold the attention of an audience. Obviously this

Figure 7.1 A modern-dress *Merchant of Venice*, staged by Peter Sellars at the Goodman Theatre, Chicago. Note the video camera recording the scene and the enlarged face on the TV monitor. (Photograph © Liz Lauren; courtesy of the Goodman Theatre.)

method of working takes up a great deal of time and is an ideal of how to work, rather than a practicable method that can be allowed to take its own course.

Some directors refuse the constraints of a script altogether and will work with the actors on a subject of their own choosing, rather than a text written and perfected by someone else. Together they develop an original performance script that reflects their explorations in rehearsals and uses their discoveries. Ariane Mnouchkine did pioneering productions of this kind with her Théâtre du Soliel in a suburb of Paris during the late 1960s and 1970s. She shaped whatever her actors found, claiming to have no knowledge before rehearsals of what the play would be. In New York, Richard Foreman started his own Ontological-Hysteric Theatre in 1968 so that he could direct productions based on ideas and experiences, rather than on a previously written script. He has continued to develop his company's shows out of exploratory work with chosen materials such as strange objects, untrained actors, stage space, fragments of dialogue, and recorded sound.

Most productions hover somewhere between these alternative ways of working. Italian director Franco Zeffirelli speaks clearly for the importance of having a "concept" before starting work on a play: "You don't need many ideas, you need one. On that you work and the idea carries you if it's right." But in practice he is more permissive than his words suggest:

> You can't force an actor. He doesn't play with his technique, he plays with his own human qualities. My job is to offer many different solutions to him, and then to

choose the right one. It may be comic or tragic, but it must be the right one *for him*. It must become part of his own blood and flesh.

Directors on Directing, eds. T. Cole and H. K. Chinoy

Even a director undertaking a free exploration of a text or subject will be guided by some controlling concept when making crucial decisions about the conditions and starting points for that work, and these early expressions of a preexisting idea will have a deep influence on the progress of rehearsals and what will be found in them. In the last stages of preparation for an audience, no director can allow the actors, or anyone else working on the show, to be entirely free; he or she may have accepted whatever they have offered earlier on, but now the director is charged with the task of taking final control and making everything work as a coherent production.

The Director as "Author" of a Production

Late twentieth-century theatre has available powerful technical resources that can support an actor's performance and also supplant it. If a director makes full use of unmistakable visual display, strong in color, form, and scale, of powerful and infinitely variable light, of amplified and multitracked sound, and of automated and synchronized transformations of the scene, their combined force is able to outdo everything else onstage and outperform even the most gifted actor. These effects can swamp the audience's ability to think for itself or to respond to any other impetus. The director who commands this technology is likely to become the only true author of the production: through the use of special effects he or she can implant a governing idea to such great effect that the director, and not the actors or the dramatist, will be ultimately responsible for the production's achievement. Directors are the new stars of the theatre, even though the audience never sees them onstage.

A director's influence used to derive from the originality and brilliance of a production concept and the skill with which the actors were cast and directed, but now the greatest mastery depends on work with designers and technicians. When the actors or an author make the strongest showing in a production today, it is either because the theatre is not equipped for modern scenography or because the director has purposefully kept that power in reserve and chosen to stage a production that relies on other resources of the theatre for its force and attractions.

Rehearsals

After basic decisions and preparations have been made regarding casting, design, music, acting style, and so forth, a production begins to develop in rehearsal. For many people in theatre, rehearsing is the most enthralling part of their work. It is like a suit of clothes being given life by being worn, or a tree being clothed with leaves, or a person, who was formerly known only from correspondence, gradually becoming known through repeated meetings. Or we may think of the play text as a painter's first sketch and the rehearsal period as the process of working toward the

Figure 7.2 *Alcestis*, a Robert Wilson production for the American Repertory Theatre with high-tech scenic effects. (Photograph © Richard Feldman.)

finished painting, following the original sketch but changing its effect by adding color, light, and texture, obscuring some details and heightening others; figures and shadows can now be added, and a perspective and background can be established where there were none before.

Rehearsals usually start slowly. Some directors tell the assembled company about why the play was chosen and outline the work plan for the production, talking about story, themes, characters, the play's relevance to contemporary life or thought, acting style, theatre space and design—whatever will set the guidelines for the work ahead. Usually the actors are shown a model of the set and sketches of costumes. Sometimes the director will have the whole company sit around in a circle and read the play together, perhaps several times over during the first few days. Other directors make the preliminary exposition as short as possible and, starting at the beginning, set the action in motion at once, the actors holding texts in hand while improvising and exploring the play in whatever ways seem possible and appropriate.

For classical plays a great deal of time may be spent disentangling the difficulties of the text, before the actors get onto their feet. Jean Vilar, who was actor-manager at the National Popular Theatre (TNP) in Paris after the Second World

Figure 7.3 Early rehearsals at the Alabama Shakespeare Festival for Penny Metropolus's production of *Light Up the Sky*. (Photograph courtesy of the Alabama Shakespeare Festival.)

War, worked on the principle that the number of rehearsals spent reading the script should amount to a third of the total:

> Manuscript in hand, seat firmly planted on a chair, body in repose: thus the deepest sensibilities will gradually pitch themselves to the desired note, as the actor comes to understand, or feel, the new character that is to become himself.
>
> *Tulane Drama Review* 3, no.2

But most directors today will leave the actors to do this study for themselves in their own time or will introduce script work by degrees as other work progresses. The double task is to help each actor both to find the impulses that will make the words necessary for the character to speak, and also to develop the means to express that inner life clearly.

Some directors will not start work on any particular scenes, but concentrate at first on establishing the characters—those other beings that the actors have to invent or compose, and then inhabit, in order to make the action of the play take place as it does. This involves finding the right posture or physical bearing for each character, the right rhythms and habits of speech and action, the right kind of connection between thought, feeling, and action. The play's text will be used to start improvisations about expectations, appetites, fears, and other driving forces; about attitudes to time, place, departure, arrival, achievement and failure; and about relations between people and reactions to all these actions. Before actors plunge into making the actual words of the text effective in performance, a considerable time will have been spent in establishing characters and motivation.

Attention must be divided between what is special to each character and often very private for each actor, and what is corporate and involves interplay between many individuals. Some directors like to deal with the group activity first, even if very sketchily, so that characters are related to each other in physical terms from the start. They want to plan appropriate movements across the stage and ensure that major groupings of characters are organized to make best use of the settings that have been built for the production. This process has been called *blocking the play*, and that phrase is sometimes doubly apt, in that working in this way can cause actors to become boxed in and settle into fixed movements too soon. Most directors want their cast members to stay open to suggestions about physical performance until late in the rehearsal process when they will have a deeper knowledge of their characters and the play as a whole. On the other hand, if a director keeps changing stage positions and movements continually, the actors may always be insecure in relationship to the set and to each other, and that is seldom good for a production.

The common task of all rehearsals is to search for what can best serve the play and the company under the present circumstances, and what is best able to hold and develop the attention of the audience. Ideally a production should use all the powers of theatre described in Chapter 1.

It is difficult to give a true idea of the gathering excitement of rehearsals: the cohesive life and assurance that begins to come through finding the true center of the work, the union of thought and feeling, and the sense of coordination operating within the time and space of the play's enactment. Only in the last week or so of rehearsals does everyone engaged in the enterprise begin to know what has been achieved. The final days are like a judgment and a celebration, for no amount of last-minute reworking, or additions or deletions, can save a bad show; the most that late modifications can accomplish is to make what is already good better.

The last weeks of rehearsals are very different from earlier ones. There is less time for searching, and most attention is paid to the task of ensuring that the best use is made of what has already been found. Usually cuts will be made in *stage business* (what actors do, as opposed to what they say) that has accumulated from early rehearsals and in movement around the stage, so that what is more central or more revealing can be developed further. Details have to be adjusted with regard to the tempo and shape of the scenes, the unfolding of the narrative, and the size and emphasis of each performance.

Moving from rehearsal room to theatre brings its own problems of unfamiliarity, and will require adjustments of scale, projection, and contact between characters. Several rehearsals of the whole play, known as *run-throughs*, are now called to show the director where balance must be adjusted from scene to scene and from moment to moment, and how to ensure continuity of interest and consistency of interpretation. Sometimes the text will be cut or modified, or occasionally added to, so that it becomes more effective in the context of this particular production; when the author is living such changes can be made legally only with his or her approval.

Dress rehearsals and technical rehearsals are scheduled, and with them come many practical problems, such as how actors should wear costumes, use props, move around the set, and take best advantage of the lights. These details are best handled at this stage, since they would have been inhibiting for the actors earlier in the rehearsal process, when they were still discovering what had to be done to create their characters and present the action of the play. Besides, in most theatres this work can only be done at a late stage because costumes, props, set, and lights will not be ready until close to opening night, and all the necessary technicians, operators, and supporting staff are not available before this time.

During the last few days, as the physical and technical tasks grow ever more complex, a director will sometimes call a *quick run* or *text rehearsal*, during which the cast moves easily through the play, simply reproducing its words and movements, with gestures and business only lightly indicated. By limiting their concerns in this way, the actors can refresh their sense of the play as a whole. In these relaxed rehearsals, surprising and eloquent new business, new relationships between characters, new sources of feeling and changes of intention, new tones of voice may yet be discovered and perhaps added to the performances.

Finally, *preview* performances before the official opening night allow the actors to gauge the effectiveness of every detail of their performances as they learn to play with and for their audiences. Tempo, balance, coordination, and, just occasionally, interpretation may be adjusted once more. In one sense the director's judgment is never more necessary than during this last tuning of a production, for a little change may accomplish a great deal, and no one else has the knowledge and authority to carry out this vital task. In another sense, at this point the director is less necessary than ever before, since as it gets ready to meet its audience, the production has a life of its own at a very basic level, and this cannot be changed: the production is *there* now, very palpably, for whatever it is found to be worth.

If you are able to attend dress rehearsals or previews, go to a number of them before the opening night of a production and make lists of the major changes that are made from night to night. Why were these changes made? Would you try to make other ones? (This is one of the very best ways to learn about how directors and actors work.)

8

Current Reading.

Thinking about Theatre

Now that the various elements of a production have been considered, it is time to ask how we can continue to think about theatre and add to what has been learned. Although we can get immediate pleasure from seeing a production, we soon come to realize how difficult it is to think and write clearly about this art. Since one of theatre's greatest strengths is to "hold a mirror up" to the whole of life, it is not surprising that trying to understand it is not unlike asking what life is all about. Another book would be needed to show what the study of theatre can entail, especially at the present time when a number of new methodologies are being developed to wrestle with its problems. Here there is scope only for practical instructions about taking the next few steps.

Criticism and Study

Most writing about theatre covers the texts of plays. This is because the words spoken onstage are the one element of theatre that can be reproduced and held steady for our attention. Take any edition of one of Shakespeare's plays and see what topics the introduction deals with. The odds are that the words of the text will be carefully considered, as well as the play's story and characters, and the ideas it raises. There will be something too about how the text echoes other plays and other books, and how it departs from them. The play may be shown to reflect the social, political, moral, and religious ideas of the times and give a picture of the life of the times. The editor will explain what, in his or her view, the play "means" or what it "does" for an audience. He or she will also record what other critics have thought about the play on earlier occasions. Some editors will tell you how the play has been staged and how well-known actors and directors have interpreted the text. These are the main means available for studying any play by any author, and there are countless books that tackle some or many of these tasks for single plays, or for the works of one or more authors. A student can access these critical writings easily through a library catalogue or on the shelves of a bookstore with a special section on drama or theatre.

Studying the play in performance and the entire theatrical experience that arises from it is a more difficult task. There is no shortage of books about individual actors, directors, or designers, or about theatre buildings and organizations, or the various techniques employed by people working in theatre, but these publications do not tackle the more difficult task of drawing all these elements together to inquire about the nature of what is achieved onstage in any one performance—the very experience that draws audiences together and lures students to study theatre. This crucial subject is most readily approached in two very different ways: through reviews in periodicals and newspapers, and through studies of the means of production.

Reviews

Reviews in newspapers and journals are the most obvious place to look for accounts of individual productions, but professional reviewers are not ideal reporters because they must emphasize the "news" element in what they have seen and need to write to catch the attention of people who may know little about theatre. The best way to learn from reviews is to see a production yourself and write your own review, and then compare your own effort with a number of published ones. You can check out reviews of productions of other plays by the same company, as well as reviews of another company's production of the same play. Slowly you build up a composite picture of a theatrical event, as one might assemble a number of sightings of a distant object, seen from different viewpoints and recorded by different instruments. Some books, often called "stage histories," record a great range of such evidence and try to make sense of it.

The Means of Production

By dealing methodically with each activity that makes up a production, a student can develop a sense of what has been achieved in any particular performance or the work of any one theatre company. Only in the last forty or so years have books been published that attempt this comprehensive approach to the study of plays in performance. A model for others was John Willett's *The Theatre of Bertolt Brecht: A Study from Eight Aspects*. This study has separate chapters on "Theatrical Practice," "Music," "Theatrical Influences," and so on, that provide an insider's view of all the processes with which this director-dramatist created a new kind of theatre. Similar inquiries are now more common: the University of Michigan Press in Ann Arbor has published a series of books linking textual criticism to stage enactment. Another series called *Theatre Production Studies* (Routledge) has published more than a dozen titles that consider specific texts in terms of theatre practice at the time of their first performances. Some modern play texts are published with an account of the production for which they were written; for example, *Unbalancing Acts: Foundations for a Theater* contains the texts of five plays by Richard Foreman accompanied by accounts of the organization, directing, acting, "visual composition," and other aspects of the plays' inception and staging (Theatre Communications Group, 1992). In general, the more recent the edition of a play, the more likely that "performance" and theatre history will be discussed.

Only since 1970, or thereabouts, have scholars begun to tackle the more general and therefore larger questions about performance, trying to define, as exactly as possible, what "signs" are given to an audience during performance and what is the nature of an audience's response. These new studies are not intended for beginning students, being too wide in reference or too concerned with debate about which terms are most generally applicable. Nevertheless, if the journal *Theatre Research International* is available in your local library, consult the following two articles to get a taste of this pioneering research: Marvin Carlson's "Theatre History, Methodology and Distinctive Features" and Janelle Reinelt's "Theatre on the Brink of 2000: Shifting Paradigms" in *Theatre Research International* 20, no. 2.

Film and Television

Most students want to know about theatre's relationship to film and television because they have been to the movies far more frequently than to the theatre. In the course of this book the topic has been touched on several times, but it needs to be addressed again in more general terms and with some attention to history.

In its early days, film seemed to have all the advantages. After all it can show sensational images of great beauty, wealth, and strangeness, and encompass both violence and gentleness. The medium can be controlled and edited, reproduced in multiple copies and distributed all over the world. Television was considered enviable too, because it can transmit images of actual events or performances as they are happening, and has a potential audience of many millions. In comparison with both media, theatre seemed disadvantaged, working within limited space, having to draw its audiences physically into one place, and being unable to reproduce its products for sale to a mass market. Toward the end of the twentieth century, however, the rival attractions of the "lens media" seem less threatening, and the very limitations of theatre have come to be seen as its great advantages.

When thinking about theatre, a comparison with film helps a student to recognize the advantages of actual live performance before an audience. Theatre, we may say, is three-dimensional, actual, and tangible; its presence is real, even when it creates an illusion of reality that is highly fantastic. A theatre audience is in direct touch with a performance: it does not have to see through the camera's lens or take an editor's selection and arrangement of what is enacted; its attention is free from any compulsion, able to make what it wishes of the event; members of an audience can even influence the performance, as the actors respond to their reception. Although some very successful theatre productions use technology that is highly controlled and very compulsive, even here the performers still face their audience, and each member of the audience has some direct contact with what is happening. Most theatre performances have the advantage of being created for particular audiences and need not be geared to what a great number of people in many and widely different parts of the world might want to see and would be able to enjoy.

In its early days, television was seen to be more like theatre than like film. It relied greatly on theatre-trained actors and transmitted dramas and debates, as well as wars and sports events, as they were actually happening and with little ability to edit or control what viewers saw. Except for continuing to show events as they happen, television has changed since the early days and has gained many of the characteristics of film; for actors and script writers, it calls for techniques suited to a camera rather than a live audience.

People who work in theatre often grow discontented with film. Antonin Artaud (1896-1948), a theatre director, actor, and visionary, believed at first that cinema would displace theatre because film can show the reality of dreams and the power of hidden impulses. He changed his mind, however, after he had worked in film and found no freedom of expression as an actor. Finally the demands of a mass market completely disabused him of his fondness for the cinema. In 1932 he wrote, "I am ever more convinced that the cinema is and will remain an art of the past. One cannot work in it without feeling ashamed" (*Collected Works*, vol. 3, trans. Alastair Hamilton).

For better *and* worse, theatre offers a precarious freedom to actors, and achievement there can be source of a very personal pride. Harold Pinter, film script writer as well as dramatist and stage actor, had this to say about acting in the theatre:

> There are no certainties in performing at all. You don't know what's going to happen next, although you try to plan. You have a curious structure available to you. But you can slip down so many keyholes, abysses, in the course of that journey. It really is an adventure. To sustain it is an extraordinary feat.
>
> Mel Gussow, *Conversations with Pinter*

Part of that adventure is the audience's: in theatre, but not in film, an audience can participate, actually, in an extraordinary feat that draws deeply and adventurously on the imagination of everyone present. In the inevitable competition with other media, theatre is more likely to thrive if it takes advantage of this unique possibility, which it has enjoyed since its very earliest days.

Training for Theatre

Thinking about theatre, it will soon become clear that anyone wishing to work in this medium will need training. In the past this was found on the job, in a formal or informal apprenticeship to a senior actor or manager, but today special courses in acting, design, stage management, direction, administration, history, and criticism are available for students as part of a general liberal arts education in schools, colleges, and universities, and also at conservatories whose whole purpose is training people for theatre.

Because the actor is basic to all theatre productions, any student of theatre in any school should learn about acting. Many types of training are available, but all have to take into account certain inherent truths about acting: it is a complex art that must mirror the complexities of personal and social life; it must be learned by practice, both individually and in groups; individual imagination and initiative are important to this craft; there are advantages to starting basic training in voice, music, and physical performance at a very early age. Added to these difficulties is the scarcity of capable teachers. Fledgling actors need to be taught by someone who is an actor—as one must be able to swim in order to teach swimming—and someone who wants to teach rather than to perform. This person must be sufficiently open-minded, generous, and sensitive to help students prepare for the physical and psychological difficulties they will meet in learning how to act, especially the fears to be overcome and the unexpected reactions that must be understood and then used. No teacher can tackle these difficulties for a student, but good teachers are aware of each pupil's lonely predicament and will show by example how similar problems have been overcome.

The question of what kind of acting should be taught is not easily answered. No student can become proficient in every style some director might require at a later date, and no one method will suit all students. The best solution might seem to be a syllabus that introduces students to several kinds of acting and then encourages a choice of one in which to specialize; but such a strategy would make courses difficult to organize, and would not guarantee that a student chose the right style for his or her own talents and temperament. (Young actors are liable to be attracted either to what is too easy or to what is too hard.) Ideally each student should be helped to find his or her own response to the essentially personal element of this art.

Because acting is the source of theatre's unique appeal, everyone who works in a theatre should know something about it. Unfortunately, this is not always possible. Costume designers, for example, have so many technical skills to learn along the way that they may complete their training without learning how to think along with actors and directors. Theatre administrators can complete their training and yet not be able to recognize the needs of the artists whose work they have to organize and support. The opposite is also true: actors should learn about the organizations and production processes within which any career must develop. More than this, some time must be found for everyone who works in theatre to learn about language, literature, the visual arts, music, history, politics, and much else. To be prepared to practice an art that can reflect life in all its aspects, people in theatre need to be prepared to train for a lifetime.

All practical aspects of theatre are best taught by teachers who practice the necessary skills and are involved themselves in making theatre. For this reason, both universities and special schools often use some part-time faculty, so that their teachers can continue to be active as theatre professionals, but such arrangements can lead to divided loyalties and uncertain scheduling. Other programs use a succession of teachers, hired for limited periods, thus ensuring that students learn to make choices between different working methods; the difficulty here is that students learning any one method need a great deal of sustained concentration, and one semester with a teacher is not enough time. Besides, many teachers are not able to do the same work as a single mentor, someone whose knowledge of a student is as complete and intimate as possible and whose interest continues throughout the training period and beyond.

How can an applicant distinguish a good school from the bad, or from the not so good? Probably there is only one reliable way, which is to ask what recent graduates are doing. If a school does not have a ready answer or tries to make small achievements seem bigger than they are, then you know that *this* school should be avoided. If the results of its teaching are obvious for all to see in what graduates have achieved seven or so years after leaving, then *that* is a school to respect. The numbers of students or the qualifications of the teachers, the physical facilities, production opportunities, or financial resources, the ambitions of a syllabus or the attractiveness of a brochure, all these are important factors to consider in making a choice, but much less so than a school's ability to turn out graduates who can find their own professional way in the world.

Figures 8.1 and 8.2   Contrasting advertisements for theatre training. (Reproduced by permission of Trinity Rep Conservatory and the Department of Theatre Arts, the University of Pittsburgh.)

At some time, most teachers of theatre will ask themselves whether they are providing too many entrants for an oversupplied profession. Far more young people want to train than can be accepted by the better schools, and, at the same time, unemployment in the profession is notoriously high while chances of success are correspondingly low. Should only a few pupils be admitted each year? My answer would be that more, not fewer, should be accepted to *start* the study of theatre and to *begin* to train as actors. Only after a year or two can talent be measured adequately; many gifted actors do not show their full potential until a final term or in the years immediately after they have left school. That is one reason why teachers should not apply the axe too early, but a more fundamental reason is that training for theatre is one of the best and fullest educations in what is often called the humanities, especially if the study is undertaken in a context, such as a university or a group of schools, where theatre students are able to mix with other students with different interests.

Training for theatre is physical as well intellectual, involving doing as well as reading and thinking. It is visual as well as verbal, cooperative as well as individual and independent. Theatre students live very much in the present, for the sake of each production as it is rehearsed and played before actual audiences. They are also in contact with the past, as they seek to re-create the finest plays of earlier ages. They must make the words of great poets in some sense their own, so that their thoughts begin to borrow the vigor and color of Shakespeare's or Sophocles'. In this way, they learn by imitation and are influenced in the deepest parts of their thinking beings. Best of all, perhaps, a theatre student cannot be overreliant on teachers; he or she must be repeatedly and responsibly alone in rehearsal and performance, each one having to make what is said and done effective in a fully achieved and uniquely personal way, and having to experiment and make decisions. In this respect, perhaps, all education should be at least a little like training for theatre.

Theatre and the Future

In earlier ages and in some parts of the world today, whole towns have stopped work so that everyone could see a theatre performance. Could that happen among us? If you were to take someone to the theatre for the first time, is it likely that he or she would want to return a second time? If the answer to either question is no, our theatre is not what it might be.

Plenty of people will say that theatre is dying, but it remains a stubborn invalid. Perhaps the main trouble is not a deadly virus or a lack of oxygen, but an unwillingness to move with the times. Because theatre is a very complicated operation, it is, by nature, highly conservative: change is always difficult. It is also a risky business, so that the people and institutions who provide financing are attracted to what has worked on earlier occasions. But theatre should mirror life, and our lives, and the ways in which we think and feel, are changing more rapidly than ever before. Theatre *has* to change if it is to thrive and draw on its natural strengths. While the past can be served by producing the great plays of earlier times, theatre must do so in ways that make these works accessible in the present. Above all, it must make its own plays that can represent all the conditions of our own times, plays that are puzzling, threatening, violent, exciting, funny, pleasurable, and entirely and marvelously new.

How can this be achieved? By trying to understand theatre afresh and finding the means to remake theatre for our own generation and for our own time. I hope this book may be of some help.

Suggestions for Further Reading

In bookshops and libraries, students of theatre need to look in several different sections. Books about plays will often be shelved under LITERATURE, and so may the plays themselves. On the other hand, both kinds may be found in a DRAMA or DRAMATIC LITERATURE section, and studies of plays in yet another labeled CRITICISM. If there is a section called THEATRE, this is where all the books relevant to our subject ought to be found, but in practice they seldom are: acting, practical stagecraft, theatre histories, biographies, and picture books may be there, but not books about plays or criticism, or theory. The situation has become still more muddled recently when newer sections have appeared, called PERFORM-ING ARTS, PERFORMANCE, and CULTURAL STUDIES. In general, the advice must be that, when searching or browsing, do not go to only one set of bookshelves.

The lists printed here give a practical selection of books for following up the interest of each chapter in the first part of this book. They exclude play texts and studies of individual dramatists because they are far too numerous and can be identified easily as need arises.

1. The Power of the Theatre

A number of highly personal books would supplement this general view of what theatre can offer. Two that are now readily available in paperback are Peter Brook, *The Empty Space* (MacGibbon & Kee, 1968) and David Mamet, *A Whore's Profession: Notes and Essays* (Faber and Faber, 1994); the one gives a director's view of how theatre can be made so that it becomes, in Brook's words, deadly, holy, rough, or immediate; the other is a dramatist's reflections on his life in theatre and film, including topics such as advice to actors, realism, and "Observations of a Backstage Wife." *Twentieth Century Theatre: A Sourcebook*, edited by Richard Drain (Routledge, 1995) is an anthology of writings by some of the most creative directors, playwrights, actors, and designers of the present time; it is also a useful introduction to contemporary practice, since the theories and manifestos found here have influenced many other practitioners.

Among histories of theatre, the best known as a college textbook, is Oscar G. Brockett's *History of the Theatre* (Allyn & Bacon); first published in 1968, it reached its seventh edition in 1995. The most recent is *The Oxford Illustrated History of Theatre*, edited by John Russell Brown (Oxford University Press, 1995); this is not the work of a single author, but of sixteen specialists each writing about the theatre he or she knows best in ways that reflect up-to-date scholarship and their own enthusiasms. Both these histories are provided with bibliographies. The most comprehensive reference book, the place to make quick enquiries about dramatists, directors, theatres, and so on, is the alphabetically arranged *Cambridge Guide to World Theatre*, edited by Martin Banham (Cambridge University Press, 1988; revised ed. 1995).

2. Plays

Aristotle's *Poetics*, which continues to influence most attempts to describe plays, is available in many paperback editions. Among books that offer accounts of how dramatic texts work in the theatre, Eric Bentley's *The Life of the Drama* (Atheneum, 1964) is especially useful in providing a full range of critical terms. An alternative basic account is Bernard Beckerman's *Dynamics of Drama: Theory and Method of Analysis* (Alfred A. Knopf, 1970). Harold Clurman's *On Directing* (Collier Books, 1972) is not strictly a book about plays, but its section on how a director should study a play text is of wider interest and very practical; also repoduced, as examples of such readings, are the notes Clurman made on ten plays he had directed. Ronald Hayman's *How to Read a Play* (Grove Press, 1977) does the same service for a reader less familiar with the ways of theatre.

What a play is, including its enacted life in time and space, is the subject of Manfred Pfister's *The Theory and Analysis of Drama* (1977), translated from the German by John Halliday (Cambridge University Press, 1988): this is not an easy book to read, but one of the very few that sets out to describe, with great care, every aspect of the complicated phenomenon that is a text acted on stage for an audience.

The critical study *Modern American Drama, 1945-1990* by C. W. E. Bigsby (Cambridge University Press, 1992) includes detailed studies of six playwrights and wider surveys of recent writing for the stage. This book, while limited to a short time span and the plays of one country, can serve as an introduction to thinking about problems of style, meaning, and dramatic genres. Books that are wider in scope are seldom able to deal with individual plays in sufficient detail to be anything more than surveys, making very general and unsupported judgments. Studies of individual dramatists or one particular kind of play are likely to be more stimulating and can be found in great variety.

Writing Your First Play (Focal Press, 1991) by New Zealand playwright and television writer Roger Hall, is based on a university course that has started numerous playwrights on successful careers. *In Their Own Words: Contemporary American Playwrights*, ed David Savran (Theatre Communications Group, 1988) is a collection of interviews concerned with the practice of playwriting at the present time.

3 and 4. Theatres and Audiences

Until recently a number of books had be sought out in order to gain an idea of how theatres have been built and used. Now Iain Mackintosh's *Architecture, Actor and Audience* (Routledge, 1993) provides both a history of theatre building and, as its title suggests, a theory of theatre architecture. It is written spiritedly, using the author's practical experience as a theatre producer, planning consultant, and play-goer. This book will help its reader to enter any theatre and make an informed assessment of its capabilities and limitations.

On how regional theatres are run at the present time in the United States, a great deal of revealing information can be found in *The Artistic Home: Discussions with Artistic Directors of America's Institutional Theatres*, by Todd London (Theatre Communications Group, 1988). Each year this can be supplemented by a pull-out section, called "Theatre Facts," which is in the April issue of same publisher's journal, *American Theatre*. William J. Byrnes's *Management and the Arts* (Focal Press, 1992) discusses the institutions alongside which theatre operates, art galleries, dance companies, and other arts organizations, and provides examples of much of the paperwork that is involved. More limited to the workings of theatre itself is the otherwise comprehensive *Theatre Management and Production in America*, by Stephen Langley (Drama Book Publishers, 1990).

Andrew B. Harris, *Broadway Theatre* (Routledge, 1993) is primarily about the production of a number of plays, but it also says a great deal about how commercial theatre has operated in New York City since the early years of the twentieth century.

5. Actors

As with plays, there are innumerable books on individual actors, and a surprising number of handbooks and manuals about learning how to act. Books about acting as an art, with its own distinct qualities, are much more rare; John Harrop's *Acting* (Routledge, 1992) is a recent attempt to fill this gap with a minimum of specialized terminology.

On particular ways of acting there are many books. Stanislavsky's were pioneering in their time and are still much used today; indeed they have provided the basic vocabulary for many later studies. The earliest of his writings and the first to be translated is *An Actor Prepares*. This is a good place to start, but one must read further to get a full view of the master's practice. The more accessible of the two that followed is *Building a Character*. Both texts were translated by Elizabeth Reynolds Hapgood (Theatre Arts Books, 1936 and 1949) and are now readily available in various paperback reprints. There are, of course, many other ways of acting. Remarks on epic acting in *Brecht on Theatre* (see below, section 4) are not as extensive as many readers would wish, but are indispensable for marking out one clear alternative to the many varieties of the Stanislavskian systems. Another alternative can be found in *Anne Bogart Viewpoints*, edited by Michael Bigelow Dixon and Joel A. Smith (Smith and Krause, 1995), which describes how to achieve a freer and more openly expressive kind of acting. An early critique of Stanislavsky is by the director, Richard Lewis, *Method-Or Madness?* (Peter French, 1958): this book is a reworking of lectures given in New York to which members of Actors Equity crowded in order to come to terms with what was, in the late 1950s, a comparatively new but extremely powerful influence in their profession. A thoughtful book on acting. which is also about working in America at this time, is Uta Hagen's *Respect for Acting* (Collier Macmillan, 1973): this sets out the actress's ideas on acting as an art and also gives instructions for beginning actors.

There are many books on specialized aspects of technique. On movement, one of the most influential has been Rudolf von Laban's *The Mastery of Movement of the Stage*, first published in 1950 and revised after its author's death by Lisa Ullmann (Macdonald & Evans, 1971). Although primarily a handbook for students, Litz Pisk's *The Actor and His Body* (Harrop, 1975) includes important passages on theory. Cicely Berry's *Voice and the Actor* (Collier Books, 1973) is used by many teachers in their classes and is recommended as a means of understanding the necessity for voice-training and its integral relationship to physical performance.

6. Stage Design

Adolphe Appia: Texts on Theatre, edited by Richard C. Beacham (Routledge, 1993) is a collection of the writings that have influenced much of modern scenography. *The Theatre of Edward Gordon Craig*, by Denis Bablet is a well-illustrated study of the other major innovator and an account of his productions that first appeared in French in 1962; its English translation by Daphne Woodward followed in 1966 and this was reissued with the present title in 1981 (Eyre Methuen). The scenography that developed with the new technology of more recent times is splendidly represented by *The Secret of Theatrical Space: The Memoirs of Josef Svoboda*, edited and translated by J. M. Burian (Applause Books, 1993). *American Set Design* and *American Set Design 2*, by Arnold Aronson and Ronn Smith respectively (Theatre Communications Group, 1985 and 1991) are well-illustrated critiques of designers active in America in the last decades of the twentieth century.

Lynn Recktal's *Designing and Drawing for the Theatre* (McGraw-Hill, 1995) is an amply illustrated handbook, with 4,600 illustrations including technical drawings; but interviews with twelve designers and its more general sections mean that it also serves as an introduction to the work of scenographers at the present time.

Douglas A. Russell's *Stage Costume Design* (Prentice-Hall, 1973) and Francis Reid's *Discovering Stage Lighting* (Focal Press, 1993) may be similarly recommended.

Sound design is a more recent development in theatre and its technology is developing at a very great rate in the production of film, television, and videos, and in the recording industry. Students with a special interest in this are probably best advised to consult the latest magazines and standard books about these other media: for example, *Sound Techniques for Video and TV*, second edition, by Glyn Alkin (Focal Press, 1989). Other new technology for stage design is the subject of *Projection for the Performing Arts*, by Graham Walne and *Control Systems for Live Entertainment* (Focal Press, 1995 and 1994, respectively).

7. Production

Peter Hall's Diaries: The Story of a Dramatic Battle (H. Hamilton, 1983) offers compulsive reading about the experience of opening the Royal National Theatre in London and gives a rare insight into the thinking of an artistic director who is also a director of plays. Peter Brook's *The Shifting Point: 1946-1987* (Theatre Communications Group, 1987) is both an acount of the life and ideas of this innovative director and a record of how much of his work has been produced outside the conventional theatre establishments. *David Merrick, The Abominable Showman: The Unauthorized Biography* (Applause Books, 1993) offers a close-up view of a financially successful Broadway producer. Bim Mason's *Street Theatre and Other Outdoor Performance* (Routledge, 1992) deals with the other end of the spectrum of contemporary theatre, describing the making of all kinds of shows that do not have the advantages (and disadvantages) of a permanent home.

Most of the books about directing are elementary textbooks or studies of individual directors; these can be found easily in bookshops and libraries. For an introduction to this branch of theatre and a means of learning how leading directors of the present time go about their work, a good place to start is *The Director's Voice: Twenty-one Interviews*, edited by Arthur Bartow (Theatre Communications Group, 1988). This can be supplemented by an earlier anthology, *Directors on Directing: A Source Book of the Modern Theatre*, edited by Toby Cole and Helen Krich Chinoy (Bobbs Merrill, 1963), and by Edward Braun's *The Director and the Stage: From Naturalism to Grotowski* (Methuen, 1982). Bertolt Brecht, one of the greatest of all directors, wrote frequently about the general principles of both directing and playwriting; the best place for the English-reading student to learn about his views is *Brecht on Theatre: The Development of an Aesthetic*, an anthology of his writings, edited, translated, and annotated by John Willett (Eyre Methuen, 1964).

There are fewer books on rehearsals, but two have appeared recently: *Directors in Rehearsal: A Hidden World*, by Susan Letzier Cole, and *Systems of Rehearsal: Stanislavsky, Brecht, Grotowski, and Brook*, by Shomit Mitter (both Routledge, 1992).

8. Thinking about Theatre

The most useful way of learning about the different nature of film and other lens-media is to consult the comprehensive anthology, *Film Theory and Criticism: Introductory Readings*, edited by Gerald Mast, Marshall Cohen, and Leo Braudy, and now in its fourth edition (Oxford University Press, 1992); a separate section deals with the relationship of film to theatre and literature, with essays by Susan Sontag and André Bazin, among others.

To learn about what courses are offered in theatre or performance at colleges, universities, and theatre schools, the obvious way of proceeding is to write to those nearest you or in which you have a special interest and ask for their syllabus and other information. One of the most influential books on the general subject is Michel Saint-Denis, *Training for the Theatre: Premises and Promises* (Theatre Arts Books [U.S.]; Heinemann Educational Books [U.K.], 1982); it includes an account of the discussions and the first formulations of a syllabus for training actors at the Juilliard School in New York.

II

Theatre Making

Theatre is an art that depends on collaboration between many specialists who are all very different from each other. It is also an extremely practical art, in that all the time, as soon as work is taken in hand, a multitude of very particular and stubborn problems have to be solved. No book that seeks to introduce its readers to theatre should try to hide the complexity that derives from these facts, because it is one of theatre's distinguishing characteristics and can be one of its most fascinating.

The second part of this book brings together many theatre people, each writing from a different perspective and with their own specialized knowledge. Few concessions have been made to uniformity or simplification because making such changes would not help to give readers a true picture of how theatre works. Some of the following pages may be difficult to understand at first, but look at them as evidence of how things are in the theatre—not always straightforward and not possible without the use of rather rare expertise. This part of the book is therefore, and very intentionally, *not* introductory; it is meant to serve as a resource as well as a springboard to launch readers on a journey to further discovery.

Section

1

Dramatists and Plays

The actual writing of a play, like all writing, is usually a very private process about which even the author knows very little, but its evolution from first draft to finished script is a process shared with many people and is more open to examination. With the help of interviews with the author, Roberta Uno provides an introduction to Jeannie Barraga's *Walls* that shows how complex the making of a play can be. This selection starts with some background on Barraga's life and then considers how theatre can reflect some of the most pressing political and moral issues of our times. The text of this play can be read in *Unbroken Thread: An Anthology of Plays by Asian American Women*.

The Making of a Play

Roberta Uno

In the late 1940s when Jeannie Barroga was born in Milwaukee, Wisconsin, Vietnam was a French colony, fighting a perennial battle for national independence. By the 1960s, however, as she came of age, Vietnam was the setting for an American war that raged at the periphery of her daily life. "I grew up with Vietnam inundating my senses through the media. It got to the point where I felt every waking moment there was something horrible happening—not just on foreign soil, but on the streets of our nation."

It was not until 1985, when she was already six years into a career as a playwright, that she began to think about the Vietnam War and its legacy as subject for a play. The notes she collected for the project were used for the basis of a play called *The Night Before the Rolling Stones Concert*, 1981, which Barroga describes as "a comedy, sort of like *The Big Chill*." When the play was given a staged reading she was surprised by the intensity of the audience response to a scene where a returning veteran confronts his friends and asks, "Why didn't you even write me while I was there?" "It was a short bit, didn't last more than two to three minutes on stage, but the reaction to those few minutes was volatile. It really surprised me that the audience should pick that one scene to get riled up about."

Barroga filed the draft of that script and pondered over the unresolved and conflicting feelings the veteran scene had raised within her audience and herself. Two years later she ran across Jan Scruggs's *To Heal a Nation*, a book of photographs with text about the Vietnam War Memorial. "I was paging through it and I just burst into tears. . . . I knew it was something I could transfer onto stage and have people feel the way I felt. . . . That's when I went into high gear and started doing the research."

While her investigation included interviews with veterans and research in the Library of Congress, she continued to return to the penetrating images in Scruggs's book. The photographs became the inspiration for several key characters and plot scenarios. The characters of Sarah and Morris, for example, were based on a photograph of a nurse pushing a disabled veteran down Constitution Avenue. "From the photos I got these 'what if' story lines. What if [Sarah and Morris] had just met at the Wall and somehow had gotten to a point where he felt comfortable enough for her to roll him down Constitution Avenue? . . . I wanted the stories to happen right in front of the Wall as opposed to peripheral areas."

As a counterpoint to the multiple scenes and subplots that occur at the Wall, Barroga chose to probe the controversy surrounding the monument's design and construction by including its architect, Maya Lin, as a character. A Chinese American, Lin was born in 1959, the year of the first American casualty in Vietnam. As a twenty-one-year-old Yale student, she competed with a national field of professional and amateur artists to have her design selected over 1,421 other entries. Her model became the center of a heated controversy, its construction opposed by veterans and veterans organizations which found its abstract lines too austere and alienating. Some wanted the competition open only to veterans, others felt the monument should be realistic and figurative.

Over sixty plays have been written by American playwrights about the Vietnam War experience including plays that deal with the veteran experience such as *Tracers* by John Difusco, *Back in the World* by Stephen Mack Jones, which details the experience of African-American veterans, and *Honey Bucket* by Mel Escueta about the participation of Asian-Americans. *Walls* is typical of this genre of American plays in that its point of view is American and its primary focus is the effect of fifty-eight thousand American lives lost as opposed to the two million Vietnamese casualties. However, Barroga adds a unique perspective through the inclusion of the Maya Lin subplot. "To me it's a woman's viewpoint on a male war. Specifically a woman of color's viewpoint on an essentially racist war which to this day I don't think people want to recognize. [In the case of Maya Lin] they reacted to a design and then a designer as if the war was still on. . . . [I]t couldn't help but be racial as much as everyone denied it. It was . . . the fact that she's Chinese, she looked like the ones they died fighting."

During her research phase Barroga attempted to contact Lin in hopes of an interview, but she received no response. In the original draft of *Walls* the Lin character's dialogue was completely invented, a decision that proved disastrous in the first reading of the play. "It just didn't ring true . . . so I went back and researched everything she ever said in interviews and devised scenes around her words." Using quotations from interviews that had appeared in *National Geographic* and the almost daily articles detailing the controversy in the *Washington Post*, Barroga devised a way for Lin to address the art war that surrounded her design while revealing the unspoken racial tension underpinning the controversy.

> Reprinted with the permission of Roberta Uno and Jeannie Barroga from *Unbroken Thread: An Anthology of Plays by Asian American Women*, edited by Roberta Uno (Amherst, Mass.: University of Massachusetts Press, 1993), 201-3. Copyright © 1993 by The University of Massachusetts Press. Jeannie Barroga is an active member of the Dramatists Guild, New York and is represented by Helen Merrill, Ltd., New York.

Some of the references in the account of *Walls* that you have just read will be unknown to you, but the nature of the dramatist's interest in them should be clear enough: her twin concerns were with her own experience and with the way in which the United States thinks about war, race, and personal responsibility. Roberta Uno's account of the writing of this play should give an idea of the research and rewriting that is often a part of writing for theatre, especially when the topic is contemporary and a matter of general public knowledge. An audience enjoys being given information.

To learn more about this dramatist and to evaluate her work, more reading will, of course, be necessary. Some questions and suggestions follow.

> *What do you think of* Walls? *Do you know what* The Big Chill *is? Have you seen photographs of the Vietnam War Memorial? Have you seen and read* To Heal a Nation? *Do you know any plays by John Difusco or Stephen Mack Jones? You can look up these titles and authors in your local library, and you may find copies of some of them at least. If none are on the shelves, you could consult* Books in Print *in any good bookstore and then you should be able to order them with help of the interlibrary loan system—ask your librarian, if you truly want to know and have time to pursue these questions. You can also look out for names in* American Theatre, Theater Week, *and other theatre journals that may be available in libraries or bookstores. You should ask similar questions throughout this part of the book, whenever you want to know more.*

This account of August Wilson's *Fences* from the autobiography of James Earl Jones gives an actor's insight into how a play found its audience and its final form. His story shows how the whole company and the producer and director, as well as the author, were all engaged over many weeks in learning about the play and their own contributions to its production. The text of *Fences* was published by Plume (an imprint of Penguin, USA) in 1986.

Fine-tuning a Play
James Earl Jones

> An actor is blessed if once in a lifetime lightning strikes him with a thunderbolt of a role. He is extraordinarily blessed if he gets struck twice, and that has happened to me, with *The Great White Hope* in 1968 and then again with *Fences* in 1987. August Wilson's play was first written in a longer version than the later one and presented at the Eugene O'Neill

Center in Waterford, Connecticut, in a stage reading in 1983. Mary Alice, that wonderful actress who was my costar in *Fences* on Broadway, took part in that initial reading. She told me that when she first read the script, she said, "These are interesting characters." But she said she did not appreciate the full power of the play until she read it on stage with other actors. Then she suddenly realized that it pulsated with a harmony of sounds and voices, and all these characters were something very special indeed.

Lloyd Richards asked me to read August Wilson's new play, set in the fifties. I have been told that August once said that sometime during the process of writing *Fences*, he began to hear me in the role of Troy. It was a role I took to immediately. I read the script, and saw right away the poetry of the writing, even though the work was still in progress, and rough-hewn in places. I reread the play, and before I read it enough times to evaluate the dramatic structure, I knew I wanted to play Troy Maxson. Here was one of those rare roles which, like Jack Jefferson in *The Great White Hope*, I knew on sight would exact a total commitment, all I could give to the stage night after night of my energy, of my imagination, of my talent.

In the winter of 1985, Mary Alice and I went into rehearsal with Lloyd, who was now dean of the Yale School of Drama and director of the Yale Repertory Theatre. Lloyd had cultivated a large, responsive black audience in the New Haven community, and they locked onto this play. When we opened in May of 1985, August Wilson was enjoying his first big success on Broadway with *Ma Rainey's Black Bottom*. In addition to Mary Alice, our cast included Ray Aranha as my friend Jim Bono, Charles Brown and Russell Costen as my older son and my brother, and Courtney B. Vance, then a Yale drama student, as my son Cory.

August was rightfully praised for his ear for black vernacular and his "genius for finding the poetry hidden in the rhythms of everyday speech." He set the play in 1957 in industrial Pittsburgh, August's own city. *Fences* tells the story of fifty-three-year-old Troy Maxson, a garbage collector; his second wife Rose; their family and their friends. As a young man, Troy was a talented baseball player, never allowed by the color barrier to make it beyond the old Negro professional leagues. Twice-married, he is an ex-con who served time in a penitentiary for killing a man in a fight. Troy is angry about his failures, especially his failure to achieve his dream of a sports career. When his son Cory is offered a college football scholarship, Troy forbids him to take it. Not surprisingly, his reasoning on race, success, and failure is complicated.

The central conflict here hinges on this tension between father and son, although there are many layers of conflict, many symbolic "fences." Troy and Rose have their heartbreaks. There is also tension between Troy and his son by the previous marriage, Lyons. Then there is Troy's brother Gabriel, irreparably injured in the war. And there is Alberta, Troy's other woman.

At the time of its first stage reading *Fences* ran about three and a half hours; but then August pared it by an hour for the Yale production.

Despite its great success at Yale, the play still had problems. Every play keeps evolving as it moves closer to Broadway, or to its final form. One of the most exciting things about the theatre is this metamorphosis of a written script into a living drama. Undoubtedly, August Wilson is a great dramatist: he is essentially a poet, and he is a brilliant editor. But his work is hampered, I think, by his inability or unwillingness to resolve the drama. I hope it is something he can learn, especially if he renders his plays into film. Lloyd and I felt the need of changes in the script, but August could not always achieve what he knew the two of us wanted.

We as actors have to dig in deep to substitute feelings for dialogue that should be in the script. There is a scene in *Fences* in which Troy has to explain to his wife Rose about his involvement with another woman. He does not say, "Forgive me." He says, "Understand why I went to the other woman." He finds himself able to do that only in baseball terminology. Troy explains it this way:

> But . . . you born with two strikes on you before you come to the plate. You got to guard it closely . . . always looking for the curve-ball on the inside corner. You can't afford to let none get past you. You can't afford a call strike. If you going down . . . you going down swinging. Everything lined up against you. What you gonna do. I fooled them, Rose. I bunted. When I found you and Cory and halfway decent job . . . I was safe. Couldn't nothing touch me. . . . I was on first looking for one of them boys to knock me in. To get me home. . . . Then when I saw that gal . . . she firmed up my backbone. And I got to thinking that if I tried . . . I just might be able to steal second. Do you understand that after eighteen years I wanted to steal second.

Lloyd and I thought August shouldn't leave it at that, but should make it very clear, if only by suggestion, what, in Troy's inarticulateness, the baseball metaphors meant to him. To leave the speech alone, by itself, was misleading, incomplete. It begged the audience to laugh it away, which some nights they did.

What is missing is the link between what Troy would have said were he an educated man, and what he is capable of saying as an illiterate man. We all know that he is trying to say something about his own value, his own worth. He is saying that he became aware of his own value only in the company of the other woman. He does not mean that he finds fault in his present wife, whom he loves very much. He just feels free to let a flowering happen with the other woman—far away from being beaten down by the duties of his daily life.

Consistently, we found that audiences began to interpret this speech to mean that Troy was simply conning his wife. Yet what he is really saying is, "With you I got to first base and with her I felt I could get to second base—and maybe get home." The original text read, "I wanted to steal second." I added the word "home" because that had a meaning to me. The audience usually laughed because that implied scoring with a second woman, not the inner psychological reality that is deeply troubling Troy. I felt we had to adjust the script in these areas if we were to clarify and enhance the undercurrents of *Fences*.

We opened at Yale Rep on April 30, 1985. Despite the great success of the Yale production, no one in the Broadway producing community wanted to touch the play. It was a drama about a black family, written by a black man, directed by a black man. That did not appear to some to be a salable commodity for Broadway. A lot of prospective producers came to see the play, and a few considered taking it on. Eventually, all of them passed.

Lucy and others kept fighting for us when we moved the production to the Goodman Theatre in Chicago. Carol Channing saw the play and encouraged a young producer named Carole Shorenstein Hays to come to see *Fences* there. Carole immediately booked us to play at the Curran Theatre in San Francisco, and then on Broadway. Other prospective producers who saw the play tended to say, "Well, it's about a black family. We don't know if that will work in the commercial theatre." Carole, to the contrary, told me that when she saw the play, she saw her own family up there on the stage.

"I realized," she said, "that no matter what your station, no matter whether you are wealthy, educated, poor, illiterate—all families wrestling with anxieties and hostilities tend to work them out the same way. All families have the power structure of parent and child. All families have rivalry." Carole comes from a wealthy Jewish family in San Francisco, but she said, "Background is irrelevant when it comes to families in crisis. The interior energy is the same in every family, no matter what the exterior circumstances, when push comes to shove."

Lucy set up a meeting with her once we finished the Chicago production, and I laid out to her all the problems I had had with the script to date. The production had been a great success in New Haven and Chicago. But reviewers saw the play as flawed, especially in the second act. This was my own sense of the play's weakness—that there was something unresolved in the second act in the scene when father and son physically confront each other. Their conflict is the crux of the play; the script's flaw rested in its void of resolution.

I could not argue the point very well without sounding as if I wanted Troy to die on stage. "What if we revive the gun?" I asked, referring to an early draft of the play which actually suggested that the father confront the son with a gun. Lloyd opposed that idea for social reasons.

"The main character, the father, ends up unresolved," I said. "You see him outcast because of his liaison with the other woman, and his commitment to raising the child—his child—she dies giving birth to. Then, suddenly, as the final scene opens, you learn that Troy is dead. He dies off stage. The audience has not seen Troy's death, much less seen him come to terms with himself. There has been no dramatic resolution of Troy Maxson's life. No one else in the play seems to resolve him. The mother tries to do it by telling the story of his life, but that does not resolve the conflict dramatically. I think the only person who can resolve it is Cory, the son. Somehow the resolution has to happen with the son."

Carole listened. I told her I had a problem with the laughter we were getting in certain places. I confided to her that at Yale and in Chicago, I would usually go home from the theatre at night depressed. I knew it was because I carried unresolved emotion home with me. I would go home to see my own young son lying there asleep. I would look at him and say, "Does this have to happen—this desperate, wordless physical confrontation between a father and a son, so choked with words they can't speak that they risk killing each other? Does this conflict between father and son have to be that brutal and deadly?"

Caught between the reality of my experience with Robert Earl and the potential of my experience with Flynn Earl, I had to have resolution of the issues between Troy and Cory. Without resolution, you had a man who does not learn anything. When you present a character who does not learn anything, there is always the even graver danger that the audience will not learn anything.

I hoped August would rewrite to achieve that catharsis. Yale gave him an ivory tower, an isolation and an insulation. Lloyd, as dean of the Yale Drama School, was determined that his new playwrights would be buffered from the pressures of commercial theatre as long as possible. He wanted to harbor them as long as he could because he felt the best creative work is done through fulfilling your own vision without yielding to the pressures of commercial theatre. August is a very private man, and I respect that. When Athol Fugard worked on new plays at Yale, he would always be available to hang out with us, to have a drink. The cast always had access to him. That was his choice. August's temperament does not seem to invite discussion.

I relied on Lloyd as the director to convey concerns to the playwright, and frankly, I preferred it that way. I didn't know how to talk to writers, particularly this one. Carole said that she would make sure we got the best production that a producer could give. Soon afterward, we had a meeting that included Carole, August, Lloyd, and myself. I thought we were going to lay our cards on the table, yet every time I said, "I have a problem with this scene, this point," August and Lloyd countered with reasons for not making changes.

I thought Carole was being stonewalled. I felt stonewalled myself, and became more and more frustrated. I left that failed meeting knowing that nothing was resolved. As frustrated as I felt, I perceived that Carole had it worse than I did. She was white, Jewish, rich, and young, and I saw something personal in the subtly negative way she was dealt with.

Early in the play, Troy is explaining to Bono how he met Rose, who is sitting on his lap: "I told her, 'Baby, I don't wanna marry, I just wanna be your man.'" And Rose says, "I told him if he wasn't the marrying kind, then move out the way so the marrying kind can find me."

They joke about how they met, and at one point Troy says, "Well, you know, so I married her 'cause I didn't want no coal black woman no way."

In the black community ever since slavery, tones of blackness have played a large role in the intricate social and political workings of intraracial conflict. There are phrases such as "The blacker the berry, the sweeter the juice" to express an appreciation of the pure blackness of a woman's skin. On the other hand, some black men choose "high yellow" women,

women who look white. It is uncomfortable to play on those themes now, but the play was set in the fifties, and August had written that negative line about being "coal black."

"I've worked too hard to bring black women into my theatre," Lloyd said. "I don't want that line to offend them." So we struck it. I raised a similar issue about another moment early in *Fences*.

"Troy is not a racialist," I said, "but he says things which suggest he is a racialist. At the very beginning of the play, I say this line—'the white man ain't gonna let you get nowhere no way.' I don't know why I should want to make the white males in the audience feel uncomfortable. Since we've already excised the lines which might offend black women, by that same logic, we should delete this line as well."

"I just want the chips to fall as they may," August answered. By now I feared that we all had different agendas.

"But Troy is not really political," I argued. "First of all, he is illiterate. He is inarticulate. He speaks only three languages—farm language, prison language, and baseball language. So what is this constant harping on the white man? It reduces him. It would seem more valid that he would say 'the man,' meaning the power structure. He lives in Pittsburgh. He is not directly confronting that polarized situation in the South. He should be larger than that. Such lines limit his dimension too much for me, especially at the beginning of the play when I want to achieve as much scope as possible with the character. I want to ensnare the audience, not repel them."

I persisted in my vision of the need for resolution. Since the father dies off stage, unresolved, something had to be resolved through the son.

I tried again for change. In the last scene, Cory has virtually nothing to say. Rose does all the talking. It is wonderful for Rose to have a final scene in which she comes into her own, but that happens at the expense of any catharsis, any resolution of the central conflict in the play. Carole promised me as we moved to San Francisco that we would resolve these issues, but she was too young to take on Lloyd, who had much more experience and who was caught between his producer and his playwright. We had good audiences in San Francisco, but critics there were not totally kind. Yet, for all of our problems, I had great faith in *Fences*. I knew it was worth a fight to make it work.

"I don't rewrite," August reportedly said. "That's it. What you've got is it." Now Lloyd was caught between his playwright and his actor. The day after we opened in San Francisco, Lloyd decided to fly back to Yale to resume his duties as dean of the Yale Drama School. Carole called him back and said, "We have work to do." She began to apply her muscle as a producer from that moment on.

When it came to the scenes Troy played in, I battled for what I believed in. I respect the writer's domain, but the actor lives out there in the words in a dimension the writer does not have to enter night after night. I think writer and actor can collaborate on honing a script for the ultimate performance. But I did not want to pull any "star" pressure tactics. For the longest time, I hesitated to speak about the one scene without Troy that troubled me more than anything else.

It was actually the epilogue scene after Troy dies. It begins with the child coming out into the garden. It ends with Troy's brother Gabriel lifting his trumpet and trying to blow his dead brother into heaven. Gabriel was hit by shrapnel during the war. Most of his brain was blown away, but he came back from death. An actor must play Gabriel as mentally impaired, but not as dumb. He is a deceptively simple character, in that he is not simple at all.

August told Frankie Faison, the actor playing Gabriel on Broadway, that his job in the family was to judge Troy as to his fitness for heaven. "You almost came back from the brink of death solely to perform that mission," August said.

Lloyd added his advice as director. "You are here to shepherd your troubled brother into heaven."

Frankie and I had worked together before; I had directed him once in a student production at New York University. He was my understudy in *Of Mice and Men*. We could talk to each other, and perceiving the difficulty he was having with directions for the scene, I discussed it with him.

"These two concepts are not really in conflict," I said. "They are really the same thing—you can be both judge and shepherd or savior. You almost trusted it one day, and you've got to go back and try to trust it again until you feel comfortable with the concept that you have one single mission on that stage." Frankie grew into that scene; it was terribly moving.

At first Carole did not want the play to end as it did. August was determined that the scene with Gabriel and his trumpet should be left in the play, and Lloyd agreed with him. I tried to be objective. I suggested that Carole needed to see the play herself a few times without that coda scene. I watched it with them, and I realized that without that scene, the play was an even more depressing experience. There still was no true catharsis written into the script, but the coda did move you beyond the depression. Carole was right that the coda was a "cop-out," but at least it was something. It enabled the audience to go away absorbing the best parts of the play.

Convinced that the resolution must come when father and son have their final confrontation, I began to focus on that scene. Troy is an "outcast" after his infidelity. Even though he is still the man of the house, he is uncoupled from everyone. His best friend does not see him anymore. His wife does not sleep with him anymore. The last person to break away from him is Cory. They stand on the brink of physical combat—then Rose intercedes. That is what is written in the script. One day I begged Lloyd to let us see what would happen, even with nothing written, if Rose does not come in. He agreed, and the scene became an improvisation—the symbolic and literal struggle between the father and son over a baseball bat. This was a symbolic sketch, not written by the playwright, and in that sense, not a legitimate part of the play.

But it worked. In that sketch, the father and son learn that they cannot kill each other. The bond between them is too strong. No one intervenes. They discover this for themselves, face-to-face. It was the first clear lesson in the whole play. They learn, and we learn, that no matter how bold or bad or desperate they are, they cannot kill each other.

From that point on, I noticed that I could leave the theatre each night absolved of carrying depression home with me. Once that sketch was accepted and woven into the performance, for the first time, I could go home and look at Flynn asleep in his bed, and feel a sense of peace.

That began to happen in the last week in San Francisco. Without any help from August, we began to refine that scene. He said he could not rewrite it, but he did agree to take the mother out of any intercession between father and son.

When the mother came on stage, I still went into the house with a burning hatred of the son, and knowing that he hated me just as fiercely. But somehow, as we wrestled over that bat and put it down, we rose above that hatred.

As a father in real life, I knew how uncomfortable it had to be to live with such animosity. Knowing my own relationship with my own father, I knew how deadly wounding it is to live with. And I went home wounded every night, until we changed that scene.

I think many black people who came to see *Fences* came in search of a hero. Black women in particular, living through the deep frustrations of our time, watched me go up on that stage and play a man who could be a hero. But eventually Troy fails—his son, his wife, himself. There is a moment when the worm turns. They found that hard to accept. Here is a man with all the potential of the wonder of mankind. There is all that potential for Troy—and for his son. And Troy, quite simply, ruins it, destroys it—and some black members of our audiences smarted from it. This story is about a man in trouble, about a whole family in deep trouble. We do not give the audience the ascendant hero and the happy ending. Some people got very upset. Stuck with the story of a "failed garbage-man," they felt betrayed.

I know I was a thorn in the flesh for August and Lloyd, but it was only because I cared so much about this play. Actor Oskar Werner observed that a good actor can bring only as much insight to a character as the playwright invests in him, while a great actor reveals more about the character than you could know if you were to encounter him in the flesh, in real life. That is the task we set for ourselves as actors. I felt I knew Troy Maxson in my bones, and I wanted to reveal him, in all his complicated humanity.

Section

2

Actors and Performances

Every teacher of actors, and every actor, has his or her own way of working. Instead of reprinting what can be read in acting manuals—and to quote much less than most of such a book would do it an injustice—this section is made up of a number of short statements that together can give some idea of the work that an actor must do.

Toward Performance: Konstantin Stanislavsky, Bertolt Brecht, Otis Skinner, Ralph Richardson, and Alan Schneider

Konstantin Stanislavsky

When Konstantin Stanislavsky was asked to address a new group of students at the school of the Moscow Art Theatre in October 1924, the acclaimed director, actor, and teacher tried to encapsulate all his advice, the "basic propositions" of what was already known as his "system":

> The *first* is this: There are no formulas in it on how to become a great actor, or how to play this or that part. The "method" is made of steps towards the true creative state of an actor on the stage. When it is true, it is the usual, normal state of a person in real life.
>
> But to achieve that normal living state on stage is very difficult for an actor. In order to do it he has to be: (a) physically free, in control of free muscles; (b) his attention must be infinitely alert; (c) he must be able to listen and observe on the stage as he would in real life, that is to say be in contact with the person playing opposite him; (d) he must believe in everything that is happening on the stage that is related to the play.
>
> To accomplish this I shall propose a number of exercises. . . . They train these absolutely necessary qualities in actors. They must be done every day just as a singer practices or a pianist does his finger exercises.
>
> Stanislavsky's Legacy, trans. Elizabeth Reynolds Hapgood

The call for an actor to "believe in everything" has become the defining mark of Stanislavsky's teaching. However he was very clear that this was not a simple instruction:

in two other "propositions," he explained that actors should create both the particular "inner" state of being and the appropriate "external" behavior that are needed to present their characters in the circumstances of a play. None of this is simple; successful work depends on thorough and constant training for both mind and body.

Bertolt Brecht

In the latter half of the twentieth century, Bertolt Brecht has been another and very different source of inspiration. He did not want an actor to "get inside the skin" of the character he or she portrayed, but to show, or "demonstrate," what takes place in a play. His description of Helene Weigel playing a servant in Sophocles's *Oedipus* provides an example of the kind of performance he sought:

> she announced the death of her mistress by calling out her "dead, dead" in a wholly unemotional and penetrating voice, [and] her "Jocasta has died" without any sorrow but so firmly and definitely that the bare fact of her mistress's death carried more weight at that precise moment than could have been generated by any grief of her own. She did not abandon her voice to horror, but perhaps her face, for she used white make-up to show the impact which a death makes on all who are present at it. . . . With astonishment she described in a single clear sentence the dying woman's ranting and apparent irrationality, and there was no mistaking the tone of her "and how she ended, we do not know" with which, as a meagre but inflexible tribute, she refused to give any further information about this death. But as she descended the few steps she took such paces that this slight figure seemed to be covering an immense distance from the scene of the tragedy to the people on the lower stage.
>
> *Brecht on Theatre*, trans. John Willett

Brecht called for the actor to be true to character and situation, but not in a way that draws attention to individual experience and feeling. Here the offstage suffering of another person dominates the performance and the fullest response to it is left for the audience to supply.

The actor's task has many aspects. Stanislavsky required a truth to life which would stop his students being overly theatrical and false, yet he also demanded truth to the circumstances of the play and an exceptional fitness and freedom in performance, both of which took the actor far beyond the confines of ordinary living.

Otis Skinner

There are many ways of saying what is required and some barely mention "truth" at all. Here is Otis Skinner on acting in comedy, written in 1938 near the end of his long career and before Stanislavsky's teachings had reached North America:

> There is no such thing as "natural acting," if by that you mean the photographic and cinematic reproduction of the individual in everyday life. It is entirely an artificial process, however colloquially presented. To a young eighteenth-century farceur who claimed that his success lay in acting as nature dictated, the old comic, Munden, retorted, "Nature? Nature be damned! You make them laugh." To my mind a performance is perfect only when the player is keyed to great and resilient elation, when his heart is beating a little faster, when the emotions of his character expose themselves clearly to his eye and color his movement. In that clarity new things born of the moment's impulse suggest themselves and become incorporated in succeeding performances.

But—and here is the paradox—possessing all these he must still be the cool-minded and alert technician whose efficiency is brought about by long study and experiment.

Theatre Arts Anthology

Ralph Richardson

Older actors are sometimes able to give the accounts of the complexities of their profession that cut through fashionable jargon. British actor Sir Ralph Richardson, experienced in theatre and film and in classic and contemporary plays, was famous for saying in a few sentences what others would need many to begin to explain. Asked about audiences, he replied:

> The actor feels the temper of the audience very swiftly, almost the moment he steps on to the stage. And, of course, it is his business to control that temper. But I don't think actors really love their audience; they are more in the nature of a lion-tamer. Perhaps the lion-tamer loves the lions, I'm not certain about that; but the actor must dominate the mood of the audience.

Questioned further about the nature of performance, he continued:

> You're really driving four horses, as it were, first going through, in great detail, the exact movements which have been decided upon. You're also listening to the audience, as I say, keeping, if you can, very great control over them. You're also slightly creating the part, in so far as you're consciously refining the movements and, perhaps, inventing tiny other experiments with new ones. At the same time you are really living, in one part of your mind, what is happening. Acting is to some extent a controlled dream. In one part of your consciousness it really and truly is happening. . . . But in my experience this layer of absolute reality is a comparatively small one.

Interview with Derek Hart, *Great Acting*

To the critic Benedict Nightingale, Sir Ralph spoke of the "beguiling frustration" of acting: "You're like a bull in a field, chasing after a cow, trying to get it by the tail, and you never quite catch it. You never quite learn to act." (*Fifth Row Center*) To director Peter Hall, he said that "acting, however beautiful a craft it is for oneself, has finally to be for *them*, the audience." (*Peter Hall's Diaries*)

Alan Schneider

In the same production two actors may use two totally different methods and yet act together to each other's advantage, as Alan Schneider's autobiography, *Entrances* makes very clear (1987). In his production of Edward Albee's *Who's Afraid of Virginia Woolf?* (1962), Uta Hagen and Arthur Hill had the leading roles. The director tells us, "Uta, of course, had ideas of her own about almost everything, although she took her time before imposing them on us." Over lunch before rehearsals began:

> she confronted me with a notebook full of her jottings, most of them totally formed in her mind and not negotiable. She did most of the talking and I listened, soon realizing that she had taken my promise to "obey" her literally.

Arthur Hill, on the other hand,

> posed for me exactly the opposite problem to Uta's. He begged for help, he demanded help, he needed help. Seemingly for every moment, every line, every move. I spent hours

in and out of rehearsal guiding him, encouraging him, making him feel that he was a match for Uta. . . . I would drill him over and over in his moves until they became part of his motor mechanism. . . . Once he had gotten them, it would take an earthquake or a tank to shake him.

As we have read an actor's thoughts about a dramatist's work on a play during previews, here we see dramatist David Mamet speaking for actors about the nature of good acting, and bad.

Acting

David Mamet

We live in very selfish times. Nothing is given away free. Any impulse of creation or whimsy or iconoclasm which achieves general notice is immediately co-opted by risk capital, and its popularity—which arose from its generosity and freedom of thought—is made to serve the turn of financial extortion.

The successful workingman's café is franchised nationwide, and the charm of its artlessness wholesaled. The energy and invention of the bohemian quarter is transformed by promoters into the marketability of "Artland." The privacy of the remote seaside resort conducive to contemplation and renewal is sold piecemeal to millions of vacationers hungry for retreat who are willing to pay for a frantic, thronged pilgrimage to a spot where retreat was once possible.

It's not a very good time for the arts. And it is an especially bad time for the art of acting; for actors, as Hamlet told us, are "the abstract and brief chronicles of their time."

There are, of course, actors whose performances are hailed as great, because critics grade (as they must, in the absence of any aesthetic criteria) on the curve. But a comparison of that which contemporary journalism lauds as great acting with the great actors of the thirties and forties (Cary Grant, Garbo, Henry Fonda, James Stewart, etc.) shows how drastically we have lowered our standards.

We expect less of our actors today because we expect less of ourselves.

Our attention is limited; and in this time of fear and anxiety, our attention is devoted to ourselves, our feelings, our emotions, our immediate well-being. This makes for very bad acting, as the more our attention is focused on ourselves the less interesting we become—think of how many fascinating hypochondriacs you know.

The laws of attention which are true off stage are true on stage. The self-concerned person is a bore and the self-concerned *actor* is a bore. And whether the actor is saying, "I must play this scene in order to be well thought of," *or*, "I must remember and re-create the time my puppy died in order to play this scene well," makes no difference. In both cases his attention is self-centered, and in both cases his performance will tell us nothing we couldn't have learned more enjoyably in a library.

Acting, as any art, must be generous; the attention of the artist must be focused outward—not on what he is feeling, but on what he is trying to accomplish.

The *organic* actor must have generosity and courage—two attributes which our current national hypochondria render in low supply and even lower esteem. He must have the courage to say to his fellow actors on stage (and so to the audience): "I am not concerned with influencing or *manipulating* you, I am not concerned with *nicety*. I am here on a mission and I *demand* you give me what I want."

This actor brings to the stage *desire* rather than completion, will rather than emotion. His performance will be compared not to *art*, but to *life*; and when we leave the theater after his performance we will speak of *our life* rather than *his technique*. And the difference between this organic actor and the self-concerned performer is the difference between a wood fire and a fluorescent light.

In a Golden Age, that which delights us on the stage (that acting we would call "art") would be the same things which delight us in our lives: simplicity, elegance, kindness, force—not that which is portrayed but that which allows us to infer; not the technical but the provocative. And in a Golden Age we would judge an actor's "character" on stage the exact same way we judge it off stage: not by his protestations and assurances but by his determination, his constancy of purpose, his generosity—in effect, his "goodness."

But we don't live in a Golden Age, and the actor, the Brief Chronicle, is an expression of and a servant to his times.

We have demanded of him and received of him little other than this: a continual portrayal and repetition of the idea that nothing very much is happening around us, that we need not worry, and that it is absolutely correct that our actions should not be determined by our perceptions.

We have demanded of the actor that he repeat to us constantly that it is fine to laugh when not amused, to cry when not moved, to beam gratitude upon the unacceptable, to condone the unforgivable, to express delight in the banal.

That most of today's acting is false and mechanical is no coincidence—it is a sign of our society's demanding that its priests repeat the catechism essential for our tenuous mental health: that nothing is happening, that nothing very bad or very good can befall us, that we are safe.

There are exceptions, of course. There are organic performances and organically directed productions and companies. But there aren't many. The actor works in a community, and the communal ideal of excellence is contagious and exigent.

Can we again ratify the Actor and the Theater which is organic rather than mechanical—which responds to our need to love rather than our need to *have*?

In this century the great and vital theaters (The Group in 1930s New York, Brecht's in 1920s Berlin, Stanislavsky's Art in 1900 Moscow, The Second City in 1960 Chicago) have emerged in response to, and signaling the end of, introverted, uncertain social periods.

For the moment, generous, organic acting can be seen occasionally in the theater (though seldom in the commercial theater), more regularly in film (generally in smaller roles), and most consistently as part of dance or opera, in performances given by those dedicated not to their performances but to the actions demanded by their material—in the work of Pavarotti or Baryshnikov, or Hildegarde Behrens, or Yuriko, or Fischer-Dieskau.

When, once again, actors are cherished and rewarded who bring to the stage or the screen generosity, desire, *organic life*, actions performed freely—without desire for reward or fear of either censure or misunderstanding—that will be one of the first signs that the tide of our introverted, unhappy time has turned and that we are once again eager and prepared to look at ourselves.

Section

3

Directors and Production

This account of rehearsals conducted by Bertolt Brecht shows how much effort and patience can be used if there is time enough and talent enough to use it. These processes were fully exploited by Brecht, but only a highly subsidized theatre could work in this way today. Nevertheless, the questions explored, the patience shown in research and experiment, and the openness to suggestion are ingredients many other directors use during rehearsals. The collaboration between director and designer is perhaps the most often copied element of Brecht's process.

Exploratory Direction: Brecht at Rehearsal

Carl Weber

I walked into the rehearsal and it was obvious that they were taking a break. Brecht was sitting in a chair smoking a cigar, the director of the production, Egon Monk, and two or three assistants were sitting with him, some of the actors were on stage and some were standing around Brecht, joking, making funny movements and laughing about them. Then one actor went up on the stage and tried about 30 ways of falling from a table. They talked a little about the *Urfaust*-scene "In Auerbachs Keller" (Mephisto brings Faust into an inn where drunken students enjoy themselves with dirty jokes and silly songs). Another actor tried the table, the results were compared, with a lot of laughing and a lot more horse-play. This went on and on, and someone ate a sandwich, and I thought, my god this is a long break. So I sat naïvely and waited, and just before Monk said, "Well, now we are finished, let's go home," I realized that this was rehearsal. And it was typical of the loose way Brecht often worked, of his experimental approach and of the teamwork the Ensemble was used to. Whatever ideas he brought to rehearsal he tried out, threw away, tried something else; sometimes 40 versions of one scene were tried, once in a while only two. Even when a production had opened, and been reviewed, he re-worked parts of it, re-rehearsed it, changed the blocking. The actors also took an experimental attitude. They would suggest a way of doing something, and if they started to explain it, Brecht would say that he wanted no discussions in rehearsal—it would have to be tried. Of course, his whole view of the world was that it was changeable and the people in it were changing; every solution was only a starting point for a new, better, different solution.

All this was—of course—not just for love of experiment. Brecht was mainly concerned with the play as the telling of a story to an audience, clearly, beautifully, and entertainingly. If he found that in an almost completed production one certain part was opaque or boring, he cut it. I have never seen anyone cut a script as mercilessly as Brecht cut his own. Brecht had another important ability: if he had worked at a scene, and then dropped it for a week, he could come back and look at it as if he had never seen it before. I remember a scene from the third act of *Caucasian Chalk Circle*, when Grusha, with her adopted child and her brother Lawrentij, arrives at the house of the dying peasant whom she is forced to marry. The scene hadn't been done for about three weeks (the play was rehearsed for eight months); he came back to it, and we all thought it was going rather well when suddenly Brecht yelled, "Stop!" He asked what the actor playing Lawrentij, who was walking across the room, was doing. Well, we answered, there's a good reason; he has to be over there for his next line, you blocked it this way. Brecht denied this angrily, saying there was no reason for such a move. "But his next line asks for it." "What line?" he barked. The actor said the line. "But that's impossible, I couldn't have written that!" We had to show him in the book that he had indeed written it, and he was furious—at us. But he rewrote the scene. He had looked at it as if it were by someone else, from a play he'd never heard of before, which he was judging as a spectator, and it failed.

The initial preparation of a play usually took about half a year, while it was discussed, and adapted (if it was a translation). The set was developed on paper and as a model during that period, as were the costumes. Then, when Brecht went into rehearsal, it could take three to four months to block the play. This blocking involved the working out of a considerable number of details. To Brecht, blocking was the backbone of the production; ideally, he thought, the blocking should be able to tell the main story of the play—and its contradictions—by itself, so that a person watching through a glass wall, unable to hear what was being said would be able to understand the main elements and conflicts of the story. To work out blocking this clear takes an enormous amount of time; he would try out every thinkable possibility—and if a scene didn't seem to work in dress rehearsal, the first thing reworked would be the blocking.

After the basic blocking was finished, we started to work on the acting detail; by this time the actors knew their lines completely, and could play around with them freely. The most meticulous attention was paid to the smallest gesture. Sometimes it took an hour to work out whether an actor should pick up a tool one way or another. Particular attention was devoted to all details of physical labour. A man's work forms his habits, his attitudes, his physical behaviour down to the smallest movement, a fact usually neglected by the stage. Brecht spent hours in rehearsal exploring how

Figure C.1 A grand theatre, opening in 1904. The Coliseum, London, seating 2,358 persons. (Photograph by Clive Barda, London; courtesy of Theatre Projects.)

Figure C.2 Model for the new Belk Theatre, Charlotte, North Carolina, seating 2,100 persons. (Photograph by Keith Krolak-Cesar Pelli and Associates, New Haven, Connecticut; courtesy of Theatre Projects.)

Figures C.3 and C.4 Interior views of the Belk Theatre, Charlotte, North Carolina, which was designed by Cesar Pelli and Theatre Projects Consultants, and which opened in 1992. (Photographs by Keith Krolak-Cesar Pelli and Associates, New Haven, Connecticut; courtesy of Theatre Projects.)

Figures C.5A and C.5B Sketch and finished set designed by Marjorie Bradley Kellogg for George Bernard Shaw's *Major Barbara*: Act I, Wilton Crescent; at the McCarter Theatre, Princeton, New Jersey. (Photographs courtesy of the artist.)

Figures C.6A and C.6B   Set designed by Marjorie Bradley Kellogg for *Major Barbara*: Act II, Salvation Army Shelter. (Photographs by courtesy of the artist).

Figures C.7A and C.7B Set designed by Marjorie Bradley Kellogg for *Major Barbara*: Act III, The Armament Works. (Photographs courtesy of the artist.)

Galileo would handle a telescope and an apple, how the kitchenmaid
Grusha would pick up a waterbottle or a baby, how the young soldier Eilif
would drink at his General's table, etc. Often paintings or other pictorial
documents of the play's period were brought into rehearsal for the study
of movements and gestures. Brecht's favourite painters were Breughel and
Bosch: their paintings told "stories" (not in the sense of the veristic nine-
teenth-century school, of course), their people were stamped by their lives
and occupations, their vices and beliefs. The influence of pictures he had
seen often could be felt in Brecht's work; certain moments of the blocking,
as well as character-images, were derived from paintings or photos.

Each moment had to be examined: for the characters' situation, for
the story's situation, for the actions going on around the character. When
all these details had been brought to a certain point, not of completion,
but of diminished possibilities, Brecht would have the first run-through.
This might be six months after the actors started work on the play, six
months of working on blocking, single beats, and small units of scenes.
The first run-through was usually a disaster—it was impossible for the
actors to pull things together so fast. But this was just what Brecht was
waiting for; in the second and third run-throughs, a rhythm began to
appear, and all the mistakes made so far emerged clearly. So then Brecht
broke the whole thing down again into short beats and small units, and
reworked every part that had been unsuccessful. After the second breakdown of the play, the final period of rehearsal usually came. This included
run-throughs—but interrupted by frequent reworking of scenes and
details. A week or more was given to the technical rehearsals. Lighting a
show sometimes took five days alone, and extras were used to walking
through all the motions, so the actors wouldn't waste their time and
energy. During dress rehearsals, details were constantly changed or developed further, including the blocking and quite often even the text. I
remember first nights, when actors would find a little note from Brecht on
their dressing-room tables, wishing them good luck and asking them to
say a new line in scene X instead of one Brecht had decided to cut, because
audience reactions in dress-rehearsals had indicated that the former line
didn't work the way Brecht intended it.

After the last dress rehearsal Brecht always did an exercise, which he
called the "marking" or "indicating" rehearsal: the actors not in costumes,
but on the set, had to walk quickly through all the actions of the show, quot-
ing the text very rapidly, without any effort of acting, but keeping the
rhythm, the pauses, etc., intact. The effect—if you were sitting far back in
the house—was very much like an early silent movie: you saw people moving
and gesturing very quickly, but you couldn't hear the words or get any kind
of emotions, except the most obvious ones. This proved to be an extremely
helpful device; it made the actors relax, helped them to memorize every
physical detail and gave them a keen sense for the show's rhythmic pattern.

Finally first night came, which in fact was a preview with audience,
after which rehearsals were used to change the production according to
audience reactions. After five to eight previews, the official "opening" with
press and invited guests took place. Brecht introduced these previews to

Germany, probably drawing on his American and English experiences. In the beginning, the German critics strongly rejected this procedure; now other theatres have followed Brecht's example. After the opening, work on the production didn't stop. The director—or one of his assistants—watched every performance, and whenever changes or a reworking were felt necessary, rehearsals were scheduled.

This sounds like a monumentally laborious process, and to some extent it was. But it took place in an atmosphere of humour, ease with experimentation, relaxation. Actors (and directors) new at the Ensemble were usually very tense, and tried to get results right away—as they must when they have only a few weeks' rehearsal time. Brecht would tell them, "Fast results are always to be regarded with suspicion. The first solution is usually not a good solution. Not enough thinking goes into it. Instinct is a very dubious guide, especially for directors."

Brecht regarded designs as of the highest importance and had worked out his methods of handling it with his friend Caspar Neher. When Neher designed a play for him, he started with little sketches depicting the important story situations—sometimes he arrived at a kind of comic strip of the entire play. He began with people, sketching the characters in relation to a given situation, and thus visualizing the blocking. When he and Brecht were satisfied with the sketches, they started to develop a set. For Brecht, for Neher when he worked with Brecht, for Otto and von Appen, who worked with Brecht in the fifties, the set was primarily a space where actors tell a certain story to the audience. The first step was to give the actor the space and architectural elements he needed; the next was to work out the set so it by itself would tell the audience enough about the play's story and conflicts, its period, social relations, etc.; the last step was to make it beautiful.

Whatever is called the "style" of Brechtian productions was always something arrived at during the last phase of production. Brecht never began with a preconceived stylistic idea, even something so "basic" as whether the production should be "period," "naturalistic," or whatever silly labels theatre convention usually pins on plays. He began with a long exploration of the intricate social relationships of the characters and the behaviour resulting from them. Their psychology was not left out, but was developed from the social relations. The designer watched, working out his ideas as Brecht rehearsed. Twice I saw about 75 per cent of a completed set—and the finished costumes that went with it—thrown away after the first dress rehearsal, because although it was beautiful it did not tell the audience what Brecht and von Appen wanted. An enormous amount of money was poured into these experiments, but certainly not wasted. One of Brecht's favourite proverbs—"The proof of the pudding is in the eating"—was always applied to his theatre work.

From the time Brecht began directing in Munich in the twenties, until the end, he liked to have people around him when he directed. He asked everyone he trusted to come to rehearsal and constantly asked their opinions; he controlled his work through their reactions. If the fifties, his productions were always team-work, and he constantly used all the people connected with a production—assistants, designer, musicians (Eisler was at many rehearsals). Brecht asked the Ensemble's technicians to attend dress rehearsals, and afterwards sought their opinions. I remember the last rehearsals of *Katzgraben* (a play by the contemporary East German novelist and playwright Erwin Strittmatter, which Brecht produced in 1953), to which Brecht had invited a group of children between 10 and 14. He spent two hours with them after rehearsal to find out what they understood and what not, trying to pin down the reasons. The discussion's result was a reworking of many scenes to achieve more clarity, a higher quality of "telling the story." Brecht believed strongly in the unspoiled and unprejudiced observation of children. They possessed the naïve and poetic quality of thought he felt so important for the theatre.

In the Ensemble, Brecht decided that the young directors should co-direct—two or even three of them as directors of the same standing. This worked well. The directors would arrive at a basic concept on which they could agree before going into rehearsal. But in actual rehearsal, beautiful things would come out of the tension between different minds working on the same problems—better solutions than any one of the directors could have arrived at on his own. In fact, many productions before and most productions after his death were directed this way. . . .

Brecht never cared how his actors worked. He didn't tell them to go home and do this or that, or to go behind the set and concentrate. He didn't give a damn about the mechanics they used, he just cared about results. Brecht respected actors and was extremely patient with them; he often used their suggestions. During breaks, he would listen sometimes to rather obvious nonsense from the actors, wanting them not to feel uncomfortable with him, wanting to gain their confidence in all matters. He himself could probably have become a great actor. He could be a marvelous clown; sometimes the actors would provoke him to demonstrate something, for the sheer joy of watching him. He did not prod the actors to ape what he had demonstrated, but rather would exaggerate enough so that while they saw exactly what he wanted, they were never tempted to copy him.

It is interesting to compare the way in which I saw Brecht direct actors with what's reported by Leon Feuchtwanger's wife (who was there) about his first directing. When Brecht was 24, and his play *Drums in the Night* was being rehearsed in Munich, the director found to his surprise that the young author was coming to rehearsals, interrupting him, yelling at the actors, and demonstrating how they should do things. Pretty soon Brecht had almost taken over the entire production, and the director—a mature man—was practically his assistant. As usual in the German theatre of that time, the rehearsal period was short, somewhat under three weeks, but by the last week the actors, some of whom were quite prominent, were trying very hard to do what Brecht wanted them to. Basically, he was attempting to wean them from the pompous, over-ambitious typical German manner of the time, to bring them back to a realistic treatment of the lines. Mrs. Feuchtwanger's report is of great interest: that very young man, who came to attend rehearsals of his first play, kept yelling at the actors that what they offered was shit. When I met him in his fifties, mellowed perhaps, but not the least weakened in his determination, he was still busy cleaning the stage (and all art) of the "sweet lies" which keep man from recognizing the world as it is.

Brecht tried to present in his theatre a real view of the world, no gold-plated images of false heroes, no "revealing" photos of rabbits, busy nibbling cabbage and humping their mates, of whatever sex. Doubt in man-made gods, doubt in man-made rules, doubt in whatever man is told to accept was proclaimed on his stage. And a profound insight into man's weakness and longing to conform, an insight, by the way, which was not without understanding, and even compassion.

Brecht used his theatre as a laboratory, to experiment with plays and players. Human behaviour, human attitudes, human weakness — everything was explored and investigated, to be exposed finally to a public which often enough refused to recognize its image in this very clear, but sometimes perhaps too well-framed, mirror. The realistic treatment of the lines, which Brecht demanded from his first hour in the theatre to the last, was more than a theatre-man's protest against the theatre's degraded conventions. For him, the stage was a model of the world—the world we all have to live in.

Few directors have been able to imitate Jerzy Grotowski, lacking the same opportunities, or not seeking them fiercely enough, or not having comparable skills. But Grotowski's work with actors, his experiments with the relationship of stage to audience, his use of theatre rituals, and his concentration on the essentials of performance rather than scenic elaboration, and, not least, his development of texts for performance have had great influence throughout the world, especially since the publication of his *Towards a Poor Theatre* (1968).

Barba had traveled from Italy to study and work with Grotowski and, soon after writing this tribute to his master, went on to found his own company, Odin Theatret, first in Oslo and then in Denmark.

With its unfamiliar references and descriptions of productions that few people living outside Europe have seen, Eugenio Barba's account of Grotowski is not easy to read, but it is packed full of practical information about this "laboratory" theatre, which sought, in Barba's words, "for new forms of theatrical magic, for new alphabets to be used by the actor-shaman." Barba's was the first extensive report on Grotowski to be published in the United States.

Director as Innovator and Author: Grotowski's Laboratory Theatre

Eugenio Barba

In 1959, in a small, provincial Polish town, Opole, a young director, accompanied by a young critic, opened a small theatre which from the very start had a specific character: a laboratory in which Jerzy Grotowski and Ludwik Flaszen experimented with actors and audiences. They were trying to build a new aesthetic for the theatre and thus to purify the art. Grotowski wished to create a modern secular ritual, knowing that primitive rituals are the first form of drama. Through their total participation, primitive men were liberated from accumulated unconscious material. The rituals were repetitions of archetypal acts, a collective confession which sealed the solidarity of the tribe. Often ritual was the only way to break a taboo. The shamans were the masters of these sacred ceremonies, in which every tribesman had a part to play. Some of the elements of primitive ritual are fascination, suggestion, psychic stimulation, magic words and signs, and acrobatics which compel the body to go beyond its natural, biological limitations.

It would have been difficult, of course, to revive these ceremonies in our day. New means had to be found to force the spectator into an active collaboration. Grotowski preserves the essence of primitive theatre by making the audience participate, but he leaves out the religious elements and substitutes secular "stimuli" for them. Grotowski uses archetypal images and actions to unleash his attack on the audience. He breaks through the defences of the spectator's mind and forces him to react to what is going on in the theatre.

The archetypes must be found in the play's text. And, in this context, *archetype* means symbol, myth, image, leitmotiv—something deeply rooted in a civilization's culture. It is a metaphor and model of the human condition. For example, Prometheus and the Sacrificial Lamb correspond to the archetype of the individual sacrificed for the community. Faustus, Tvardovski, and Einstein (in the imagination of the masses) correspond to the archetype of the shaman who has surrendered to the devil and in exchange has received a special knowledge of the universe. The essential task is to give life to an archetype through the staging of a play. It is what the poet Bronieski called "the expression by the voice and the body of the very substance of man's destiny."

Several examples from Grotowski's work will illustrate this.

The Ancestors by Mickiewicz has been treated as a ritual drama. The audience is a collective group participating in the action. Spectators and actors are scattered through the whole room. The actors speak to everyone who is there. They treat the audience as fellow actors and even invite them to become active participants. The last scene of the play tells the story of Gustav-Konrad who, from a Czarist jail, rebels against the established order. He is the rebel with whom Poland, torn and conquered, identifies. Ordinarily this scene is presented as a metaphysical revolt and played with great pathos. In the Theatre Laboratory it demonstrates the naïveté of the individual who believes himself to be a saviour. The long soliloquy has been changed into the Stations of the Cross. Gustav-Konrad moves among the spectators. On his back he carries a broom, as Christ carried his cross. His grief is genuine and his belief in his mission sincere. But his naïve reactions are shown to be those of a child who is not aware of his limitations. Here the director used a specific dialectic: entertainment versus ritual, Christ versus Don Quixote. The meaning of the production becomes clear in this final scene, where the individual revolt aimed at effecting a radical change is shown as hopeless.

Kordian, by Slovacki, is another example of Grotowski's methods.

It is a Polish classic, as well known to Poles as Peer Gynt is to Norwegians. It takes place in the divided Poland of the nineteenth century. A young aristocrat, Kordian, wants to sacrifice himself for his country and free it from Russian rule. An attempt against the Czar's life fails and, after being committed to a lunatic asylum, Kordian is judged sane and condemned to death. Grotowski considers the scene in the hospital the key to the play. Hence, the entire play is set in the hospital. All of Kordian's experiences, the people he meets, the plots he organizes, the women he loves, are presented as hallucinations. An evil doctor who turns into the Pope, then the Czar, and finally an old sailor, brings about the hallucinatory crises. In the original text, Kordian recites a solemn soliloquy on the top of Mont Blanc. There he offers his blood to Poland and Europe. In Grotowski's production, the doctor takes a blood sample: dialectic of derision and apotheosis. The sufferings of Kordian are real, but the reasons for his suffering are imaginary. His sacrifice is noble, but naïve.

"It is not the first time that our Laboratory presented a heroic personality obsessed with the idea of saving mankind," said Flaszen. "The director analyzed the meaning of an individual act in an era where collective action and organization are the guarantees of success. Today, the man who tries to save the world alone is either a child or a madman, and I am not sure that in our world he could even claim the charm of Don Quixote."

Or, as Grotowski said:

> No rule is sacred, not even the rule that a single archetype must be represented. Ordinarily there are several archetypes in a text. They branch out and intermingle. One is chosen as the pivot of a play. But there are other possibilities. One could, for example, present a set of archetypes all of which would have the same value in the play. It is by means of the archetype that the dialectic of derision and apotheosis attacks a system of taboos, conventions, and accepted values. In this way, each production has a "multiface mirror" effect. All the facets of the archetype are successively destroyed; new taboos rise from the destruction and are, in turn, destroyed.

Five years of work and experimentation have brought success to the theatre. The point is no longer to present convincing characters, but to use the text as a catalyst setting off a violent reaction in the spectator. "Not to show the world as separated from the spectator, but, within the limits of the theatre, to create with him a new world." The main problem of the Laboratory was to find new means of expression. "Many people are surprised that our productions have nothing in common with literary theatre," Grotowski said.

> Faithful recitation of the text and illustration of the author's ideas are the goals of the traditional theatre. We, on the contrary, believe in the value of a theatre that some have called "autonomous." For us the text is only one of the play's elements, though not the least important. The "peripe-

tia" of the plays (as we do them) do not correspond to the text. They are expressed through purely theatrical means. The director takes liberties with the text. He cuts, he transposes. But he never indulges in personal interpolation. He lovingly preserves the charm of the words and watches carefully to see that they are spoken. The text is artificial and composed, but it is the author's text.

This free treatment of the text is the first decisive step in liberating the theatre from literary servitude. The director uses the playwright's text as the painter uses landscape motifs and as the poet uses semantic material accumulated by his civilization. As a text undergoes transpositions and scoring, it acquires new interpretive possibilities. It becomes the experimental ground on which the creative director works. Of course, the reborn text has only limited powers if it is not supported by a completely new acting technique.

Grotowski begins with the assumption that "everything which is art is artificial." Pushing this to its extreme expression, he has come up with the following:

> *No technique is sacred.* Any means of expression is permitted, provided that:
>
> 1. It is functional, justified by the logic of the production. Walking on one's feet demands the same justification as walking on one's hands. The logic of life cannot be substituted for the logic of art.
> 2. It has been deliberately chosen. It can no longer be changed, except in certain scenes where limited improvisation is permitted.
> 3. It is "built," composed. Theatrical techniques form a structure whose parts cannot be altered.

We are especially interested in an aspect of acting which has seldom been studied: the association of the gesture and intonation with a definite image. For example, the actor stops in the middle of a race and takes the stance of a cavalry soldier charging, as in the old popular drawings. This method of acting evokes by association images deeply rooted in the collective imagination.

According to Grotowski, there are three kinds of actors. First, there is the "elementary actor," as in the academic theatre. Then there is the "artificial actor"—one who composes and builds a structure of vocal and physical stage effects. Thirdly, there is the "archetypal actor"—that is, an artificial actor who can enlarge on the images taken from the collective unconscious. Grotowski trains this third type of actor. In developing his actors, Grotowski instills in them certain principles which are characteristic of the Theatre Laboratory:

> *The deficiencies of the actor are used, not hidden.* An actor's handicaps are as important as his qualities. An old actor can play Romeo if he emphasizes his limitations. That is, if he situates his part within a definite composition. The part then becomes that of Romeo in his old age reminiscing with Juliet.
>
> *Costumes and props are the actors' partners or they are "artificial extensions of the actor."* The actor gives life to the prop by treating it as a living thing.

It is friendly or hostile to him. The "partner" may be a costume—in that case there is a contrast between the two: the actor is young and handsome and the costume is ugly: or the situation is poetic and the costume is vulgar and coarse. When used as extensions of the actor, costumes and props accentuate the gestures by inhibiting them. For example, a sleeveless costume prevents the actor from using his arms. In any case, the accessories must not be used as ornaments. Their only function is to increase the actor's power of expression. In Kordian, for example, the hospital beds are used as acrobatic parallel bars.

Each character is depicted most purely by vocal or physical effects. The actor gives concrete expression to his desires, passions, thoughts, etc., by a physical action (gymnastics, acrobatics, or pantomime) or a vocal action (incantation, production of associated sounds, etc.). To make the effect properly suggestive, it must be done in a trance (concentrating all the physical energies). To achieve communication, it must be a sign which awakens associations buried in the audience's unconscious. The sign must be a revelation which starts a train of reactions and brings to consciousness latent feelings linked to individual or collective experiences. These experiences will be related to the culture, history, and folklore of the country.

There must be direct contact between the actors and audience. There is no stage. The actor speaks directly to the spectator, touches him, is around him all the times, startles him by frequent surprise effects. There is individual contact between one actor and the whole audience and there is collective contact between a team of actors and the audience. There are several forms of collective contact. In Byron's *Cain* the spectators are descendants of Cain. They are present but remote and difficult to approach. In Kalidasa's *Sakountala*, they are just a crowd of monks and courtiers. In Mickiewicz's *The Ancestors*, they are made to participate in the crop and harvest ritual. An actor becomes the Chorus Leader and the audience the Chorus. In Kordian the spectators are patients in the asylum; as such they are the doctor's enemies. In Wyspianski's *Akropolis* they are completely ignored, because they represent the living while the actors are ghosts. The actors speak while gliding between the spectators, but there can be no contact.

Theatrical magic consists in doing publicly that which is considered impossible. For example, the actor transforms himself into another man in full view of everyone. Or else he becomes an animal or an object. Acrobatics liberate the actor from the laws of gravity.

Makeup is unnecessary. Makeup does not accentuate the physical characteristics of the actors. The actor can change the expression on his face through control of facial muscles. Lighting, sweat, and breathing transform his muscles into a mask.

The spectator's unconscious is deliberately attacked. The actor does not give a visual representation of the archetype—this would be familiar and banal. Through his techniques he evokes and attacks a collective image. In the improvisation in *The Ancestors*, Gustav-Konrad does not look like Christ and he does not carry a cross. But with his ridiculous broom and quixotic outbursts he collides with the popular representation of Christ: hence the shock value. A faithful reconstruction of either Gustav-Konrad or Christ would have been familiar and boring.

Figure S3.1　The use of space for *Kordian*. As in the circus, there is much simultaneous action. The black figures are the actors.

The artificiality which Grotowski strives for must stem from reality, from the organic necessity of the movement or the intentions. Deformation must have a value as form, or else everything becomes a frivolous puzzle or, even worse, pathology. Artificiality is tied to life by an unbreakable umbilical cord. A few examples will help to show what is meant:

Every gesture must be composed. A short series of motions is a micro-pantomime which must illuminate the character. There can be no complication for its own sake. The actor must be able to shift the spectator's attention from the visual to the auditory, from the auditory to the visual, from one part of the body to the other, etc. This is the skill of magicians.

There must be theatrical contrast. This can be between any two elements: music and the actor, the actor and the text, actor and costume, two or more parts of the body (the hands say yes, the legs say no), etc.

Parts are exchanged during performance. Romeo becomes Juliet and Juliet becomes Romeo.

The actor metamorphoses. An actress is a secretary, then a mistress, then the boss, then a telephone, typewriter, table, sofa, etc. This was done in Mayakovski's *Mystère-Bouffe.*

Characters are built on several levels. A doctor is in fact the devil who becomes the Pope, then the Czar, and then an old sailor (*Kordian*).

Figure S3.2 The use of space for *Faustus*. The spectators are Faustus' guests. The acting takes place on the banquet table.

Styles change rapidly. The same scene is played by the same actor in artificial, naturalistic, pantominimic, improvisational, and other styles.

Physiological manifestations are used. In the improvisation of *The Ancestors*, for example, Gustav-Konrad is exhausted and drips with sweat. He does not try to hide it. His gestures suggest that it is the blood that Christ sweated.

The word is more than a means of intellectual communication. Its pure sound is used to bring spontaneous associations to the spectator's mind (incantation).

Each day the actors work their way through a series of exercises:

1. Diction, vocal work, artificial pronunciation (incantation). They shift from one timbre to another, chant, whisper. These exercises are always accompanied by breathing exercises. The secret of good diction is breathing. The experiments at the Laboratory investigated the part played by the brain in the formation of sound; the importance of the throat muscles for an appropriate opening of the larynx; how to determine the proper pauses for a specific role; harmony between breathing and the rhythm of a sentence; breathing as a dramatic effect (where it is abdomen and chest; usually only the abdomen is considered necessary); simultaneous use of the cranial and thoracic sounding boards; loss of voice as a result of psychological problems or faulty breathing.

2. Plastic motion following the Delsarte method and others. Simultaneous activity of different parts of the body, each at a different rhythm (the arms move fast, the legs slowly, the actors speak at different speeds); muscle control; instant relaxation of the muscles not engaged in motion (Hatha-Yoga is used).
3. Study of mime, both artificial and naturalistic.

This training results in a decidedly anti-naturalistic style in which rhythm and dynamism are as strictly fixed as in a musical score. The actor must be highly skilled and rigorously trained to control a technique which governs each gesture, each breath, each voice tone, and which uses acrobatics and gymnastics. The actor must provoke and fascinate the audience. To do so he must play his score correctly—but in a trance of concentration—while deliberately attempting to subjugate the spectator. As a shaman, he must create a magic action and prod the spectator into participation. He must force the audience to drop its social mask and face a world in which old values are destroyed without offering in their place any metaphysical solutions.

A struggle therefore ensues between performer and spectator. The one tries to fascinate the other and overcome all defences; the other fights against the spell of gestures and words, grasping at old logic and seeking shelter in a social shell. According to Grotowski, the director shapes the two groups, actors and spectators. They both must become aware of being part of the ritual-spectacle. It is this very awareness that distinguishes theatre from film. The future of the theatre depends upon this close contact between spectator and actor, which makes possible an act of collective introspection. Of course, putting the audience on stage (there is no "stage," but the action takes place in the space where the audience sits) presents problems. A new theatre architecture is needed. From the moment when Grotowski eliminated the stage, he was involved in architectural problems. A young architect, Jerzy Gurawski, has joined the company to help with these investigations.

The Theatre Laboratory rejects the eclecticism which has cancerously eaten away at the modern theatre. It is foolish to try to "modernize" the theatre by using electronic music, abstract settings, and clownish makeup. These are only superficial copies of what an audience can see at a concert, art exhibit, or circus. These elements are not essential to the theatre, which needs only the physical and vocal expressions of the actors. Theatricality could be defined as a deformation and/or reformation of life with its own autonomous aesthetic. Movies and television have taken over the social function of the theatre and the only way for the theatre to survive is for it to exploit its unique characteristic: the direct contact between actor and audience. The actor, each night, faces the live critical audience; he recites his part *at* a public eager to note his slightest mistake. Every night he must find new ways to fascinate and control the audience; and every night it is a different audience challenging him. The Theatre Laboratory is looking for new forms of theatrical magic, for new alphabets to be used by the actor-shaman. Much is written, but little is done because directors and actors must make money. What madman would dare finance an experiment so eccentric, so shocking by its aggressiveness, and

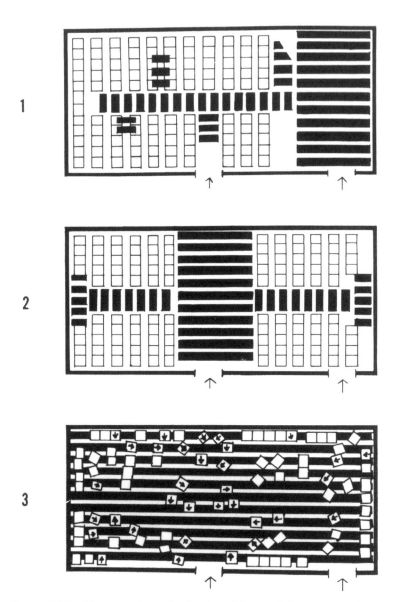

Figure S3.3   The space dynamics for three Theatre Laboratory productions. The areas in black represent those places where the action takes place. The productions were Byron's *Cain*, Kalidasa's *Sakountala*, and Mickiewicz's *The Ancestors*.

demanding so much skill from its actors? The Polish government has understood the necessity and has proven its goodwill by supporting Grotowski's experiments. Will others follow suit in other countries?

Reprinted by permission of the author, from Eugenio Barba, "Theatre Laboratory 13 Rzedow," ed. and trans. Simone Sanzenbach, *Tulane Drama Review* 9, no. 3 (1965): 153-65. Copyright © 1965 by Tulane Drama Review.

When she published the following account of her working methods, Anne Bogart had been a director for nearly twenty years, working in regional theatres across the United States and in New York City, at festivals in America, Europe, and Japan, and in small experimental theatres both with her own companies and as guest director. She is well acquainted with European master directors and with Suzuki Tadashi in Japan, but her own work is centered in the United States where she is a leading figure among a later generation. She has served as president of Theatre Communications Group, which is based in New York.

From "Terror, Disorientation and Difficulty"

Anne Bogart

Every time I begin work on a new production I feel as though I am out of my league; that I know nothing and have no notion how to begin and I'm sure that someone else should be doing my job, someone assured, who knows what to do, someone who is really a professional. I feel unbalanced, uncomfortable and out of place. I feel like a sham. I usually find a way to make it through the table work on the production, where the necessary discussions, analysis and readings happen, but then always the dreaded moment arrives when it is time to put something onto the stage. How can anything be right, true or appropriate? I desperately try to imagine some excuse for doing something else, for procrastinating further. And when we do begin work on the stage, everything we set out to do feels artificial, arbitrary and affected. I'm sure that the actors think that I am out of my mind. Every time the dramaturg steps into the rehearsal hall I feel that what I am doing with the actors reflects none of our dramaturgical discussions. I feel unsophisticated and superficial. Fortunately after a stint with this dance of the absurd, I start to notice that the actors are beginning to transform the idiotic staging into something I can get enthused about and respond to.

I have spoken with a number of theatre directors and found that I am not alone in this sensation of being out of my league at the beginning of rehearsals. We all tremble before the impossibility of beginning. It is important to remember that a director's work, as with any artist, is intuitive. Many young directors make the big mistake of assuming that directing is about being in control, telling others what to do, having ideas and getting what you ask for. I do not believe that these abilities are the qualities that make a good director or exciting theatre. Directing is about feeling, about being in the room with other people—with actors, with designers, with an audience—about having a feel for time and space, about breathing and responding fully to the situation at hand, being able to plunge and encourage a plunge into the unknown at the right moment. David Salle, the painter, said in an interview, "I feel that the only thing that really matters in art and life is to go against the tidal wave of literalism and literal-mindedness to insist on and *live* the life of the imagination. A painting has to be the experience instead of pointing to it. I want to have and give *access to feeling*. That is the riskiest and only important way to connect art to the world—to make it alive. The rest is just current events."

I know that I cannot sit down when work is happening on the stage. If I sit, a deadness sets in. I direct from impulses in my body responding to the stage, the actors' bodies, their inclinations. If I sit down I lose my spontaneity, my connection to myself and to the stage, to the actors. I try to soften my eyes, that is, not to look too hard or with too much desire, because vision is dominant and eviscerates the other senses.

When I am lost in rehearsal, when I am stymied and have no idea what to do next or how to solve a problem, I know that this is the moment to make a leap. Because directing is intuitive, it involves walking with trembling into the unknown. Right there, in that moment, in that rehearsal, I have to say, "I know!" and start walking toward the stage. During the crisis of the walk, something *must* happen: some insight, some idea. The sensation of this walk to the stage, to the actors, feels like falling into a treacherous abyss. The walk creates a crisis in which innovation must happen, invention must transpire. I create the crisis in rehearsal to get out of my own way. I create despite myself and my limitations and my hesitancy. In unbalance and falling lie the potential of creation. When things start to fall apart in rehearsal, the possibility of creation exists. What we have planned before, what we have in our mind in that moment is not interesting. Rollo May wrote that all artists and scientists, when they are doing their best work, feel as though they are not doing the creating, they feel as though they are being spoken through. How do we get out of our own way in rehearsal?

The vitality, or energy, in any given work is a reflection of the artist's courageousness in the light of her own terror. For me, the essential aspect of a work is its vitality. The creation of art is not an escape from life but a penetration into it. I recently saw a retrospective of Martha Graham's early dance works. I was astonished that pieces such as *Primitive Mysteries* are now fifty years old and *still* risky and exposed. Graham once wrote to Agnes DeMille:

> There is a vitality, a life-force, a quickening that is translated through you into action, and because there is only one of you in all time, this expression is unique. And if you block it, it will never exist through any other medium and be lost. The world will not have it. It is not your business to determine how good it is; nor how valuable it is; nor how it compares with other expressions. It is your business to keep it yours clearly and directly, to keep the channel open. You do not have to believe in yourself or your work. You have to keep open and aware directly to the urges that motivate you.

Vitality in art is a result of articulation, energy and differentiation. All great art is differentiated art. Our awareness of the differences between things around us touches upon the source of our terror. It is more comfortable to feel similarities, yet we need to accept the terror of differences in order to create vital art. The terrible truth is that no two people are alike, no two snowflakes are alike, no two moments are alike. Physicists now say that nothing touches, nothing in the universe has contact; there is only movement and change. This is a terrifying notion given our attempt to make contact with one another. The ability to see, experience and articulate the differences between things is differentiation. Great artworks incorporate this notion of differentiation in varying ways. An exceptional painting is one in which, for example, one color is highly and visibly differentiated from another, in which we see the differences in textures, shapes, spatial relationships. What made Glenn Gould a brilliant musician was his openness to high differentiation in music, which created the ecstatic intensity of his playing. In the best theatre, moments are highly differentiated. An actor's craft lies in the differentiation of one moment from the next. A great actor seems dangerous, unpredictable, full of life and differentiation.

> Reprinted by permission of Smith and Kraus, Inc., from *Anne Bogart: Viewpoints*, ed. Michael Dixon and Joel A. Smith (1995). Copyright © 1995 by Actors Theatre of Louisville.

The following extract from a feature article on Jo Anne Akalaitis quotes the director's own words about her approach to staging classic texts and her determination to create a theatre that is "real" for her own times. In two ways it reflects on important topics raised in the first part of this book: the story of the Mabou Mines illustrates how new theatres can be started (see Chapter 7, "Producers and Artistic Directors"); and the dispute with Samuel Beckett questions the nature of a director's responsibility to an author (see Chapter 7, "The Script").

A Director and a Text

Simi Horwitz

As a founding member of Mabou Mines, an artistic collective, Akalaitis has her roots firmly grounded in the counterculture's theater movement. Mabou Mines' signatures emphasizes the visuals and merges movement and music to create a total theater experience. In fact, in its early years, the company performed in universities' art and music departments, and museums. Akalaitis says it was way ahead of its time.

"I don't think we had a particular mission," she adds. "There was tremendous diversity in the company and it was an interesting dynamic. But what we all wanted was to control the theater we were part of. Operationally we had a socialistic structure. All decisions were made by consensus and everyone got the same salary. There was no competition."

Akalaitis resigned from the company last spring after working with the group for more than twenty years. Throughout the two decades she also accepted freelance directing assignments at the Guthrie, Goodman, and American Repertory Theater, among others. Many of her productions aroused debate. Her own controversial hallmark is a striking visual sense that freely combines a potpourri of theatrical styles and historical eras.

"I'm interested in creating a world, a look, a sense of place. I'm not interested in sets, costumes, or lighting. That's unimportant. Most Shakespearean productions have no idea about place. The look is modernist, minimalist, or classical. It's dull to me."

No one can accuse Akalaitis of dull work. Even her detractors acknowledge the memorable elements in her anti-literal vision. In *Henry IV*, Part I: a gargoyled fountain spewing forth blood to foreshadow the upcoming war; or Poins, a member of Falstaff's gang, played by a Hispanic clutching a TV set (are we to assume it's stolen?) right out of a sitcom about El Barrio life; or, most vivid, a bawdy tavern scene staged to suggest an eighteenth-century mental institution inspired by Peter Brook's *Marat Sade*, and painted by Breughel.

"Shakespeare belongs to us. We can create any world we want to," says Akalaitis. "When Poins comes in and sees Falstaff surrounded by crushed beer cans—I'm not saying it's 1991, but rather the morning after. We respond to the world we're familiar with. I place *Henry IV* in a historical frame, but contemporary touches make the play more real." Akalaitis pauses. "We know we're in a theater. Art is invention."

Invention has landed Akalaitis in hot water, and not just with the critics. Her production of *Endgame* at the American Repertory Theater in Cambridge some years ago enraged playwright Samuel Beckett who tried unsuccessfully to put an end to the production. Among other things, he objected to her setting the piece in a subway station, instead of the bare room he explicitly describes in his stage directions. He also objected to Philip Glass's music—he wanted none. The black actor Akalaitis cast as the son also angered him on the ground that it raised issues of miscegenation.

"Directors channel a work through their own artistic vision," Akalaitis responds. "What I was doing was no different from what other directors do. Simply because a stage direction says, 'a blonde actress on a purple sofa'—does that mean a director is obliged to stage the scene that way!"

"Frankly, I was disappointed the whole thing didn't go to court," Akalaitis continues. "But it was too expensive on all sides. The lawyers finally came to an agreement: Beckett's name would be taken off all ads and the program. He wrote a statement that was published in the program. Robert Brustein [artistic director] responded—also in the program. Unfortunately, all of it became a filter through which the audience saw the play."

Akalaitis makes it clear that she still believes *Endgame* was one of the most thrilling theatrical projects she was ever involved in. "*Endgame* is a modern masterpiece," she says. "I don't think what we did was wild and wacky."

Reprinted from *Theater Week*, March 18, 1981, by permission of Simi Horwitz and the publishers. Copyright © 1981 by Theater Week.

Section

4

Scenography: Stages and Audiences

Theatre Projects Consultants, one of the world's leading theatre design consulting firms, has been responsible for over five hundred projects in thirty-six countries around the world. In this specially written article the company's chairman sets out his view of the task of designing theatres at the end of the twentieth century. Richard Pilbrow is also a lighting designer and theatre producer.

The Magic of Theatre Design
Richard Pilbrow

Theatre is a magical place. Its mysteries have held their fascination for thousands of years. Despite the ever growing competition from cinema, radio, television, video, and who knows . . . virtual reality . . . generations of theatregoers have been captivated time and again. But what role does the design of the theatre space—the physical building that houses the live performance—have in the theatrical experience?

Theatre buildings are complex places. They contain a stage for the performers and a auditorium to seat the public in comfort and safety. Backstage is both a factory for the preparation of the show and a home for the actors. The auditorium is supported by foyer and lobbies, box office, and other facilities for the entertainment and hospitality of the audience.

There are many different types of theatre for different types of performances. Large opera or ballet houses, touring theatres for musicals, smaller theatres for drama stand alongside a wide variety of less formal venues for more pioneering performances. A concert hall is in fact a theatre specially built for classical music performance. There is also no absolute form for any of these theatre types. The most common is the end stage, which places the stage at one end of the theatre facing its audience, sometimes behind a proscenium arch; but other forms such as the arena stage place the stage in the middle of the audience, and the thrust stage is surrounded on three sides by the public.

Modern theatres usually employ scenery, lighting, and sound effects to create an environment around the actors. Some types of performance require sound amplification. Modern technology includes video and projection, and computers are often employed to control lighting, sound, and sometimes scenery. All this technology has to be housed in the stage and auditorium together with the necessary technical infrastructure. The unobtrusive integration of technology into the theatre space without adversely affecting the audience's enjoyment presents a challenge to the designer.

Finally theatre is always changing. Styles of production alter far more quickly than does the theatre building, which may last for decades or even several centuries. A fine theatre must allow the creative artists, directors, and designers sufficient freedom and flexibility to explore changing styles and fashions.

There was a boom in building theatres in early years of the twentieth century. Many theatres in New York, London, or the touring theatres in England and America date from this time. They are characterized by their often baroque decoration, multiple balconies, and enwrapping boxes on the side walls. But from the time of the depression until after the Second World War the world turned instead to the enormously popular cinema, and few new theatres were built. Those that were constructed were heavily influenced by movie house design. Side seats and wraparound balconies were inappropriate for viewing a flat cinema screen.

By the 1960s when the growth of regional theatre began a renewed demand for modern theatre buildings, only a few new theatres had been built in England or America for several generations. Furthermore most theatre people looked down upon the often cramped backstage working conditions of the older theatres and ignored their positive qualities. Architects planning new theatres sought to reinvent the form, overcoming the perceived limitations of the past, hoping to improve acoustics and to provide much better sight lines and more sophisticated technology.

Throughout an explosion of theatre building during the next twenty years, buildings indeed became more functional, but they often seemed to disappoint both performers and audiences. Few seemed to possess the character, or popularity with players and spectators, of theatres of the past. Even mighty efforts on such projects as the National Theatre of Great Britain proved problematic. Despite a brief conceived by the greatest figures in contemporary British theatre working with an outstanding architect, the complex proved hard for actors and directors to use; and hard for audiences to enjoy. Michael Conveney wrote in May 1994 of Tom Stoppard's *Arcadia* transferring to the Haymarket: "It benefits from being seen in a proper theatre, as opposed to the concrete mausoleum of the Lyttleton." In the United States few theatre people prefer the vast expanses of the Los Angeles Music Center or New York's Lincoln Center to the more homely and older theatres of Broadway. The recently despised heritage of our ancestor's theatres grows more charming in retrospect—or is it perhaps in actuality?

People have built theatres all through history. In the olden days we must assume that a theatre manager, actor or entrepreneur would hire an architect, explain what type of theatre he required, and expect the architect to get on with it. The promoter's technical staff would probably have assisted the architect to understand the particular needs of theatrical oil lighting or scenery rope and capstan rigging. (Sound was perhaps less technically daunting before the age of electronics!) The architect studied the well-established precedents of building a successful theatre or concert hall and got on with it. Architectural standards and approaches were usually clear. For example, Victorian or Georgian architectural standards were universally accepted by their contemporary societies.

There were outstanding theatre architects. Over the ages the Bibiena family in Germany and Italy; Inigo Jones, C. J. Phipps, and Frank Matcham in England; and J. B. McElfatrick, Herbert J. Krapp, and Thomas A. Lamb in the United States were masters at creating theatrical space. Most of them also became theatre specialists and were responsible for practices turning out a large number of theatre commissions.

Today few architects have the opportunity to practice on a number of theatre commissions. Indeed, Sir Denys Lasdun was selected for the National Theatre of Great Britain because of his theatrical "innocence" and lack of preconceived notions. Michael Hopkins (Glyndebourne) and Jorn Utzon (Sydney) were two architects both new to opera house design. Yet despite the involvement of famous architects, experienced in theatre or not, and despite the involvement of the wisest of theatrical minds, too many modern theatres lack some almost intangible quality.

The theatre consulting profession is a new one. Many people will be certain of the architect's contribution to a building, and many will be familiar with an acoustician's role, but comparatively few will know what on earth the theatre consultant actually does. There are "star" architects, even "star" acousticians; seldom does the theatre designer receive significant credit.

Initially theatre consultants were almost solely concerned with technical and programming issues. They came from a theatre background; some were lighting designers—used to dealing with most aspects of theatrical production—and were called in to explain to architects the practical need for box offices, lighting bridges, and dock doors.

It soon became obvious that this was not enough. There's little point in a fine technical installation in a theatre that fails to meet its first objective: the creation of an exciting and stimulating environment for lively theatre.

What is that special environment? Theatre is different from cinema. A movie proceeds irrespective of the audience's reaction. Alone among the storytelling media, theatre is alive. The actor is real and together in the same room with you, the audience. The audience's participation in the live event is crucial to its success. This quality of emotional involvement is critical. It is not enough to see. It is not enough to hear. Spectators must be emotionally connected, turned from a group of individuals into that singular animal, malevolent or benevolent: "the audience."

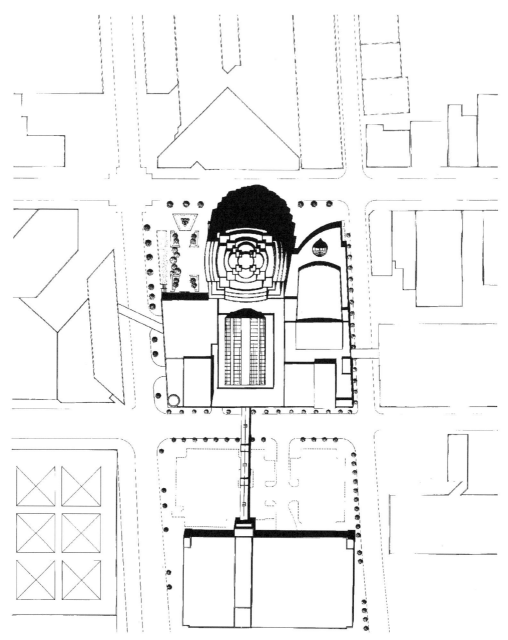

Figure S4.1   Site plan for the Belk and Booth Theatres, North Carolina Blumenthal Performing Arts Center. (Reproduced courtesy of Theatre Projects.)

That is the element missing in so many modern theatres: Emotion. Acoustics are only a part. Sight lines are only a part. The magic of turning individuals into a collective—the psychological imperative of enthusing emotional response—lies at the heart of successful theatre.

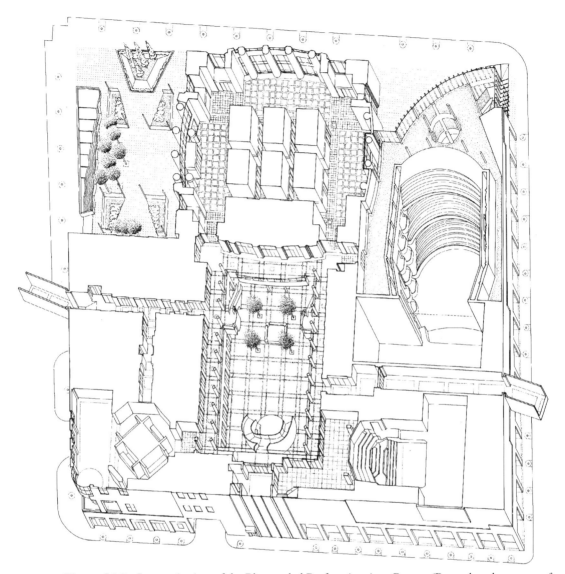

Figure S4.2 Isometric view of the Blumenthal Performing Arts Center. (Reproduced courtesy of Theatre Projects.)

Our ancestors built upon tradition. They knew what worked and built upon it. Only in the twentieth century has architecture tried to reinvent the wheel. Modern architecture stripped off the gilt and baroque decoration that had previously excited the imagination. Influenced by decades of movie palace architecture, theatre people led the move to get rid of "inefficient" side box seating and multiple balconies. This was often justified as a search for more social equality. The result was the barren, characterless, cinema-style fan-shaped "auditoria" with towering blank side walls, that have passed as theatres for decades.

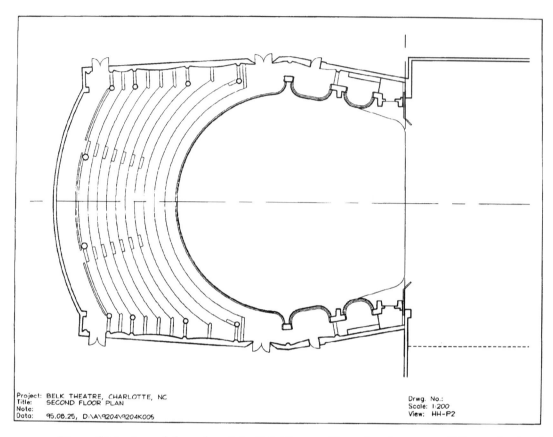

Project: BELK THEATRE, CHARLOTTE, NC
Title: SECOND FLOOR PLAN
Note:
Data: 95.08.25, D:\A\9204\9204K005

Drwg. No.:
Scale: 1:200
View: HH-P2

Figure S4.3   Second-floor plan of the Belk Theatre. (Reproduced courtesy of Theatre Projects.)

The wheel has turned. A very few architects sensed that all was not well. Some theatre consultants extended their work beyond technology into the design of the theatre space itself seeking to find a way to assist the architects' rediscovery of the excitements in "real" theatre.

In 1981 I gave an address at the United States Institute of Theatre Technicians' annual conference. My theme was "Back to the Future," suggesting that we must learn from theatres of the past in building for tomorrow. It was received with polite disbelief. Thirteen years and dozens of projects later, there are almost no cinema-style theatres left on the drawing boards. Everywhere balconies and boxes are back in vogue, and architects and designers are reinventing a modern form of three-dimensional theatre, a theatre that tries to place the performer at the heart of a tightly woven web of participating humanity that creates a place of meeting, a place where lively audiences meet alive performers, a place where emotion and excitement can explode.

The task of the theatre designer is to create space for lively performance. To do this we must take onboard the paraphernalia of performance technology and acoustics. We must study in detail the performing arts in action; we must be aware of other spaces past and present; we

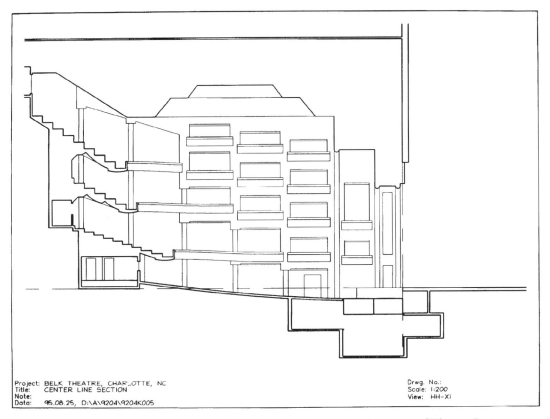

Figure S4.4   Center line section of the Belk Theatre. (Reproduced courtesy of Theatre Projects.)

must strive to capture the dynamics of lively communication—what it is to realize the magic of live theatre. The extraordinary subtleties of the relationships between both stage and audience, and, as importantly, among all the members of that audience with each other, must be made evident. Only when those dynamic relationships are clear can the architect add his vital vision of architectural "place" to create great and theatrical space.

At Theatre Projects we're proud that our design for the National Theatre's third space, the Cottesloe, has made that space the epitome of flexible experimental theatre in the world. We're proud of our role in creating the Royal Exchange Theatre, Manchester, the Tricycle Theatre in London or Steppenwolf in Chicago, and many other modern three-dimensional theatres of exceptional intimacy and theatrical excitement. We're proud of our theatres at Derngate, Northampton and Cerritos, California, which like their smaller kin, the many courtyard theatres now around the world, combine classic three-dimensional intimacy with twentieth-century flexibility of staging opportunity. The enormous popularity of the "megamusical" has rekindled a need for large-scale theatres. These, too, can benefit from combining the opportunity for spectacle onstage with as intimate an auditorium

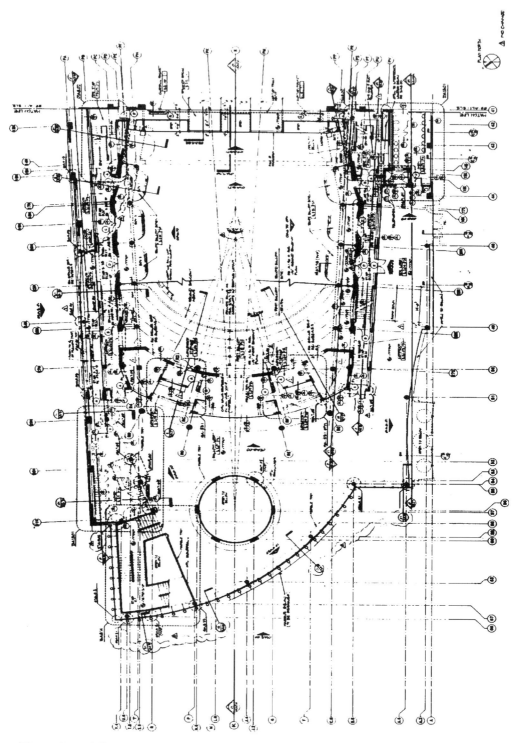

Figure S4.5   The complications of theatre planning: working plans (greatly reduced in scale) for level 2 of the Belk Theatre. (Reproduced courtesy of Theatre Projects.)

as possible, as personified by the Ohio Center for the Performing Arts in Cincinnati or the Charlotte North Carolina Center for the Performing Arts.

We're also proud that our design for an opera house for Michael Hopkins at Glyndebourne has been hailed by audiences, singers, and press as "thoroughly traditional." Only ten years ago such respect for tradition would have been most unlikely. The *Architectural Review* writes: "Intimacy has been achieved, apparently effortlessly." It actually was quite an effort: a road that we have been pursuing for nearly thirty years. It involved a rediscovery of the essence of theatre: a meeting place for people and a rediscovery of magic.

Lee Simonson was one of the designers who in the nineteen-twenties brought European innovations in set design (see Chapter 6, "Varieties of Stage Design") to the United States. His *The Stage Is Set* (New York, 1932), from which this account is taken, was widely read and is still influential.

The Ideas of Adolphe Appia

Lee Simonson

The Plastic Elements

The aesthetic problem of scenic design, as Appia made plain, is a plastic one. The designer's task is to relate forms in space, some of which are static, some of which are mobile. The stage itself is an enclosed space. Organization must be actually three-dimensional. Therefore the canons of pictorial art are valueless. The painted illusion of the third dimension, valid in the painted picture where it can evoke both space and mass, is immediately negated when it is set on a stage where the third dimension is real.

The plastic elements involved in scenic design, as Appia analysed them, are four: perpendicular painted scenery, the horizontal floor, the moving actor, and the lighted space in which they are confined. The aesthetic problem, as he pointed out, is a single one: How are these four elements to be combined so as to produce an indubitable unity? For, like the Duke of Saxe-Meiningen, he was aware that the plastic elements of a production remained irretrievably at odds if left to themselves. Looking at the stages about him he saw that the scene-painter of his day merely snipped his original picture into so many pieces which he stood about the stage, and then expected the actor to find his way among them as best he could. The painted back-drop was the only part of an ensemble of painted scenery that was not a ludicrous compromise. Naturally the scene-painter was interested, being a painter, in presenting as many stretches of unbroken canvas as possible. Their centre of interest was about midway between the top of the stage and stage floor at a point where, according to the line of sight of most of the audience, they attained their maximum pictorial effect. But the actor works on the stage floor at a point where painted decorations are least effective as painting. So long as the emphasis of stage setting is on painted decoration, the inanimate picture is no more than a coloured illustration into which the text, animated by the actor, is brought. The two collide, they never meet nor establish any interaction of the slightest dramatic value, whereas, in Appia's phrase, they should be fused.

"Living feet tread these boards and their every step makes us aware of how meaningless and inadequate our settings are." The better the scenery is as painting, the worse it is as a stage setting; the more completely it creates an illusion of the third dimension by the pictorial conventions of painting, the more completely an actually three-dimensional actor destroys that illusion by every movement he makes. "For no movement on the actor's part can be brought into vital relation with objects painted on a piece of canvas." Painted decorations are not only at odds with the actor but also with the light that illuminates them. "Light and vertical painted surfaces nullify rather than reinforce each other. . . . There is an irreconcilable conflict between these two scenic elements. For the perpendicular, painted flat in order to be seen, needs to be set so as to catch a maximum amount of light." The more brilliantly it is lighted, the more apparent the lack of unity between it and the actor becomes. "If the setting is so placed as to refract some of the light thrown on it its importance as a painted picture is diminished to that extent."

For Appia there was no possibility of compromise by keeping actors away from perspective back-drops where doors reached only to their elbows, or by warning them not to lean on flimsy canvas cut-outs down stage. He denied painted simulation of the third dimension a place in the theatre with a finality that gave his analysis the air of a revolutionary manifesto. He was the first to banish the scenic painter and his painted architecture from the modern stage. To Appia the actor was *massgebend*— the unit of measurement. Unity could be created only by relating every part of a setting to him. He was three-dimensional, therefore the entire setting would have to be made consistently three-dimensional. The stage setting could have no true aesthetic organization unless it was coherently plastic throughout. Appia's importance as a theorist is due to the consistency and the practicability of the methods he outlined for achieving this result.

One began to set a stage not in mid-air on hanging back-drops, but on the stage floor where the actor moved and worked. It should be broken up into levels, hummocks, slopes, and planes that supported and enhanced his movements, And these were again not to be isolated—a wooden platform draped with canvas here, a block or rock there, planted on a bare board floor, a "chaise-lounge made of grass mats." The stage floor was to be a completely fused, plastic unit. Appia in this connection thinks in terms of sculpture. In order to make a model of a stage floor as he described it one would have to use clay. He considered the entire space occupied by a stage setting as a sculpturesque unit. The solidity achieved by setting wings at right angles to each other to imitate the corner of a building seemed to him feebly mechanical. He conceived much freer stage compositions where the entire area could be modelled as a balance of asymmetrical, spatial forms, a composition in three dimensions, that merged imperceptibly with the confining planes that bounded the setting as a whole.

Appia expressed in dogmatic form much of what the Duke of Saxe-Meiningen had demonstrated pragmatically. But in promulgating his theory of a stage setting he completed its unification by insisting on the plasticity of light itself, which no one before him had conceived. He demonstrated in detail, both as a theorist and as a draftsman, how stage lighting could be used and controlled so as to establish a completely unified three-dimensional world on the stage. Appia distinguishes carefully between light that is empty, diffuse radiance, a medium in which things become visible, as fish do in a bowl of water, and concentrated light striking an object in a way that defines its essential form. Diffused light produces blank visibility, in which we recognize objects without emotion. But the light that is blocked by an object and casts shadows has a sculpturesque quality that by the vehemence of its definition, by the balance of light and shade, can carve an object before our eyes. It is capable of arousing us emotionally because it can so emphasize and accent forms as to give them new force and meaning. In Appia's theories, as well as in his drawings, the light which in paintings had already been called dramatic was for the first time brought into the theatre, where its dramatic values could be utilized. Chiaroscuro, so controlled as to reveal essential or significant form, with which painters had been preoccupied for three centuries, became, as Appia described it, an expressive medium for the scene-designer. The light that is important in the theatre, Appia declares, is the light that casts shadows. It alone defines and reveals. The unifying power of light creates the desired fusion that can make stage floor, scenery, and actor one.

Light is the most important plastic medium on the stage. . . . Without its unifying power our eyes would be able to perceive what objects were but not what they expressed. . . . What can give us this sublime unity which is capable of uplifting us? Light! . . . Light and light alone, quite apart from its subsidiary importance in illuminating a dark stage, has the greatest plastic power, for it is subject to a minimum of conventions and so is able to reveal vividly in its most expressive form the eternally fluctuating appearance of a phenomenal world.

The light and shade of Rembrandt, Piranesi, Daumier, and Meryon was finally brought into the theatre as an interpretive medium, not splashed on a back-drop, as romantic scene-painters had used it, but as an ambient medium actually filling space and possessing actual volume; it was an impalpable bond which fused the actor, wherever and however he moved, with everything around him. The plastic unity of the stage picture was made continuous.

If one looks at reproductions of stage settings before Appia—and the history of stage setting might almost be divided by B.A. as history in general is divided by B.C.—they are filled with even radiance; everything is of equal importance. The stage is like a photograph of a toy theatre; the actors might be cardboard dolls. In Appia's drawings for the

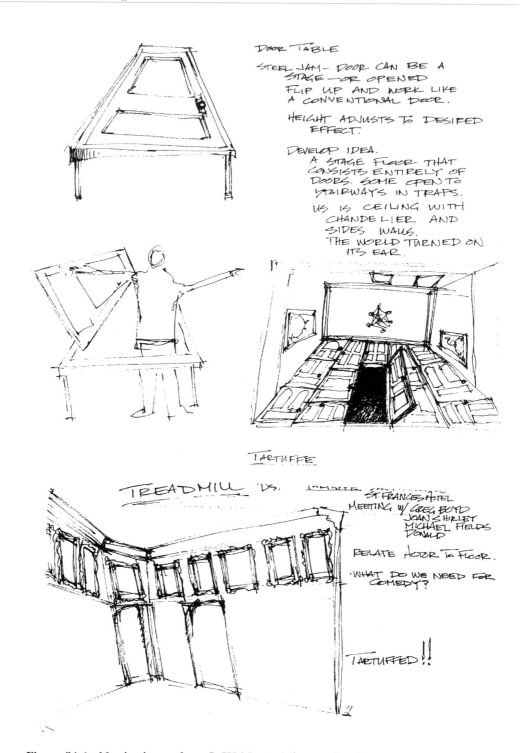

Figure S4.6   Notebook page from G. W. Mercier's design of Molière's *Tartuffe* at the Alley Theatre Houston, Texas. (All illustrations of *Tartuffe* photographed by G. W. Mercier, and reproduced by his courtesy.)

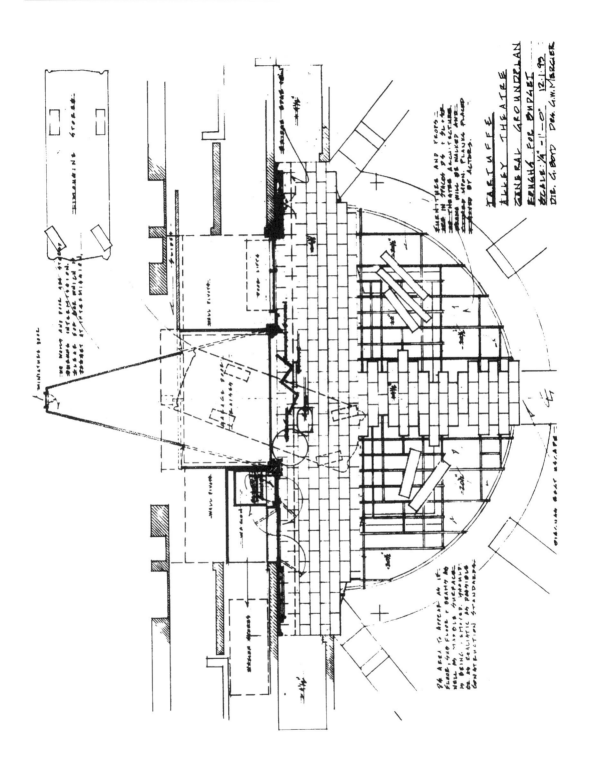

Figure S4.7 First stage plan for G. W. Mercier's design of *Tartuffe* at the Alley Theatre.

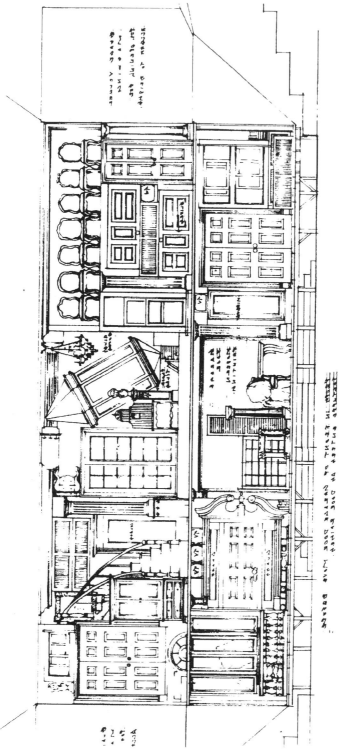

Figure S4.8 First elevation for G. W. Mercier's design of the set of *Tartuffe* at the Alley Theatre.

Figures D.1 and D.2 First and second models for *Tartuffe* at the Alley Theatre; G. W. Mercier, designer.

TARTUFFE
#1

MORMAN DISGUISE

Two CRISP WHITE
POLY/COTTON
SHIRT

BLK POLY TIE

BLK. POLY
SLACKS
(NO CUFFS)

PRACTICAL TIE
SHOES

TARTUFFE
#3 I, ii

HIGH STYLE
SUIT
DOUBLE BREASTED

FLASHY TIE

Figure D.3 Costumes for Tartuffe in *Tartuffe* at the Alley Theatre; G. W. Mercier, designer.

Figure D.4 Costumes for Damis and Cleante in *Tartuffe* at the Alley Theatre; G. W. Mercier, designer.

Figure D.5 The completed set for *Tartuffe* at the Alley Theatre, Houston; G. W. Mercier, designer.

Opened February 1994
Tartuffe by Moliere
Alley Theatre, Houston TX
directed by Gregory Boyd, Michael Fields, Donald Forrest, Joan Schirlee
set and costume design by G.W. Mercier

Photos came out pretty good. I sent them with the negatives so you can choose what suits your purpose; if you like them. One is a 1/4" rough paper model (11-1/4"w. x 5-1/4"h.)which I used to communicate with the director and work out proportions. The second is a 1" scale painted model (45"w. x 20"h.) that was for paint information and the technical director to understand the design, as well as the actors in rehearsal. I decided to make an inch scale finished model because the set has so many working parts (all the doors and windows function, walls slide, etc.) and I wanted to use some dollhouse furniture and architectural pieces as I wanted the actual set to have this slightly chunky quality. I built the models in New York in my studio and they were shipped to the Alley Theatre in Houston, Texas.

This was an interesting show. I was approached by the Artistic Director of the Alley, Gregory Boyd, who had seen several productions that I designed, to design an original adaptation of the Moliere script, yet to be written. The writing and directing collaborators were the Dell'arte Players (A contemporary comedia troupe that toured original work and was based in an old theatre in Blue Lake, California). After my agent negotiated the contract, I flew to Houston to see the theatre. A few weeks later I flew to San Francisco to meet with the four writer/directors. The theatre rented us a work suite and rooms and we had four days of intensive meetings. I sketched ideas, which they responded to and by the fourth day, we had a direction. The script was then written to accommodate the visual goals. It was to be a very physical production and the set needed to embody obsticals as well as provide an informative environment of place and time. The clothes needed to support the comedy as well as withstand the physical stress. We determined to set the show in Texas and Tartuffe as a new age mystic of the "Mens Movement" preyed on the very wealthy and searching new rich. Sort of Ross Perot meets Robert Bly.

I was interested in the excess that people with new money often partake--conspicuous consumption. The house became a pile of expensive and beautiful things, architecture, furniture, art and sculpture. Doors and windows rarely functioned normally, they flipped, spun, opened from the top or bottom, the central painting was a garage door that opened exposing Tartuffe's lair, filled with his plunder--money, art and expensive things.

Each member of the cast was an extreme character. Argon was modeled after Colin Powell, Elmire a billionairess socialite, Madame Parnelle a female impersonator, CIA agents, etc. They were all heightened characters, in a contemporary comedic tradition without being cartoons.

Figure S4.9 G. W. Mercier's notes concerning designing *Tartuffe* and the illustrations reproduced in this book.

first time the stage is a microcosm of the world. It seems to move from "morn to noon, from noon to dewy eve," and on through all the watches of the night. And the actors in it seem living beings who move as we do from sunlight or moonlight into shadow. Beneath their feet there is not a floor but the surface of the earth, over their heads not a back-drop but the heavens as we see them, enveloping and remote. There is depth here that seems hewn and distance that recedes infinitely further than the painted lines converging at a mathematical vanishing point. In attacking the conventions of scene-painting Appia created an ultimate convention. For the transparent trickery of painter illusions of form he substituted the illusion of space built up by the transfiguration that light, directed and controlled, can give to the transient structures of the stage-carpenter. The third dimension, incessant preoccupation of the Occidental mind for four centuries, defined by metaphysicians, explored by scientists, simulated by painters, was re-created in terms of the theatre, made actual. The stage more completely than ever before became a world that we could vicariously inhabit; stage settings acquired a new reality. The light in Appia's first drawings, if one compares them to the designs that had preceded his, seems the night and morning of a First Day.

Reprinted from *The Stage Is Set* (New York: Routledge, 1932), by permission of the publisher.

Current design is illustrated here by models, drawings, and stage sets by Marjorie Bradley Kellogg and G. W.Mercier. In these the task was to provide stage settings for specific texts. Side by side with this practice a new form of design has been developed for which designer and director, and often author, are one and the same person and everything is geared to the actors' work in rehearsal. Richard Foreman is a leading exponent of this form of theatre, and here, in an extract from his *Unbalancing Acts* he explains the nature of his involvement.

Scenery that "Is in Many Places at Once"
Richard Foreman

As the texts of my plays became increasingly fragmented in order to echo the truth of psychic life, I wanted the scenery to do the same. I wanted it to make reference to the various locales suggested on the page, but without my having to make set changes every three minutes. I wanted scenery that was in many places at once, like the mind. The spectator should ask: Am I in a living room, or in a bizarre factory where art (this play) is being produced? In all of my sets, I try to create a space which suggests something is being manufactured; it could be a laboratory, a factory, a meditation chamber, or a kitchen. The sets are not dreamy, poetic landscapes, but they become evocative because they give concrete form to the tension between different levels of reality. How can you be in something that seems like a factory and yet, at the same time, seems to be like your living room? Where are you really? It should make your head spin, because it echoes your real situation in life: you are in your living room relaxing, but at the same time your living room is a kind of factory where, even when relaxing, you are in the process of manufacturing your life. Moreover, the actions performed on the set should echo this same kind of tension. For instance, the performer's elbows might be askew, as if at work making something in a factory, while the rest of his body is balanced in a pseudo-relaxed position, semiprone against a pillow, which suggests the couch he rests upon in his living room.

From *Unbalancing Acts* (New York: Theatre Communications Group, 1992, p. 62).

Technology has brought a new kind of designer to theatre, one who creates a very variable, pervasive, and powerful "world" of sound in which a play may be performed and by means of which the audience's attention can be caught and controlled. In the September 1994 John Istel described the resultant "Sonic Boom" in *American Theatre*.

Sound Design: "American Theatre Gets Wired"
John Istel

The irony's rich. A generation of theatre artists creating cacophonous "noises off"—the whir of helicopters circling, the earthquaking entrance of angels, the ripple of history wrenching open—has quietly tweaked the craft of sound design into an art form. And no one has sounded so much as a fanfare, flourish or alarum.

The most visible venue for the recognition of American theatrical accomplishment—the Tony awards—despite repeated requests, refuses to add a category for sound design. Nevertheless, in the past twenty-odd years since *Hair* and *Jesus Christ Superstar* introduced rock music to Broadway, sound has become a fourth design discipline, elbowing its way down the aisle to join the familiar trio of sets, costumes and lights.

Sound effects, of course, have embellished theatre productions for centuries, as has live musical accompaniment. Shakespeare's storms, for example, were created by stagehands manipulating devices similar to the wind machines, thunder sheets and split-pea-filled rain-makers common in theatres until after World War I. And, until the invention of recorded sound, effects were primarily the responsibility of the property department. Then, in 1890, a few years after electricity first fully illuminated Victorian theatres, an English farce used a backstage phonograph to effect a baby's cry on cue. Nevertheless, for the next fifty years, theatre artists' abilities to manipulate and distribute light far exceeded their capabilities to do so with sound. While a sign appeared outside a Broadway house in 1921 crediting "lights by Abe Feder," it wasn't until 1971 that Abe Jacob identified himself as the first "sound designer" on Broadway, for his contribution to *Jesus Christ Superstar*.

Sound's bastard position among the disciplines isn't because of lack of artistic vision. Imagine Jean Cocteau's frustration in Paris in 1917 trying to stage his "surreal ballet" *Parade*, which featured Picasso's scenic design and Erik Satie's music. Cocteau's text, obviously inspired by Russoli's Futurist experiments, assigned each character a "sonic costume" of key sounds—whistles, drums, clappers, and so on—and called for a "noisecape" of machines—airplanes, typewriters, sirens—to accompany Satie's compositions. Unfortunately, Cocteau didn't even have a reel-to-reel tape machine, the single major technical innovation in sound reproduction to have come along since the unwieldy backstage phonograph.

Now, at the end of the twentieth century, the Machine Age finally has been reconfigured and rewired, and it's time theatregoers and practitioners said hello to the digital era. Hartford Stage Company's resident designer David Budries insists that sound design has only become an art form because of the digitization of sound. A knowledgeable designer sitting at a digital audio work station may create, compose and manipulate a huge assortment of aural elements—samples of pop songs, multilayered synthesized effects, echoes of actors' voices—as easily as a playwright manipulates dialogue on a word processor. More important, a single cue (which could contain Satie's music and trigger "sonic costumes" for any character Cocteau wanted) can be played back precisely the same way at each performance. Digital sound, many designers assert, has affected their discipline as profoundly as the invention of electricity enhanced the art of the lighting designer.

In autumn 1993, two events crowed the dawn of this new era. For one thing, sound designers were admitted for the first time into the design program at the Yale School of Drama instead of into its technical crafts division. Although a simple administrative change, the move symbolizes the way sound increasingly is approached—not as a technical science, but as its own design element.

Budries heads Yale's graduate program and believes the increased use of sound reflects a growing appreciation for more expressionistic texts. "When I first came to Yale ten years ago, there was no sense that sound was important," he recalls, "especially with the drama school's emphasis on naturalistic playwriting." Center Stage of Baltimore's artistic director Irene Lewis concurs: "As the theatre movement has moved away from naturalism—thank God!—you wind up with much more abstract settings, and sound paints the stage very effectively."

Although experimental playwrights and directors—Robert Wilson, Anne Bogart, Richard Foreman, JoAnne Akalaitis and others—have always demanded a full range of sound and noise, such work now appears more frequently at resident and off-Broadway theatres, and budding designers must be masters of the aesthetics of sound as well as the physics. For Budries, "the tools are easy to teach," but what a superior sound designer requires is "a thirst for exploration and a need to use the imagination."

The same September that Budries's students began classes at Yale, Abe Jacob, the godfather of Broadway sound design, had a big breakthrough in New York. As the first and only president of Local 922, chartered in 1986 as the sound design chapter of IATSE, the stagehands' union, Jacob negotiated the first standard labor contract for Broadway and Broadway-tour sound designers. Although its minimum design fee of $2,500 pales in comparison to Broadway fees for lighting designers (which can range from $4,500 to nearly $15,000 for large-scale, multi-set musicals), Jacob felt the compromise worth the League's belated acknowledgment that sound indeed was a legitimate fourth design discipline. Now, Jacob feels future negotiations will yield more rewards: "The contract's something to build on."

Of course, because of the nature of Broadway and its emphasis on musicals, the forty-odd designers in Local 922 concentrate on "reinforcement" (Jacob prefers the euphemism "enhancement"). Their skill at boosting the volume of God-given vocals has changed the terms of the debate in the last two decades from whether amplified sound has *any* place in the theatre to *what* role it should occupy. Sophisticated sound systems allow producers to charge more for the "nose-bleed seats"—musical theatre audiences in the back balcony may not see the action but they will *hear* it as if they were sitting fifth row center. Now more and more money goes to elaborate systems, conceived by audio wizards like Jonathan Deems, the Las Vegas-based designer whose computerized program for Jack O'Brien's Broadway production of *Damn Yankees* marks one of the first times a show's complexity of sound cues has been controlled by computer.

This frenzy of invention and spending makes the three rental shops servicing Broadway very upbeat. ProMix, for one, is doing booming business. A pilgrimage to the company's Westchester warehouse last spring revealed a marvel awaiting lift-off: the mixing board for Tommy Tune's short-lived *The Best Little Whorehouse Goes Public*. ProMix employee Simon Nathan explained its significance: "It's an automated console that has a limited amount of computer built in, so the engineer can program the complete play cue-to-cue. A single 'next cue' will not only turn channels on, turn channels off and reassign channels, but even reassign different subgroups to different channels on a cue-to-cue basis—and at the same time trigger effects or a DAT (digital audio tape player), and simultaneously activate motorized faders that will send that cue to different parts of the theatre." Now you know how the helicopter lands in *Miss Saigon*.

The speed of change makes even insiders' heads spin. ProMix cofounder Bob Rendon recalls, "We used six wireless mikes on *Dream Girls* and thought that was a lot." Last spring, *Showboat*'s producers requested a price quote for forty-four mikes. DigiCarts, computerized hard drives that stack sound cues and play them at a press of a button, have rendered tape decks obsolete. Designer John Gromada says he expects reel-to-reels to disappear at most major theatres within five years.

Only recently has theatre sound begun to mirror society's reality. For digital sound not only emanates from your favorite CD, but from speakers built into theme park roller coasters, museum installations, supermarket aisles, church choir lofts, cineplexes and airport lounges. The result is that Americans' rich digital sound diet has spoiled theatre audiences. Commercial producers, therefore, must protect their multimillion-dollar investments by competing in these sonic sweepstakes.

Nevertheless, outside the commercial arena, most sound designers remained unaffected by the events of last year. Invariably autodidacts without graduate instruction, most resident theatre and experimental sound designers stumbled into a college or a resident theatre and wired their musical training to the speakers, decks and synthesizers laying around. Each must continually reinvent his or her own "program" as new technologies become available.

And while some resident theatre directors take sound design aesthetics seriously, the designers contacted for this article bemoan those who remain ignorant of sound's changing role in the digital era. Like some mysterious club or guild, designers thrive on the Zen-koan-like conundrums they encounter.

Sound's mystical qualities, in fact, may account for its presence in humanity's most profound questions: "Does a tree falling in the middle of the woods make a sound if no one's there to hear it?" Or the familiar Zen koan designed to provoke enlightenment: "What is the sound of one hand clapping?" Such questions are fundamental to the aesthetics of sound design; both are different ways of asking the same oxymoronic question Simon and Garfunkel addressed: What are "the sounds of silence?" The reason for its profundity, as the late maestro of found-sound John Cage obviously believed, is that "silence" doesn't exist or, at least, is a relative term. In fact, Cage proved, by making concert audiences listen to "it," that silence is filled with an infinity of possible noise. And so, the irony in the theatre is that sound designers are the conscience and keepers of silence. They understand that without silence their work is unintelligible.

Darron West's ninety-something sound cues for Anne Bogart's production of *The Medium* at the Saratoga International Theater Institute and New York Theatre Workshop—including samples of TV's *The Dating Game* ditty, the theme song from *The Valley of the Dolls*, and assorted statics, hisses and roars—fill most of the show's running time. "Maybe there's five minutes we've logged through without any cues," West explains. "With so many cues, the silences are a *big deal*—you have to plot where they are going to be."

Without the budgets of their colleagues on Broadway, these designers depend on their ability to manipulate limited resources to create "sonic environments" that embellish their productions with effects and underscoring that is simultaneously ethereal and expressive, abstract and concrete, all the while offering audiences answers to impossible questions.

Reprinted by permission from the April 1994 issue of *American Theatre* magazine, published by Theatre Communications Group, September, 1994, pp. 15-17.

Section

5

Administrators
and Finance

All artistic organizations in the United States have been short of money at the end of the twentieth century and theatre is no exception; perhaps it suffers more than most. Every year *American Theatre* magazine, published by the Theatre Communications Group (TCG) in New York, surveys the current situation. The article reprinted here refers to 1991, a year chosen as one in which the crisis seemed clearer than usual; it considers what needed to be done then, as well as what had happened during earlier years. Its author, Peter Zeisler, was then executive director of TCG.

Ill Winds

Peter Zeisler

In a field that for thirty years has grown exponentially (horizontally but not vertically), we find ourselves today with many trees, but with shallow root structures. Like trees, theatre institutions have no real stability without deep roots—shallow roots will not withstand strong winds of change. And today's winds are approaching gale proportions.

The extent to which theatres are now suffering from the impact of the recession becomes all too clear in "Theatre Facts 91," TCG's latest annual survey of theatres nationwide, which appears in this issue. While it is premature to proclaim our Last Hurrah, the report should be required reading for everyone who is involved in, or who cares about, the American theatre. Artists in particular have an enormous stake in these economic trends, for they threaten the resources they need to engage in the research and development that will keep the art form living and growing. Audiences across the country also stand to lose, as theatres are forced to close doors, or curtail programs.

Only time will tell if these trends augur even worse times to come; in the meantime, the report offers an opportunity for the theatre community to ponder collectively what interim measures might be taken, or whether a radical rethinking is necessary if the field is to survive and flourish in the future.

Of the 184 theatres that participated in this year's survey, half posted operating deficits for the year. Because very few theatres have a sufficiently strong financial base that can absorb a deficit year, ill winds easily escalate to storms. We can unfortunately point to the 25 theatres that have closed in the past five years as proof of the field's continued fragility. To compound the problem, our sample group reported that for the first time since we began the surveys in 1973, attendance declined. After years of steady audience growth, a sudden reversal, caused by curtailed performance activity, reduced marketing resources, rising ticket prices and the public's lack of disposable income. The recession is clearly taking a toll on efforts to develop new audiences for the future.

To compensate for dwindling capital and cautious audiences, there was a significant increase in presenting special productions and booked-in events. While the strategy demonstrably assisted box-office revenue, it put the brakes on artistic research and development. Sadly, what was curtailed were the workshops, the staged readings—the laboratory work of theatre. If the brakes continue to be applied, and repertoires become more formulaic to reduce risks, not only will the theatre be less challenging and inviting to artists, but the services theatres are providing to their communities may be decreased to protect balance sheets. If so, it will be much harder to make the case for theatre as an essential social service, like schools and libraries, instead of institutions that must earn their way as part of the "entertainment industry."

There are external forces over which the theatre community has little control. But there are internal forces that we can try to channel. As our economy flags, there will be increased competition for funds. Smaller theatres tend to have much less access to corporate, foundation and individual funding; now that government funds are rapidly disappearing, many of these companies are really struggling. "Big is better" has never been a motto for theatre. Some of the most important and exciting work is developing in smaller venues, and we need to be sure in times of fiscal austerity that we protect and nurture the more fragile sectors of our constituency.

The larger and relatively stable theatres can reach out to smaller companies by offering residencies, bookings or co-productions—or assisting with some of their administrative needs. In this issue, Alexis Green describes how museums are supporting and sheltering performance artists. The Indiana Repertory Theatre has developed a relationship with MAPI Rep, a local African-American theatre company; the New York Shakespeare Festival is providing space for three "homeless" New York companies.

As we asked how much can we compromise, streamline or minimize, we must also remember that there is a point of diminishing artistic returns. Perennially undercapitalized, theatre has always been just a little too adept at operating on a shoestring, and that is why it is so vulnerable in hard times.

The most troubling trend in "Theatre Facts 91" is the precipitous decline in the number of full-time and full-season employees, and the simultaneous increase in part-time and jobbed-in personnel. The ability of theatre professionals to earn a reasonable annual living is becoming less possible every year, and what is politely referred to as a "talent drain" could very easily become an artistic "black hole."

In this issue you will see an announcement of the Pew Charitable Trusts' grant to TCG to develop and administer a National Theatre Artist Residency Program. The program is a direct response to the principal findings of TCG's 1988 report, *The Artistic Home*, which focused on the need to strengthen relationships between institutions and artists. The residency program is a new approach to developing partnerships between artists and theatre companies. We are enormously grateful to Pew for listening well to the theatre field and for making a significant move to enable the field to help itself—at a time when such help is sorely needed.

Reprinted by permission from the April 1992 issue of *American Theatre* magazine, published by Theatre Communications Group, p.5.

The following self-appraisal by a flourishing regional theatre seeks to explain priorities and achievements. It should be read in conjunction with the financial details provided in Figure S5.1.

Background: Seattle Repertory Theatre

Some of the best playwrights in America have been trying to set up tents under the roof of the Seattle Rep. . . . The Rep has moved Seattle into the forefront of the resident theatre renaissance.

—*New York Times*

Founded in 1963 by a group of prominent civic leaders, the Seattle Repertory Theatre stands as a legacy of the 1962 World's Fair. The Rep, as it has become known, performed twenty resident mainstage seasons in the Seattle Center Playhouse, while its second-stage series and support operations were spread throughout the city. With the opening of the Bagley Wright Theatre in 1983, the Rep consolidated its operations in the new facility. Since then, it has flourished by presenting six mainstage productions annually at the 856-seat Bagley Wright Theatre, as well as three Stage 2 works and two to four New Play Workshops in the 133-seat PONCHO Forum each year. Through these productions, along with a comprehensive series of Education and Outreach programs, the Rep serves approximately 170,000 audience members annually, including more than 30,000 students.

In 1993, The Rep's Board of Trustees approved the following mission statement for the theatre:

To create living theatre with the highest standard of artistic excellence; to develop a body of work by the finest playwrights, directors and actors; to challenge and entertain our audience with plays and productions that reflect the human experience in all its complexity.

This mission statement is supported by the following objectives:

Develop and stage the work of emerging and established playwrights.

Establish a resident acting company of national distinction.

Offer education and community outreach services to all ages.

Create a supportive environment that nurtures collaboration among all artists and staff.

Foster the growth and freedom of the artist's and the audience's imagination.

Develop and balance the resources necessary to maintain artistic and financial integrity.

Under the leadership of artistic director Daniel Sullivan and managing director Benjamin Moore, The Rep has achieved international acclaim for its leadership role in developing new works and nurturing both new and established playwrights. Highly regarded as one of the foremost stage directors in America, Sullivan has played a major role in developing such plays at Herb Gardner's *Conversations with My Father* and *I'm Not Rappaport*, Lanford Wilson's *Redwood Curtain* and Bill Irwin's *Largely/New York*, among others. Each of these has moved from The Rep to Broadway, as have Wendy Wasserstein's *The Sisters Rosensweig* and her Pulitzer Prize-winning *The Heidi Chronicles*. These are just a few of the accomplishments which led the Rep to receive the coveted Tony Award for Outstanding Regional Theatre in 1990.

The Rep is proud of its distinguished reputation and its steadfast commitment to excellence. Its achievements and its promising future are the result of an outstanding commitment from our regions' public and private sector, to support the full range of work presented on our stages and in our outreach programs. The Rep is pleased to work with more than three thousand donors—including individuals, corporations, foundations and government agencies—to make our performances and programs accessible to the broadest possible base of audiences. Leading that effort is the Rep's sixty-member board of trustees, composed of the region's corporate and civic leaders. The Seattle Repertory Theatre is a not-for-profit, tax exempt organization, Tax Identification Number 91-075-6535.

Reprinted by permission of Seattle Repertory Theatre.

"Theatre Operations" reproduced opposite, gives opportunity to ask questions about the theatre's policy: for example, Why are administration costs almost two fifths of total expenditure? or Who are the people whose donations keep the theatre going in the style to which it has become accustomed? or How much is spent on publicity and promotion for each $20 ticket, and should it be more? Figure S5.2 shows how many people attended performances, but does not show which shows were the more successful.

By any standards, theatres playing to over 90 percent capacity are highly successful operations and should be able to afford an occasional risk-taking production. The 101 percent capacity for the smaller Stage 2 performances suggests room for development. Does the theatre lack the human resources to take advantage of this, or are the possible financial returns too low to encourage initiative?

Consult the annual reports of theatres in your own town or district, and compare them with those of the Seattle Rep. Seek reasons for the more notable differences.

What further questions would you like to see answered in a mission statement or annual financial report?

THEATRE OPERATIONS

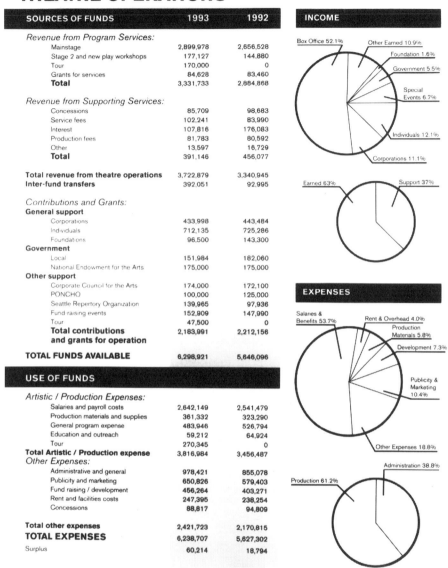

SOURCES OF FUNDS	1993	1992
Revenue from Program Services:		
Mainstage	2,899,978	2,656,528
Stage 2 and new play workshops	177,127	144,880
Tour	170,000	0
Grants for services	84,628	83,460
Total	3,331,733	2,884,868
Revenue from Supporting Services:		
Concessions	85,709	98,683
Service fees	102,241	83,990
Interest	107,816	176,083
Production fees	81,783	80,592
Other	13,597	16,729
Total	391,146	456,077
Total revenue from theatre operations	3,722,879	3,340,945
Inter-fund transfers	392,051	92,995
Contributions and Grants:		
General support		
Corporations	433,998	443,484
Individuals	712,135	725,286
Foundations	96,500	143,300
Government		
Local	151,984	182,060
National Endowment for the Arts	175,000	175,000
Other support		
Corporate Council for the Arts	174,000	172,100
PONCHO	100,000	125,000
Seattle Repertory Organization	139,965	97,936
Fund-raising events	152,909	147,990
Tour	47,500	0
Total contributions and grants for operation	2,183,991	2,212,156
TOTAL FUNDS AVAILABLE	6,298,921	5,646,096

USE OF FUNDS		
Artistic / Production Expenses:		
Salaries and payroll costs	2,642,149	2,541,479
Production materials and supplies	361,332	323,290
General program expense	483,946	526,794
Education and outreach	59,212	64,924
Tour	270,345	0
Total Artistic / Production expense	3,816,984	3,456,487
Other Expenses:		
Administrative and general	978,421	855,078
Publicity and marketing	650,826	579,403
Fund raising / development	456,264	403,271
Rent and facilities costs	247,395	238,254
Concessions	88,817	94,809
Total other expenses	2,421,723	2,170,815
TOTAL EXPENSES	6,238,707	5,627,302
Surplus	60,214	18,794

INCOME

Box Office 52.1%
Other Earned 10.9%
Foundation 1.6%
Government 5.5%
Special Events 6.7%
Individuals 12.1%
Corporations 11.1%

Earned 63%
Support 37%

EXPENSES

Salaries & Benefits 53.7%
Rent & Overhead 4.0%
Production Materials 5.8%
Development 7.3%
Publicity & Marketing 10.4%
Other Expenses 18.8%

Administration 38.8%
Production 61.2%

Figure S5.1   Financial Statement concerning the 1993 season at Seattle Repertory Theatre.

Education and Outreach and Special Events Programs at Seattle Repertory Theatre, 1992-1993

Our thirtieth season saw continued growth in a broad variety of programs that touch the lives of students, educators, audiences, and artists. These

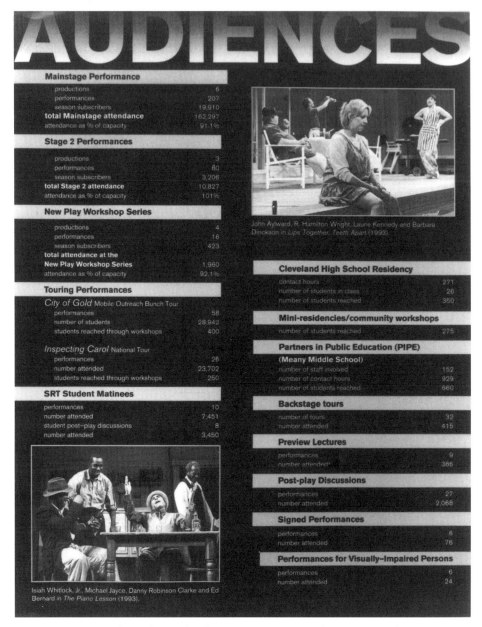

Figure S5.2   Attendance figures for the 1993 season at Seattle Repertory Theatre.

programs became more a part of our daily lives, enriching and informing our work and providing us with a new sense of our community. Whenever the daily demands of our work have begun to isolate us from that community, the contact made through education and outreach has become our window on the world.

Seattle Rep's relationship with Meany Middle School through Partners in Public Education (PIPE) has become the cornerstone for our education and outreach efforts. We not only teach theatre as an art form and include the students as audience members, but demonstrate how to use theatre as a tool to explore all aspects of education. The Rep's "Shadow Day" program, in which students spend half a day with staff, one-on-one, learning firsthand about working in the theatre, doubled in attendance this year. More staff members than ever eagerly signed up to speak in Meany's career classes. The Rep also welcomed students and teachers to matinee performances in the Bagley Wright Theatre, continued teacher training with SRT staff, worked with the school's Drug Intervention Specialist, and offered special season subscriptions to students and teachers. Residency activities, in which students focus on particular plays, including studies of *Julius Caesar* and *The Piano Lesson* for the bilingual studies program and an examination of *The Piano Lesson* for a language arts class.

The Mobile Outreach Bunch (MOB) completed its eighteenth season of touring with the encore presentation of *City of Gold* by Charles Smith. Commissioned by SRT, *City of Gold* chronicles the waste and destruction left in the wake of Christopher Columbus's voyage to the New World. Over 28,942 students at fifty-eight schools experienced this touring production, sponsored by the Cultural Enrichment Program of the Washington State Arts Commission. The six-week tour opened dramatically with a performance at Chief Leschi School for 250 Native American students, part of a four-day residency sponsored by the United Puyallup Tribe revolving around the meaning to Native Americans of Columbus's arrival in this hemisphere. From there, the tour went on to middle and junior high schools across the state, including a special performance at Echo Glen Childrens Center, a detention facility for youthful offenders. A number of these performances were attended by staff and board members. On the Quincentennial day itself, October 12, 1992, the Rep's touring company joined Red Eagle Soaring, a Native American theatre group, for a program at the Langston Hughes Cultural Center. Called "Celebration of the First People," it was an evening of traditional and contemporary Native American music, dance, poetry, and drama dedicated to indigenous peoples everywhere.

Traditional theatregoing experiences for young people were also made available. 7,451 students attended student matinees of *Julius Caesar*, *Inspecting Carol*, *Heartbreak House*, and *The Piano Lesson*, after teachers had prepared them with the help of the Rep's study guide. Over 45 percent of the students also participated in postplay discussions with members of the cast and crew following each performance. It became an energizing break in the work day for many staff members to slip into the back of the house during these performances and discussions to observe the lively reactions and comments of the students.

Students' involvement with Rep plays went beyond seeing them at the theatre. Seattle's Cleveland High School presented two performances of *Beyond Caesar*, a theatre piece based on their reactions to the Rep's production of *Julius Caesar* by William Shakespeare. This freshman English class traced the entire production process of the play while working with Rep artists to explore the themes and issues in the play.

The MOB tour was not the only show sent on the road by SRT. Our production of *Inspecting Carol* by Daniel Sullivan and the Resident Acting Company toured for five weeks, delighting audiences around the states of Washington and Colorado, Illinois and Ohio. A highlight of the tour was a two-day stop in Bremerton, just across Puget Sound. This presentation was unique for the involvement of the local high school students who participated fully in mounting the production, from marketing tickets to loading in the set. The Seattle Repertory Theatre remains one of the only resident theatres in America to tour its plays. The Rep's Professional Arts Training Program provided 24 interns, 5 acting fellows, a Drama League of New York Fellow and an Arts International intern with comprehensive work training and experience in their areas of interest. In addition, participants had the opportunity to explore the workings of the entire organization and the Seattle arts community.

The Rep's other outreach programs include:

Audio descriptive performances for the visually impaired (presented by Arts and Visually Impaired Audiences).

American Sign Language-interpreted performances for the hearing impaired.

Discount tickets for students, seniors, hearing- and visually impaired patrons, and audience members with limited financial resources.

Half-price and group sales programs.

Scholarship tickets for young people.

Special Events.

Every season, many events are held to support the Rep and its programs, events that bring contributors and the community closer to the theatre and add lustre to its image.

The Rep's Thirtieth Anniversary Season was marked by the annual gala fund-raising ball. One of Seattle's most popular events, the Gala brought together hundreds of the Rep's most dedicated supporters, including patrons, playwrights and performers, in the stunningly decorated Grand Ballroom of the Westin Hotel. Entertained by the Seattle Men's Chorus and the Stan Keen Orchestra, the guests toasted the Rep's birthday and reveled past midnight.

In appreciation for our corporate sponsors, The Rep hosted a special reception and private performance of *Inspecting Carol* for executives from more than forty of Seattle's leading companies on Corporate Night. Some of the organizations in attendance were SAFECO, Washington Mutual, Graham & Dunn, the Shunju Club, American Airlines, Seafirst Bank and The Boeing Company, among many others.

This year, The Rep was proud to offer its scene shop on the opening night of *The Piano Lesson* as the setting for a special benefit dinner for the African American Heritage Foundation. The event brought together new communities and began what will likely be a long relationship between The Rep and the African American Heritage Foundation. *The Piano Lesson* playwright August Wilson attended as a special guest.

Throughout the year, The Rep hosted receptions for Producing Partners and Associates of the Mainstage, and Playwright's Circle pre-play dinners on selected opening nights.

Calendar 1992/93

October
> The Trustee and Alumni Reunion
> The Spirit of Washington Dinner Train
> Halloween murder mystery fund raiser, cosponsored by Applause

November
> The Thirtieth Anniversary Gala

December
> Corporate Night for the Rep's corporate sponsors

March
> Night in the Spotlight in recognition of the Rep's donors
> SRO Nordstrom Fashion Luncheon

April
> African-American Heritage Foundation Fund-raising Dinner on opening night of *The Piano Lesson*

May
> The Best of the Rep Education and Outreach Program Benefit

June
> SRO Elegant Elephant Rummage Sale

Reprinted by permission of Seattle Repertory Theatre.

Section

6

The Public: An Audience Survey for Studio Arena Theatre, Buffalo

Theatre's necessary collaborator is its public, but assessing popular demand, special interests, and the reputation of any theatre among its theatregoers is a difficult task. Audience surveys can give useful information, as illustrated here by the summary and conclusions of one undertaken in 1993 for Studio Arena Theatre in Buffalo, New York. A second performance space had been proposed in order that the company could serve its community better and satisfy its artistic aspirations.

Management Summary

Two focus groups were conducted recently to assess reaction to a second stage offered by Studio Arena Theatre. One of these focus groups was conducted with individuals who frequent cultural events more than twelve times a year—Heavy User group. The other focus group was conducted with individuals who frequent cultural events six to twelve times a year—Moderate User group. Slightly less than half of the participants were recruited from lists of season-ticket or single-ticket buyers provided by Studio Arena.

In briefest form, the results of these focus groups show the following:

Theatre in general, and Studio Arena in particular, is considered one of the major and best-liked entertainment options facing Heavy and Moderate Users.

Both Heavy and Moderate Users would like to see more theater options in western New York State. Heavy Users tend to view these options more in terms of Broadway productions, while Moderate Users think of improvement more in terms of more current and more off-Broadway productions.

While Moderate Users tend to think of thought-provoking or risky plays as something currently unavailable in the area, Heavy Users believe that such material is already being offered at Studio Arena Theatre.

Of the terms which could be potentially used to describe second-stage plays, the most positive overall reception was given to: thought-provoking, addresses important social issues, a play that takes chances, and adventuresome. The terms that received the most negative reception were radical, risky material, adult themes, and unconventional.

Photo personification tests in both groups identified second-stage prospects as young professional men, young professional women, and active young couples with no children.

While both groups reacted favorably to the idea of a second stage, Moderate users showed much more interest in attending its productions, but were concerned about production quality and ticket cost.

Summary Observations and Conclusions

Based on the findings and comments reported in previous sections—a number of summary observations and conclusions can be made. These are:

Entertainment

Theater, and Studio Arena Theatre in particular, is considered one of the major entertainment options facing Heavy and Moderate Users of cultural activity.

While Heavy Users show no signs of reducing cultural entertainment activity, Moderate Users, who tended to be younger, showed signs of cutting back because of their economic situations.

Gusto is the major source of entertainment information for Heavy and Moderate users of cultural activities.

Cultural entertainment activity is almost always planned as opposed to being spontaneous.

Studio Arena Theatre ranks among the top entertainment options that come to mind on an unaided basis, and ranked as the favorite among the highest number of focus group participants.

Theater in General

Heavy Users and Moderate Users of theater indicated that they would like to see more theater options in Western New York.

Moderate Users point to lack of funds or lack of topic interest as reasons that they do not frequent theater attractions to a greater degree.

Heavy Users tend to think of improvement in theater in terms of the production capabilities of a New York or Toronto versus a Buffalo theatre, while Moderate Users think of improvement in terms of more current and off-Broadway productions becoming available in Buffalo.

Printed with permission of Studio Arena Theatre, Buffalo, N.Y.

Consider what other issues are raised by this survey, besides whether or not to create a new, smaller performance space. What does it reveal about the composition of the theatre's audience? What further sections of the public might be attracted to the theatre, and by what means? Make a list of the plays you would like to see and ask whether they would be likely to draw an audience at Studio Arena, with or without a second stage.

Glossary

This list provides short definitions of theatrical usages which may not be familiar to all readers. The numbered references give the pages on which further information can most readily be found; they are not intended as an index to the book.

absurd, theatre of the (30) Name given to plays of the 1950s and 1960s that abandoned realism and regular narrative for fantasy and disjunction; many were intellectually paradoxical or provocative. Eugène Ionesco and Fernando Arrabal were leading playwrights developing this form of theatre.

act Major and distinct structural unit in drama. Customarily plays have from one to five acts; they are often devised to build to a strong conclusion so that an intermission may be taken between them. Time, place, or mood will often change between acts, and the narrative will advance notably. An act may include several or many separate scenes.

actor manager (129) Leading actor in a company who is also in charge of it, and may sometimes own it; technical and administrative complications of twentieth-century theatre and the possibility of parallel careers in film and television have increasingly made such a task impractical, so that few attempt it now, except in a very small scale.

agitprop theatre A term of Russian origin to describe drama intended as political agitation and propaganda.

arena-stage theatre (56-57) As the alternative name of *theatre-in-the-round* indicates, the stage in this theatre is surrounded on all sides by the audience.

aside Stage direction indicating that a character speaks to his- or herself, or to the audience, not addressing other characters onstage.

audition Meeting in which a *play director* and *producer* test an actor for a role or position in an acting company; major roles are almost invariably decided (or "cast") on the strength of prior achievements, without recourse to auditioning.

backstage (69) That part of a theatre building that supplies the needs of a play in performance, including dressing rooms, "green room" (where actors can meet and relax before or during performances), workshops, wardrobes and stores, offices, and so on.

black-box theatre (63) More like large rooms than conventional theatres with a permanent division between stage and auditorium, they are painted black to avoid light reflections. They are provided with an overall grid on which to hang lights; the acting area can be shaped and placed to serve the needs of each new production.

blocking (142) Process used by some *directors* whereby actors are shown where to move onstage at an early stage in rehearsals.

bookkeeper (110) Name for the person who kept order *backstage* in theatres of Shakespeare's time; he literally "held" the manuscript (few plays were in print when performed) in which all entries, exits, and stage business were clearly marked.

Broadway The major commercial theatres, many dating from the 1890s, grouped around Broadway as it crosses streets in the Forties and Fifties in central Manhattan, New York City.

choreography The art of arranging dances, fights, and large-scale movements on stage, or the arrangement of these features as used in a particular production.

chorus Group of (often nameless) characters who comment on a play's action and themes or represent the people amongst whom its leading characters are presented as living. Sometimes it fulfills both functions, as notably in ancient Greek plays and others written in imitation of them. In Elizabethan plays, the chorus is usually a single spokesman addressing the audience on behalf of the dramatist or acting company. In most twentieth-century musicals, a large chorus, by singing and dancing, will support the performances of leading actors and help to establish situation and mood, as required for individual *scenes*.

chronicle See *history play*.

classical acting (91-93) Used not only of actors in ancient Greek theatres but also of contemporary actors who pay particular attention to the demands of dialogue in verse and nonrealistic, non-naturalistic prose.

clown Comic character in a drama, often pretending to be more stupid than other people and so getting the better of them. A clown appears on his or her own, or with other clowns, in circuses and other popular entertainments.

comedy (24, 26, 27) Variously defined as a play ending happily, or causing laughter, or being performed in a spirit of carnival and revelry.

commedia dell'arte (104) A form of comedy originating in Italy during the sixteenth and seventeenth centuries among companies that maintained a *repertoire* of plays using a number of basic characters, such as young lovers, old pedant and miserly father, bragging soldier, innocent fool, and so on. Their actors were both skilled in particular roles and *"lazzi"* or pieces of comic business, and were possessed with talent for improvisation in speech and bold physical performance.

concept, production (134, 137) Idea chosen and defined by some *play directors* as a means of giving unity and specific meaning to a production.

cue Signal for the entry of actors or for a light or sound change, etc., during the run of a play.

curtain Screen hanging between stage and auditorium in *picture-frame* or *proscenium* theatres; also used as a *stage direction* to indicate the end of a *scene* or *act*.

designer, light, set, sound (107-108) Person who works with the *director* to devise and superintend these stage effects for a production.

developed play (32) Production that is not based on a play text but devised during company research and rehearsals, often without help from a dramatist.

development officer Member of a theatre company responsible for raising money from public and private sponsorship.

dinner theatre (75) Theatre performances at which meals are served, usually both before a play and during an intermission.

director, artistic (129-132) Person who is responsible for the choice of productions and is in overall charge of all work on them at a particular theatre or for a particular company.

> **managing, producing** (129-133) Person in financial and administrative charge of a theatre company.

> **play** (134-139) Person in charge (under an *artistic director*) of the preparation of a specific production, from casting and design through to performance.

documentary drama   Plays seeking to present evidence onstage about real-life events of major importance, often based on research and exploratory work in rehearsals, sometimes without the help of a dramatist.

dress rehearsal   (142-143) Rehearsal of a production immediately prior to public performance; the first time that actors are in costume and provided with all *props* and most of the stage effects.

end stage   See *open-stage theatre.*

ensemble acting   (103-105) Style of acting that is developed between a group of actors working together consistently, usually under one particular director, and over a considerable period of time. Its strength lies in group effects rather than star performances.

epic acting   (93-95) Style of acting developed by Bertolt Brecht in opposition to a conventional and debased form of *classical acting*. It seeks to demonstrate the facts of a situation, rather than to develop highly charged and emotional performances or to exploit the attractions of individual star performers.

epic theatre   (29) Name used by Bertolt Brecht to define the kind of play he wrote. He aimed at making the audience think rather than feel, observe rather than sympathize or identify with any of the characters.

Equity, Actors'   Association that defends its actor-members' rights and seeks to promote the good of their profession. The separate British and American Equities attempt to protect national as well as more local and artistic interests.

eurythmics   (116) Means of teaching movement for the stage that was very influential in the 1920s and 1930s.

expressionist theatre   (29) Plays that seek to show the nature of human existence, rather than individual stories or dilemmas. They often have many scenes and characters representative of types of persons in contemporary society. The style was especially favored between the two world wars.

extravaganza   (113) Spectacular, fantastic and, often, burlesque entertainments, popular in Britain in the nineteenth century.

farce   (27) *Comedy* in which the action becomes wildly improbable. The word's original use was for food that is "stuffed" and thereby not entirely natural.

flies; fly-loft   Space over the stage in a *picture-frame theatre* in which pieces of *scenery* are stored so that they can be lowered into position onstage between *scenes* or, sometimes, during the action of a play.

fool   Character, often confused with a *clown*, who uses verbal and sometimes physical wit as a means of self-promotion and criticism of others.

footlights   Sources of light placed along the front of the stage in a *picture-frame theatre*. They are going out of use in the second half of the twentieth century, except for occasional special effects.

front of house   (67-69) That part of a theatre building used to receive an audience before its members take their seats and also during intermissions. It includes *box-office*, rest rooms, bars, restaurants, and all public areas.

gods, the   (73) Uppermost of several balconies in theatres of the eighteenth and nineteenth centuries where the cheapest seats and, often, the noisiest members of the audience were located. The word was used partly in irony and partly because the highly vocal judgment of "the gods" had important consequences for the success of a production.

history; history play   (25) Form of play, based on published *Chronicles* of a nation's history, popular in theatres of Shakespeare's time. He was its most productive and successful exponent.

marionette   (see also *puppet*) Doll, used for theatre performances, that is manipulated by strings from above.

mask   (88, 89) Covering for the face (or a part of it) depicting another face; used by actors as a disguise and as a means of characterization, especially when an appearance is required that is very different from the actor's own, such as that of a god, an excessively old or ugly person, a baby, or an animal.

melodrama   (29) Literally meaning a "song drama," the term is used to describe plays with highly sensational and strongly emotional action. Characters are usually simply motivated and strongly opposed to each other.

method acting   (102-103) Style of acting developed (chiefly by Lee Strasberg) from some parts of *Stanislavskian acting*, at Actors Studio in New York City in 1950s and 1960s. Although widely influential in theatre, it was perhaps more successful in film.

mime   (13) Silent acting, often attempting an eloquence of gesture to take the place of words as a means of communication onstage and from stage to auditorium.

miracle play   See *mystery play*.

multimedia show   (33) Theatre production making use of modern technology to merge theatre with film, pop-music presentation, "virtual reality," and much else; light spectacles, multiple projectors and screens, complex sound tracks, powerful music reproduction, laser beams, computerized control—all have their parts to play.

musical   (29, 75-76) Play in which music is given a basic role, often using full orchestra, large singing and dancing *chorus*, popular lead singers, and (increasingly in the last decades of the twentieth century) lavish, automated stage spectacle. Devised by a team of director, choreographer, designers, lyricist, music director, composer, dramatist, and producer, most musicals are extremely costly and therefore designed to appeal to the widest possible audience and to run for many years in a number of large theatres around the world.

mystery play   (25, 61) Narrative drama, usually presenting the Bible story and played (chiefly by amateurs) in open places throughout early Christian Europe; occasionally revived from the early twentieth century onward.

neoclassical   Term used (from the fifteenth century onward) for drama and other works of art created in imitation of those of the ancient world and following its "rules" and methods.

off-Broadway; off-off-Broadway   Small and usually impecunious theatres situated well away from the center of commercial theatre on *Broadway*.

open-stage theatre   (52) Its "end stage" is without any frame or other barrier between itself and the auditorium.

pantomime   Originally synonymous with *mime*, the word was used in the nineteenth century of light-hearted and spectacular dance dramas. Later it was reserved for family Christmas entertainments in Britain, based on well-known fairy stories.

performance artist   (31) Actor who performs, often solo, in dramas devised to suit his or her own capabilities and idiosyncratic experiences.

picture-frame theatre   (49-52) Its stage is surrounded by a (*proscenium*) frame that marks a clear separation from its auditorium.

pit   (73) Central area of early modern theatres. Admission was cheap because its seats, when provided, were benches, close together and at a lower level than the stage or those in balconies around the auditorium. Toward the end of the nineteenth century, the benches were replaced by "stalls," and the floor of the auditorium was tiered to give a better view, so that only the very back seats under the first balcony were called the "pit"; now even these no longer exist.

platform stage   (59) That part of a stage in a *picture-frame theatre* that projects beyond the frame into the auditorium; or a simple stage that can be dismantled and erected with ease and so placed in any open space.

preview   (143) One of a number of performances given between *dress rehearsals* and the "first night," usually at reduced prices or entirely free, to give opportunity for adjustments to be made after a production has met its first audiences.

producer   (129-132) Person financially and administratively responsible for a *production*. For expensive commercial productions, the task may be shared between several persons or syndicates.

production   (129) The word used of the everything that is combined in the staging of a play at a particular time and place.

prologue   Speech or short episode prefixed to the play about to be offered; it usually flatters its audience and explains or excuses (often ironically) what is to follow.

props   (43) Articles used by the actors onstage during a performance.

proscenium   (49-52, 59) Literally "what is in front of the stage." In the later seventeenth and throughout the eighteenth century, entries could be made onto it through proscenium doors, often two on each side. When stage lighting was rudimentary, it was here that the main action of a play took place, close to important members of the audience sitting on the stage or in "side boxes" and illuminated by the candelabra suspended over *the pit*. Now the word is also used to refer to a structural frame in front of the entire acting area of a stage and separating it from the audience.

puppet   (21) Doll representing a human or other creature. Puppets can be used for all the characters in a play (for example, in the Bunraku theatre of Japan) and also in regular productions for special characters, such as babies, gods, fairies, animals, and so forth.

rendering   (107) A *designer*'s word for a drawing of a stage *set* or costume.

repertory; also repertoire, rep.   (71-72, 131) A number of plays performed by a single theatre company during a season or when *touring*; sometimes used to name the parts that have become associated with a particular actor or actress.

scene   (49) Originally a word for the stage, it is now used to describe a continuous but separate and distinct part of a play, usually with its action taking place in one time and place. There may be any number in a single *act*.

scenery; also setting, set   (59, 107) What is placed onstage to represent or suggest the location and time of a play's action. Scenery often changes in the course of the play, as required by the narrative.

scenic artist   Painter of stage sets.

scenographer; scenography   (107-109) Words popularized by the Czech designer, Svoboda, to denote the art of setting a play in a theatre for a particular production. It involves not only designing scenery but also the use of the theatre building, costumes, lighting, sound, acting style—every visual element of a production.

soliloquy   Solo speech in a play, in which a character speaks to himself or the audience, usually with no other character onstage.

soundeffect; also *soundtrack*   Means of making the sounds appropriate to any particular moment in a production, other than those made onstage by the actors themselves or by musicians.

stage direction   Words in the text of a play that are not to be spoken but indicate what is done onstage or the manner in which the words should be spoken.

stage manager   Person in charge of the practical running of rehearsals and subsequent performances. He or she sees that everything is in place at the start of each performance and that each *cue* to actors and technicians is given clearly and exactly on time.

Stanislavskian acting   (98, 99, 100, 101-103) Style of acting derived from the teachings of the Russian actor and director, Konstantin Stanislavsky, and especially concerned with expressive and naturalistic performance.

studio theatre   (63) Small theatre, often a *black box*, with minimal facilities for accommodating audiences—certainly not large ones—and simple equipment. Work done in a studio theatre is more experimental, risky, or specialized than that found in full-scale theatres where production expenses are greater. Some studios are used only for "laboratory" work, with little or no thought of finalizing a production or attracting audiences.

subtext   (15, 40, 96) That which makes the character say what he or she says in a play; the unspoken thoughts underneath those that are voiced and easily recognized. *Subtext* is a word commonly used when actors are working on a role according to *Stanislavskian* acting techniques.

symbolist drama   (29) Plays that seek to express the hidden essence of life, using poetic language and atmospheric settings. Notable writers of this movement originating in Paris were the Belgian Maurice Maeterlinck and the Irish poet, W. B. Yeats.

technical director   Person in charge of the entire technical side of a production or theatre company.

technical rehearsal; also **tech**   (142) Rehearsal, during the last stages of preparation for a production, that concentrates exclusively on getting scenic, light, sound, and other technical effects correct and on *cue*.

thrust stage   (52-56) Stage jutting out from a backstage wall so that the audience sits on three of its sides.

touring   Taking a *production* or a *repertory* company on a series of visits to different theatres. Until recently a "tour" would usually precede an opening on *Broadway* or in the *West End*. Now several touring productions, created in imitation of the original one, may follow a successful, big-city run.

tragedy   (24, 27) General name for plays ending in the death of their principal characters. These are usually of high status and have important responsibilities or they possess exceptional personal qualities. A tragedy is said to provoke both pity and terror in an audience.

tragicomedy   (27) Variously defined as plays that bring their leading characters close to death or that mix elements of *comedy* and *tragedy*.

traverse stage   (57-59) Acting space with audience sitting on two opposite sides, facing each other; usually long and narrow in shape.

truck   (or **wagon**) Platform on wheels or rollers, and sometimes moving along tracks set into the stage; used to bring large *props* or *scenic* units onto center stage.

tryout   Performance, usually taking place on *tour* or in a small *studio theatre*, used to test a play text or production before venturing it in a more expensive and critically important venue.

West End   District around Shaftesbury Avenue in central London where most of the principal commercial theatres are situated.

Index